H. D.'s POETRY

H. D.'s POETRY

"the meanings that words hide"

essays edited by

Marina Camboni

AMS Press
New York

Library of Congress Cataloging-in-Publication Data

H. D.'s Poetry: "the meanings that words hide". Essays / Edited by
Marina Camboni.
  p. cm – (AMS Studies in Modern Literature; no. 24)
  Includes bibliographical references and index.
  ISBN 0-404-61594-5 (alk. paper)
  1. H. D. (Hilda Doolittle), 1886-1961—Criticism and
interpretation.   2. Women and literature—United States—
History—20th century.   3. H. D. (Hilda Doolittle), 1886-
1961—Language.   4. Feminist poetry—History and
criticism.   I. Camboni, Marina.   II. Series.
PS3507.O726 Z718   2003
811'.52—dc21   2002026237
                                                                      CIP

All AMS books are printed on acid-free paper that meets the guidelines
for performance and durability of the Committee on Production
Guidelines for Book Longevity of the Council on Library Resources.

AMS Press, Inc.
Brooklyn Navy Yard, Bldg. 292, Suite 417, 63 Flushing Ave.
Brooklyn, New York 11205
U.S.A.

MANUFACTURED IN THE UNITED STATES OF AMERICA

To my daughter
Eva
For the New Millenium

Would she have been Rose
If her name had not been Rose
　　—Gertrude Stein

Contents

vii

Acknowledgments

Publication of this volume has been made possible by research funds from the University of Macerata and by the factive help of Elvira Crema, Renata Morresi, and Samuela Marcozzi. I also wish to thank the individual contributors for the energy and creativity they put into the whole project, and particularly wish to thank Diana Collecott, Kathleen Fraser, and Eileen Gregory for their critical and linguistic support.

Introduction

In the past fifteen years or so a new crop of critical essays and volumes has been devoted to H. D.'s oeuvre, marking a fresh turn in the understanding and appreciation of the poet's contribution to twentieth-century literature and to the shaping of a female poetic voice. Though a great number, if not the majority, concentrate on her poetry, not many have taken her poetic language as a privileged ground of investigation. I have always felt this lack and the necessity of an in-depth analysis of the less-known poems, both of her middle and of her last years.

Coherently, the essays here assembled are all devoted to a textual, linguistic, and rhetorical analysis of H. D.'s poetry, from her early lyrics to her late poetic sequences. It is within this perspective that the contributions of a philosopher of language like Marina Sbisà, and of a philologist like Patrizia Lendinara—and the specific methodological lenses which they use to magnify aspects of the poet's linguistic search and choices—become relevant to the critical work.

The essays gathered in this volume are the outcome of each contributor's long involvement with H. D.'s poetry. There was, however, a single event that set them off: a one-day colloquium on H. D.'s poetic language that took place at the University of Macerata in the spring of 1998. Eileen Gregory had come to Rome to teach. We had corresponded when she was directing the *H. D. Newsletter* and I was translating the *Trilogy*. She had just published her wonderful *H. D. and Hellenism* and I was thrilled at the idea of finally

getting to know her personally. We met around Christmas and together visited the Museo Nazionale Romano at Palazzo Altemps,
which had opened the day before. In it the Ludovisi Collection was
beautifully displayed, and we sat in silent contemplation of the
famous Ludovisi throne, the rose-cream frieze of marble where, in
bas-relief, Venus is shown in the act of coming out of the waters,
gently helped by two young maids. The piece exercised a sort of
subtle fascination. We thought of H. D., of her passion for Greek
art and poetry, imagining she would have liked to be there with us,
sharing our experience and the magic of the piece.

We started to think of ways of getting together and sharing ideas
about H. D.'s work. When we learned that Diana Collecott—who
was then finishing her *H. D. & Sapphic Modernism*—would come to
Italy the following spring, I decided to create an occasion for a
critical exchange between them and other Italian H. D. scholars,
Americanists like Raffaella Baccolini and Paola Zaccaria, and lin-
guists like Marina Sbisà, with whom I had worked in a research
project on the *Trilogy*, and Patrizia Lendinara, whom I had involved
in H. D.'s work a few years earlier, at the University of Palermo. I
knew that the poet Kathleen Fraser, who spends a few months every
year in Rome, would return with the swallows and the spring. As
an innovative writer and professor of modernist poetry in several
American university programs, she had written essays on H. D.
from the perspective of a working poet and would add that element
of "practice" to our discussion.

The dialogue, which started during that colloquium, has continued in the intervening years as a reflection on critical ways of responding to and representing a woman poet's art and poetics. All
this shows in the essays that have been contributed to the volume.
Each is also an "essay" in criticism.

The three sections of the volume, though apparently governed by
a chronological sequencing that goes from H. D.'s early lyrics to her
reception by a contemporary poet, develop around formal rhetorical, and thematic cores. In the first, " 'Intricate songs' lost measure':
The Early Lyrics," H. D.'s poems are read in the context of their
affiliative or antagonistic relationship with a chosen poetic tradition
(Sappho's, the Pre-Raphaelites) or elective female or male masters
(Isadora Duncan, Sigmund Freud). Their form, language, and rhetoric are shaped by H. D.'s need to express the sense of a self moving
away from confining spaces of growth and self-realization, finding

in the process figures and models capable of guiding her toward an expression of her own desires and her own voice.

Both Collecott and Gregory focus their contributions on Sappho's presence in H. D.'s early lyrics, developing their interpretations around two distinct key aspects: H. D.'s rhetorical tropes of transformation and her use of lyric as a subversive genre. Camboni explores the connection of visual and rhetorical figures while tracing both H. D.'s lifelong fascination with the Pre-Raphaelites and her construction of an autonomous authorial self. Zaccaria investigates the palimpsestic layering of personal and mythical aspects in two poems by H. D. written at the time of her analysis with Freud.

Sappho, Collecott writes, was for H. D. what Homer was for Pound and Dante for T. S. Eliot. The more than fifty fragments H. D. embodied in her lyrics attest to both her elective textual genealogy, honoring and continuing what H. D. believed to be an occluded tradition, and the dialogic relationship she establishes with the Greek poet upon whose authority she relies to voice her own plea as woman artist. If the presence of a vocabulary traceable to Sappho marks the textual places where the Greek and the modernist texts overlap, what Collecott points out is the fact that H. D.'s Sapphic intertextuality takes readers not only to the heart of Sappho's Eros, but to the cutting edge where her own poetry takes place.

H. D.'s two rhetorical tropes on which Collecott focuses her attention, the oxymoron and the chiasmus, are interpreted both as the embodiments of Sapphic expression and as H. D.'s linguistic rendering of the cutting edge where opposites meet and where complication—but also transformation—may take place. The oxymoron, analyzed in terms of the tradition of "signifying" in the Afro-American community, is for Collecott a figure that allows for double-talk, that foregrounds ambivalence, as she shows in her analysis of "Eurydice," and is an early instance of transformation transcending paradox, which will eventually lead to H. D.'s mature project of conciliation of opposites. Chiasmus, a legacy of lyric as well as epic poetry, is on the other hand a figure of the crossroads, of creation through reversal and revision, where the mirroring function is one of its possibilities, the enveloping form also recalling the "folded texts" and hidden meanings of the ancients. Though Collecott does not explicitly say so, these figures should be considered early instances of H. D.'s hermeticism, of uses of language and rhetoric that at one time reveal and veil. If, by choosing to be part of the Sapphic tradition, H. D. claims a context where her values are recognized and supportive of the creative poetic act, the poet's deathlessness is, at the same time, both revealed and contained in her own words.

Focussing on the lyric as a literary genre—first asserting, against common wisdom and the Romantic lyric tradition, that the lyric form is a radical and potentially subversive genre—Eileen Gregory argues that H. D.'s lyrics belong within a tradition of resistance to orthodoxy and participation in desire. She traces this tradition back to those lyrics by Sappho in which the Greek poet defies the public acceptance of values of war and conflict, opposing to them the intimate value of love and the lover's presence. One further and fundamental element, according to Gregory, makes the lyric potentially dangerous. That is its capacity to persuade the reader to imagine the world from the vantage point of feeling and desire. In keeping with the above, Gregory finds that H. D.'s dialectical struggle with consecrated values is most visible in those lyrics, like "Epitaph," in which one or more censoring voices are present, articulating moral and aesthetic norms that stand for confinement and deathliness. While exploring the complexity of H. D.'s play with the censor, Gregory also points out the ways our poet engages the reader in the dialectic, entrapping one in a pact with the poet. "Adonis" is one such poem, which Gregory acutely analyzes, showing how the reader is involved in the text and invited to see himself or herself as a divine body, one with the God.

Whereas Collecott points out the visual and transformational value of H. D.'s rhetorical figures, Camboni's semiotic analysis explores the interpretive possibilities inherent in the multiple reference of the word "figure" which, while suggesting a spatial form, spans the visual and verbal art mediums. Camboni's starting point is H. D.'s claimed genealogy, her acknowledgment that Pre-Raphaelite and Decadent art nourished her beginnings. She then proceeds to illustrate how, in line with contemporary radical feminist representations of self-awareness and self-determination, H. D. moves away from her early models and projects her sense of self in figures that are the poet's "subjective correlatives," embodying her dialectic of *being* and *living*, of change and permanence. Thus, in "Pygmalion" and "Eurydice," the two mythical figures, though bearing the same names as their canonical and more recent representations, refer to substantially different entities that are also figures of the poet as author and woman. In these poems the act of reflection, the images of self as double and their rhetorical equivalent, the chiasmus, are central. "Eurydice" moreover stands for H. D.'s awareness that her authorial quest originates in a state of loss, that is in a sense of misconstructed and misrepresented cultural identity, which is the black hole of hell Eurydice must climb out of in order to start her true search. Camboni traces such movement in the poet's late works (*Trilogy* and *Bid Me To Live (A Madrigal)*), in which images of women correspond to her increasing sense of authority as a poet and her growing belief in the social significance of poetry.

By focusing on the palimpsest as the figure that bespeaks temporal, cultural, and psychosexual transformations, in her "sentient-sensitive" understanding of H. D.'s multilayered discourse, Zaccaria corroborates Camboni's reading of the use of figures. In H. D.'s poetry, Zaccaria maintains, words are the carriers of a form of understanding in which facts and experiences are perceived as superimposed, "things under things," related among themselves as well as to the author, and conveyed as a combination of language, thought, and vision. Wordplay and word-punning, homophony and double meaning—as Collecott has also shown—but also neologisms and compounds, as Lendinara points out, are fundamental linguistic tricks H. D. uses to shed monological meaning, speaking for a plural subject and its ambivalent, playful multivolcality. In her examination of two key poems, "The Dancer" and "The Master," written at the time of H. D.'s analysis with Freud, Zaccaria brings evidence of the way they grow out of the layering of figures wherein personal and mythical aspects combine. Both poems reveal a poetical writing practice where prosody and the unconscious work together in the service of poetry; both center on Rhodocleia, a goddesslike figure. If in "The Master" Rhodocleia is seen in her relation with the father-god figure—H. D.'s poetic incarnation of Freud—in "The Dancer" her dancing, love-making, sensual body is desire made poetical discourse, which allows for the incessant flow between the physical and the symbolic.

In the essays gathered in the second section of the volume, "Write, write, write or die': The Late Poetic Sequences," writing itself occupies center stage as a figure of the woman writer who aims to be a creator and transformer of culture. Writing, synonymous with the transgressive act of inscribing woman within the text of Western written culture, stands also for H. D.'s own will to break with tradition and with patriarchal authority alike, to shape her own, and new tradition, moving away from the "crystal and air" of her early lyrics, as well as from a self-reflexive identity, to enter the arena of the world in search of personal and collective salvation. *Trilogy*,

Helen in Egypt, By Avon River, Vale Ave, Hermetic Definition are all texts born out of a critical dialogue with the key texts that shaped our culture. Though H. D.'s emphasis on language—on words and names capable of excavating cultural history and at the same time of showing its layers—begins much earlier, it is not until the *Trilogy* that it joins forces with her will to shape a mythical world not only and simply personal, but outright human. It is this peculiar quality that makes H. D.'s work much closer in development to that of William Carlos Williams and his *Paterson* than that of Pound and Eliot in the same years. And this may also be one of the reasons Kathleen Fraser, a writer in the more experimental American tradition of Williams and Olson, could feel inspired by H. D.'s late poetics. Joining in her work the most daring linguistic experimentation, a scientific precision and a visual quality, and wanting to give form to a woman's experience of self and the world in innovative ways, Fraser is in many ways radically different from H. D., but her work with words, dreams, and images taps the mythical dimension of the experience of the present.

Trilogy is the first of H. D.'s long poetic sequences where her quest for an authoritative female subject is yoked to her exploration of the language of the new. It is only pertinent, then, that the two essays by Marina Sbisà and Patrizia Lendinara be devoted to *Trilogy* as the rich mine of H. D.'s textual and linguistic experimentation.

Marina Sbisà interprets H. D.'s representation of subject and gender in *Trilogy* from the joint perspective of a philosopher of language and a feminist. After first establishing the methodological ground of her analysis, Sbisà concentrates on the enunciating subjects in *Trilogy*, illustrating how subjectivity develops throughout the poem from forms of dialogue and intersubjective confrontation, to forms in which the authorial subject firmly expresses her wants, either directly or through the staging of subordinated enunciators, like Mary of Magdala in *The Flowering of the Rod*. Sbisà calls attention to a specific strategy H. D. uses to construct subjectivity, transcend patriarchy, and attain higher levels of authority in her enunciation: the dialogue with, and appropriation of, the Word of God in the Bible, expressed in the intertextual insertion of italicized quotations. She also shows how all through the poems in *Trilogy* the subject stages a kind of knowledge rooted on sensing or feeling (*Walls Do Not Fall*) and on visual, purely ostensive experience (*Tribute to the Angels* and *The Flowering of the Rod*). Turning from enunciation to the enunciated discourse, Sbisà focuses on gender representation in *Trilogy*. She points out how, refusing the androgynous as fusional totality of the sexes and in accordance with her appreciation of individual ways and differences, H. D. subverts gender expectations by assigning traditionally feminine attributes to male characters and traditionally masculine attributes to female ones. Moreover, by aligning the author as narrator in *Flowering of the Rod* with the male character Kaspar, H. D. exemplifies acknowledgement of that autonomous feminine subjectivity, which as author she has pursued and practiced throughout the poem.

In her investigation of H. D.'s creation and use of an extremely high number of compound words in *Trilogy*, Patrizia Lendinara uncovers H. D.'s play with tradition and innovation, with time and myth sedimented in language. By splitting prefixes and suffixes from the words they are attached to, by creating daring syllabifications and misspellings ("dev-ill" but also "Par-Isis") H. D. manages to open up words, reveal hidden words, and thus complicate their reference. In this way, inner and outer experiences mix, while a multilayered historical, mythical, and dream world takes shape. What is relevant in Lendinara's work, which doggedly and carefully tracks down and subdivides all instances of compounding, is the evidence it brings to other critical analyses and to what goes under the overall name of H. D.'s re-visionary practice. On the one hand, H. D.'s splitting of words seems to respond to a need to re-visualize and temporally re-define the reality they create, breaking away from automatic associations, or creating new ones, as with "paw-er." On the other hand, her newly created compounds, like "bird-claw" or "bird-beak," seem to respond to a more complex need than that of giving visibility to a specific part of the bird. It seems, rather an antieconomic linguistic gesture, which creates a figure that is the exact reversal of metonymy. In these compounds the part and the whole stick together while the alliterative sound stresses the sharpness of the image and the wilfulness of the bird. Many of H. D.'s neologisms are the result of her compounding two or more words into a higher semantic unity. This emphasizes the processual aspects of inner or outer experience, as in "self-out-of-self," or "Water-to-be-changed-into-wine." Lendinara points out how in *Trilogy* H. D. creates compounds to complicate the play between lexical meaning and textual sense and make this last capable to convey the multilayered, mythical, historical, and personal quest of her poetic subject(s).

Moving on in time and concentrating on *Vale Ave* within the context of H. D.'s late works, Baccolini reads in the poem a confessional shift where personal past experiences are perceived as part of a larger universal design, just as, according to M. L. Rosenthal, confessional poetry fused the private and the culturally symbolic. Baccolini finds that, though coherent with the autobiographical character of most of her prose, the autobiographical shift in *Vale Ave*, where the persona and the poet often seem to share the same voice, is new in H. D.'s poetry, making it diverge from her early lyric poetry, as well as from *Trilogy*, with its play of roles between the persona and the author articulately illustrated by Sbisà. Tracing a pattern of meeting and parting, of acceptance and repudiation—which she sees central to *Vale Ave* and to most late poems—Baccolini points out how memory, love and sexual desire, writing and identity are indissolubly linked. Memory in *Vale Ave*, she maintains, is "the main structural device and theme," its centrality being derived from psychoanalysis but also from H. D.'s reading of Dante's *Vita Nuova* as a model of recollection and interpretation leading to a higher form of knowledge.

In Baccolini's essay most of the thematic threads spun in the previous essays are woven into a pattern showing persistence and variation within H. D.'s poetic discourse. Old themes like erotic desire, the poet's quest, her revisionist mythology and language, reappear transformed in old age and adapted in the construction of the woman as quester of spiritual and personal identity and creator of a world governed by Love. In this way, the erotic desire of H. D.'s early lyrics and the subject's desire for personal and human salvation in *Trilogy* are, in her late works, made more concrete and pervasive; they are transformed as well, being recontextualized in the mystical tradition of the Church of Love, of Dante's *Divine Comedy* and his search of knowledge and salvation.

There are other aspects, and words, that connect many of the essays in the volume. Reference to "figures," whether rhetorical, mythical, or imaginary and visual, returns over and over, (see Collecott, Camboni, Baccolini, Zaccaria)—twice in the title of the essays—and runs as a blue thread, pointing out the highly visual and symbolic quality of H. D.'s language. Also, throughout all the essays the thematic connection of poetry and identity forms a textural continuum, from Gregory's reading H. D.'s poetry within the lyric tradition as emblematic of a highly subjective desire, to Sbisà's articulate declension of the language of subjectivity in *Trilogy*.

Kathleen Fraser stresses the support she found in the "persistent quest for the as yet unmapped interior life" within H. D.'s work. Her contribution, in the third section of the volume, further testifies to the belated but very powerful impact H. D. had on contemporary poets. H. D. scholars know of Robert Duncan's lifelong engagement with H. D.'s esoteric facet; of Adrienne Rich's "discovery" of her *Trilogy* and the impact it had on her own poems, collected in *The*

Dream of a Common Language. Not many critics, however, would associate Kathleen Fraser's highly experimental poetry and poetics with H. D.'s.

Fraser herself acknowledges that in her formative years as a poet she seldom encountered women poets as models. In the sixties, avoiding the self-centeredness of dominant poetries, she found in visual art, in the poetics of the New York school, in the "energy fields" of the Black Mountain poets an answer to a de-centered sense of a self no longer credibly unitary. Only in the eighties, she admits, did she discover in H. D.'s work "a kind of female en-spiriting guide that I'd been lacking."

The blank page, as the title of her essay clearly indicates, is the point where H. D.'s poetics and Fraser's own work meet. What she learned from H. D. is not a pattern for her poetic lines, but the stubbornness acquired to insure the empowering process of a female voice and vision of the world as it moves onto the written page of a text and becomes capable of shaping a new culture. Connecting the blank page with myth, and finding in this connection the master lesson she learned from H. D., Fraser tells us that myth provides a route of independent travel, a large page on which to engraft perceptions and experiences retrieved from a female life. To exemplify this, Fraser tells of the process that led to her own poem "Etruscan Pages." Having gone to visit an Etruscan site armed with traditional guidebooks, she found—once there—that the emotions and internal echoes the place activated in her were different from anything she had read or anticipated. This simple fact opened her up to a direct contact with the places' historical and mythic encrustations, as their details were retrieved for her own "empty pages." Although what came out of this is nothing like H. D.'s lines, all the same, her page "wanted to be inscribed as it were a canvas" appropriating the Etruscan inscriptions and other texts and dreams that had filled the days of her writing—and quite intentionally recording an alternative vision from D. H. Lawrence's, although finding points of alignment when later comparing her notes with his *Etruscan Places.*

Fraser writes of the shaping hand of influence, of the prevailing standards of judgment, and how the effects of gender-specific valuing, editing, and explication can make a difference in the continuing life of the working poet. I believe the effort of all the contributors to this collection goes in that direction—the shaping of gender-specific valuing and critical perspectives that help both writers and critics to find their voices.

Marina Camboni

PART I

"Intricate songs' lost measure": The Early Lyrics

"She too is my poet": H. D.'s Sapphic Fragments

Diana Collecott

A rose is a rose?

At the start of H. D.'s published work—on the first page of her first volume—is the poem "Sea Rose":

> Rose, harsh rose,
> marred and with stint of petals,
> meagre flower, thin,
> sparse of leaf,
>
> more precious
> than a wet rose
> single on a stem—
> you are caught in the drift.
>
> Stunted, with small leaf,
> you are flung on the sand,
> you are lifted
> in the crisp sand
> that drives in the wind.
>
> Can the spice-rose
> drip such acrid fragrance
> hardened in a leaf?
> (*Collected* 5)

Eileen Gregory has commented on this poem: "The sea rose is a
sign in terms of which a poetic voice presumes power and opens a
circuit with the reader, who is thus implicated in a transtemporal
project—making the rose out of language, interiorising the rose in
an allegory of desire" (*H. D. and Hellenism* 136). "Sea Rose" belongs
(as Gregory points out) in a long lineage of English poems. We can
supply our own favorites: mine is Edmund Waller's "Go, lovely
rose," which Ezra Pound quoted in the *Cantos*. But beyond and
behind all these are the roses that Sappho loved and associated with
love; by analogy, I propose that behind H. D.'s poetic are the poetics
of a Sapphic Eros.

What survives of Sappho's poetry from circa 600 B.C. are mere
quotations and translations, scraps of parchment and papyrus, "torn
petals," to adapt an image that H. D. applied to the isles of Greece.
Nonetheless, these fragments were enough to endorse Sappho's reputation as the greatest lyric poet of antiquity. Her work came down
to H. D. directly from the Greek and also in versions made by
Victorian poets such as Swinburne, who said: "Shakespeare is the
best dramatist who was also a poet, but Sappho is simply nothing
less . . . than the greatest poet who ever was at all" (quoted in Greer
146). There was sufficient indication of this quality in the mere fragments that lasted into the Hellenistic period for Meleager to include
Sappho in his *Garland*, and to praise her surviving poems thus:
"few . . . but they are roses" (Peter Jay, ed., *Greek Anthology* 375).

In her essay entitled "The Wise Sappho," H. D. rejected this as
faint praise. She suspected that Meleager was presenting Sappho's
lyrics as merely decorative, and she resisted the implication that
women's work was in any sense superficial or ephemeral. This is
what she wrote:

> I think of the words of Sappho as these colours, or states rather,
> transcending colour yet containing . . . all colour. And perhaps the
> most obvious is this rose colour, merging to richer shades of scarlet,
> purple or Phoenician purple. To the superficial lover—truly—roses!
>   Yet not all roses—not roses at all . . . but reading deeper we are
> inclined to visualize these broken sentences and unfinished rhythms
> as rocks—perfect rock shelves and layers of rock between which
> flowers by some chance may grow[,] but which endure when the
> staunch blossoms have perished.   (*Notes on Thought and Vision* 58)

Just as H. D. resisted Meleager's reading of Sappho, so she resisted
the rose-imagery of the dominant masculine tradition. In this critical
and historical context, the poem "Sea Rose" belongs with H. D.'s

larger project, that of a woman poet in a culture that has long excluded or belittled or suppressed the female voice. Eileen Gregory is surely right to see this poem as an annunciation of creativity, even an appropriation of power. I read it also as a sign of Sappho's presence in H. D.'s poetic.

Others, more expert than I, have recognized this Sapphic presence as a source of energy for the modern writer. Susan Gubar connected it with the "eroticized female relationships that, quite literally, empowered [her] to write"(47). Eileen Gregory has demonstrated Sappho's central significance in H. D.'s recovery of "an archaic lyric tradition in which the voice of the woman poet has distinct potency" ("Rose Cut in Rock" 527). My own close reading of H. D. has persuaded me that this engagement between the two poets is persistently textual. There are no exact lexical echoes of Sappho in "Sea Rose," but its conceptual basis is in the Lesbian poet's famous oxymoron *glukupikron.*[1] (This is usually translated into English as "bitter-sweet," but it actually means "sweet-bitter", suggesting that the effects of love come in that order—first sweet, then bitter—as most of us can testify). H. D.'s "harsh rose" undercuts the usual attributes of the garden rose: it is not sweet-scented, nor soft-petalled, nor full-blown. Paradoxically, it is "more precious" for being *marred, meagre, thin, stunted,* and *hardened.* These adjectives also apply to a poetic that survives under conditions that hardly nourish it; hence the poem's metonymies become metaphors for the poetry itself: "with stint of petals . . . sparse of leaf. . . ."

H. D.'s Imagism certainly had a tenuous existence after the florid abundance of Keats and Tennyson. Like her "Sea Violet," its "grasp is frail / on the edge of the sand-hill" (*Collected* 26); like her "Sea Iris," its condition is both "sweet and salt" (*Collected* 36). As Louis Martz has pointed out in his introduction to the *Collected Poems,* a crucial boundary in H. D.'s writing is between sea and land. Her "Sheltered Garden" is oppressive because it is inland, cultivated, unexposed to keener, wilder elements:

---

1. References in the text to Sappho's poems and fragments are here identified by the numbers assigned to them in Campbell's recent Loeb edition (which largely correspond with those in Lobel and Page's earlier Oxford edition) and in Wharton's edition used by H. D. *Glukupikron* occurs in Campbell 130, Wharton 40. Fuller details of the fragments discussed here will be found in the Appendix to my book (Collecott 266–72).

there is no scent of resin
in this place,
no taste of bark, of coarse weeds,
aromatic, astringent—
only border on border of scented pinks
(*Collected* 19).

In contrast to these cloying scents, and that of the "spice-rose," H.
D.'s "Sea Rose" has pride of place, signing her work with its "acrid
fragrance"—bitter-sweet.

"Eros is an issue of boundaries," writes Anne Carson, "like
Sappho's adjective *glukupikron*, the moment of desire is one that
defines the proper edge" (30). Far from seducing H. D. into the
luxury of Lesbos as imagined by decadent poets such as Baudelaire
in his *Les Fleurs du Mal*, Sappho's example hones the cutting edge
of her new poetic. Carson continues: "As Eros insists upon the edges
of human beings and of the spaces between them, the written consonant imposes edge on the sounds of human speech and insists on
the reality of that edge, although it has its origin in the reading and
writing imagination" (55). True to its Imagist origins, H. D.'s writing
is consonantal in this sense. In "Sheltered Garden" and "Sea Rose,"
we find sharp expressions like "scent of resin," "caught in the drift,"
and "lifted / in the crisp sand." These aptly occupy the line end-
ings, at the edge of articulation, marking the spatial interface between print and page. Much of H. D.'s early poetry is poised, like
her "Cliff Temple," between *rock ledge* and *world-edge* (*Collected* 26).
This world is alive with intersections: of elements, of textures, of
colour and light. Its rhythms are adapted from the turning movements of the Greek chorus—*strophe* and *antistrophe*—which approach, meet, retreat. The space in which her poetry takes place
is thus one of contiguity and crux; it is also a place of continual
transformation from literal to figurative.

Sapphistry

"H. D. saw herself as a writer in Sappho's tradition and as a Sapphic
writer," says Rachel DuPlessis; nowhere is this more evident than
in the improvisations on the numbered fragments that this critic has
described as "coming out" texts and also as *tours de force* of poetic
invention (*H. D.: The Career* 24–25). Nevertheless, the editors of a
recent anthology entitled *Sappho Through English Poetry* dismissed

H. D. from consideration, asserting that she avoids "creative dialogue" with Sappho, and simply uses some surviving fragments as
"points of departure for poems which move in completely non-
Sapphic directions" (Jay and Lewis 25). My research shows, however, that far from merely "alluding to Sappho in epigraphs to a
handful of poems," as these editors suppose (24), H. D. embodies
actual fragments of Sappho in more than thirty poems and embeds
many more in her prose. Following on the scant but telling traces
found by other readers, I have identified over fifty distinct fragments
in H. D.'s *Collected Poems*, together with her essay "The Wise Sappho." These examples also indicate that despite her familiarity with
Wharton's *Sappho*, H. D. worked directly from the Greek, resisting
previous translations and engaging with newly discovered material.

Susan Gubar wittily described this aspect of H. D.'s poetic practice
as "Sapphistry." Only at its most obvious does it take the form of
direct quotation with variation, as in the poems numbered from H.
T. Wharton's bilingual edition of Sappho, which H. D. owned.
Among these, "Fragment 113" ("*Neither honey nor bee for me*") has
hidden depths, both sexual and textual. As Gregory comments, the
title announces a specific textuality which the text resists, just as the
poem itself enacts "voluptuous denials of voluptuousness" (*H. D.
and Hellenism* 152). Beginning with one fragment,[2] "Fragment 113"
ends with several; here are the final lines:

> neglect the lyre-note;
> knowing that you shall feel,
> about the frame,
> no trembling of the string
> but heat, more passionate
> of bone and the white shell
> and fiery tempered steel.
>   (H. D., *Collected* 132)

These lines stress the firmness of the *frame* (a term applied to the
human body, as well as the musical instrument), the structural hardness of *bone*, *shell*, and *steel*, rather than the softness of flesh. They
also echo the moments when Sappho spoke of, or spoke to, her lyre,
calling it a "divine shell."[3] It comes as no surprise that H. D. was
later drawn to the lyrists of the English Renaissance, especially Tu-
dor lutanists, who performed their poems to music and addressed

---

2. Campbell 146, Wharton 113. (Discussed by Gubar 53–55).
3. Campbell 118, Wharton 45.

their instruments as Sappho did. In her tribute to Shakespeare, *By Avon River*, she twice cites Sir Thomas Wyatt's song "To His Lute" (72, 78). Moreover, the expression "no trembling of the string but heat" recalls Sappho's famous references to the way desire sets one trembling and starts fires in the body.[4] These references resonate with phrases found on a piece of papyrus from the third century A.D.: "strike the strings . . . receiving the *olisbos*."[5] This fragment, of uncertain ascription and dubious transcription, has been interpreted both as "strings which welcome the plectrum," and also as "women who use the dildo" (Campbell 125n3). Hence the Sapphic intertextuality of "Fragment 113" extends well beyond its innocuous epigraph translating a single fragment; it engenders a conceit that takes us to the heart of Sappho's Eros, and to the complicated relationship between the art of a singer and the life of a woman.

Beyond the specific fragment, H. D. often uses a vocabulary that is traceable to Sappho and may well revive her values. For example, in "Halcyon" (a poem addressed to the young Bryher) she alludes to a line of Sappho's that reads, in a literal translation, "You seemed to me a small, graceless child."[6] When H. D. describes Bryher in these terms as "small" with "hardly any charm," "a child" with "no Grace" (*Collected* 271, 275, 273), she is applying the Greek term *acharis* ("without grace") to mean, in Jane Snyder's words, "not yet subject—in Sappho's way of thinking—to the charms of Aphrodite and the Graces" (86); hence not merely awkward, but undesirable. According to this interpretation, an entire aesthetic may be transmitted by a single word—fortunately, in view of the almost complete destruction of Sappho's writings. H. D.'s English usage supports this; for instance, in "A Note on Poetry" she uses "fragrant" to connote the sensual delicacy of a Sapphic sensibility (73). In a poetic so crystalline, a mere word or phrase can serve as what Pound called the "luminous detail" (*Selected Prose* 23): the part contains the whole, the fragment the poem. H. D. identified the power of this aesthetic as Sappho's wisdom, saying: "She constructed perfect and flawless . . . the whole, the perfection . . . of goddess, muse or sacred being from the simple grace of some tall, half-developed girl" (*Notes on Thought and Vision* 65). We can see from this slight example that in contrast to the sometimes perfunctory preservation of Sappho's art in the prose of classical grammarians and rhetoricians, H. D.'s

---

4. For example, Campbell 130, Wharton 40; Campbell 31, Wharton 2.

5. Campbell 99; not in Wharton.

6. Campbell 49, Wharton 34. (Echo first noticed by Swann 34).

remembering of Sappho also serves to reincorporate her writing in
a lyric context, a lesbian poetics.

Signifyin(g)

Before turning to further traces of Sappho in H. D.'s early poetry, I
wish to suggest a terminology that will allow us to recognize, and
more precisely describe, this impact of her writing practice. Two
terms have helped me especially: the first is *palimpsest*, a word of
Greek origin that H. D. herself used as the title of a work of fiction.
Aware of the "precious inch of palimpsest" on which Sappho's
songs might be traced (*Notes on Thought and Vision* 69), she defined
ηαλιμφηστοζ as "a parchment from which one writing has been
erased to make room for another" (*Palimpsest* [1]). Hence the idea
of a *palimpsest* or over-written text, consisting of erasures as well as
fresh inscriptions, of previous as well as subsequent writings, becomes a metaphor for the collective process of reading and rereading. Snyder has applied it to the presence of Sappho's writing within
and beneath H. D.'s, saying: "the Greek poets, especially Homer,
Sappho, and Euripides, continually float up from the underlying
surface on which she layers her meanings, and layer interacts with
layer to create an ever-shifting pattern of text" (137). We have seen
this fluid process at work in "Fragment 113."

The second term that I have found useful is *signifying*. Historically, this African-American expression refers to forms of wordplay
and indirect speech used by slaves. Those excluded from the dominant community—ethnic, religious, and political minorities,
women, lesbians, and homosexuals—have also used double-talk to
elude punishment, censorship, or denigration. Such forms of discourse may conceal meaning from one listener, and reveal it to
another. Hence they are vital to what Gary Burnett has called the
"mysteries" of H. D.'s poetics. Henry Louis Gates spells the term
"Signifyin(g)," to distinguish it from de Saussure's notion of *signification*, and defines it as "a mode of formal revision, [that] depends
for its effects on troping . . . is often characterized by pastiche, and
. . . turns upon repetition of formal structures and their differences"
(*Signifying Monkey* 52).

We have seen how such a revisionary mode serves H. D.'s purposes in "Halcyon"; I later show how her poem "Fragment Thirty-
six" deploys the repetition of formal structures inherent in Wharton's version of the original Greek. In "The Wise Sappho," H. D.

translates another fragment: "I think no girl ... will ever again ... be as wise as you are";[7] she then tropes it, inverting the verb, to ask playfully of Sappho "was she wise?" (*Notes on Thought and Vision* 63, 64). Rhetorical questions and name-calling are just two of the language games that H. D.'s Sapphistry shares with African American speech. Gates asks himself why black people in the U.S.A. "talk about talking," and he replies: "they do this ... to pass these rituals along from one generation to the next. They do it to preserve the traditions of 'the race' " (*Signifying Monkey* xi). In Black culture, therefore, Signifyin(g) is as self-conscious as the use of literary allusion, parody, and pastiche by male modernists such as Eliot, Joyce, and Pound. Both lines unite in the complex art of Ralph Ellison and Toni Morrison, but whereas the white writers' rhetoric often undermines the very tradition on which it signifies, the black writers are intent on sustaining their culture. Similarly H. D.'s linguistic rituals honour what she perceived as an occluded Sapphic tradition.

According to Shari Benstock, "the Sapphic ... exists in another realm ... and when it finds a medium through which to speak, it radically restructures the rules of the cultural game" (193–94). While Benstock's essay on expatriate Sapphic modernism privileges white writers—Willa Cather, Gertrude Stein and Virginia Woolf, as well as H. D.—she partly owes her understanding of the *Sapphic* to the black writer Audre Lorde's understanding of the *erotic*. In "Uses of the Erotic, the Erotic as Power," Lorde wrote:

> The erotic is a resource within each of us that lies in a deeply female and spiritual plane, firmly rooted in the power of our unexpressed or unrecognized feeling. In order to perpetuate itself, every oppression must corrupt or distort those various sources of power within the culture of the oppressed, that can provide energy for change. For women this has meant a suppression of the erotic. . . .
>
> (*Sister Outsider* 53)

Depoliticizing Lorde's theory, Benstock identifies the Sapphic as "a source of artistic creativity" that is simultaneously remembered by the artist and suppressed by the culture (193). Most writers agree that Sappho and her sister-poets flourished before patriarchal power was fully institutionalized, and in a partially preliterate culture. Glimpsed through traces as limited—yet as telling—as Sappho's own fragments, the Sapphic can thus be sited in the prehistory of our owners: a place both "forgotten" and "remembered," as in Benstock's formulation.

---

7. Campbell, 56, Wharton 69.

Eurydice

H. D.'s poem "Eurydice" has had a marginal existence; first published in *The Egoist* in 1917, it was reprinted in the American *Collected Poems* of 1925, then forgotten for over half a century, until Louis Martz's new collection in 1983. Rachel DuPlessis has read this poem, in relation to H. D.'s autobiographical novel *Bid Me to Live*, as an instance of the woman writer's "struggle for cultural authority" (*H. D.: The Career* 104). She also describes it as "a reconstruction of the [Orpheus] myth that puts the woman as hero at the centre of the story" (*Writing Beyond the Ending* 70), and hence as a preparatory sketch for the large-scale work of H. D.'s maturity. "Eurydice" may be all that remains of the "Orpheus" sequence criticised by the D. H. Lawrence figure in *Bid Me To Live*—if that ever existed outside her fiction. I intend to show how this poem's strength as a growing-point for H. D.'s later work derives, at least in part, from the way it signifies on Sappho.

Like "Fragment Forty-one" and "Fragment Sixty-eight,"[8] "Eurydice" alludes to Sappho's bridal-songs. It explores the possibility of a new marriage between Orpheus and Eurydice, when he and his ravished bride have escaped from Hades to the "upper earth" (*Collected* 52). Lawrence used as similar myth in his later poem "Bavarian Gentians," to celebrate Persephone's return to the underworld and her forced marriage with its ruler Pluto: he envisaged Persephone as "darkness invisible enfolded in . . . / . . . the arms Plutonic, and pierced with the passion of intense gloom" (*Complete Poems* 697). Whereas Lawrence, obliterating Persephone as the "lost bride" of Pluto in a context both phallic and patriarchal, would signify on Milton ("darkness visible"), H. D. signifies on Sappho. She also recalls the matriarchal myth of Persephone and Demeter (the earth-mother), as Eurydice reflects on her lost chance of being restored to the world of light:

> What had my face to offer
> but reflex of the earth,
> hyacinth colour
> caught from the raw fissure in the rock
> where the light struck,
> and the colour of azure crocuses

---

8. Campbell 131 and 55 respectively; H. D.'s poems take their titles from Wharton's numbering.

and the bright surface of gold crocuses . . .
(*Collected* 52)

"Hyacinth colour" translates a phrase from a Sapphic fragment describing Leda's egg;[9] "gold crocuses" may allude to Sappho's praise of her daughter Cleis.[10] Other references to colour and light in "Eurydice" indicate an elaborate signification on tropes from Sappho's Epithalamia; for instance, she celebrates a bride honoured by Aphrodite thus: "Your eyes [are] gentle, and love streams over your lovely face"; a similar expression is used (perhaps mockingly) of a bridegroom: "spread abroad the grace in your eyes."[11] By contrast, H. D.'s Eurydice asks:

> what was it that crossed my face
> with the light from yours
> and your glance?
> what was it you saw in my face?
> the light of your own face,
> the fire of your own presence?
> (*Collected* 52)

This poem is far from a celebration of marriage; it gives voice to a woman whose abandonment by her husband has enabled her to see through a situation that Virginia Woolf described as follows: "Women have served all these centuries as looking-glasses possessing the magic and delicious power of reflecting the figure of man at twice its natural size" (*Room of One's Own* 37). H. D.'s poem counterpoints Orpheus' disastrous backward glance at his wife with Eurydice's hindsight on the sexual politics of their relationship. Its intertexuality with Sappho represents not only a recovery of the female voice, but also a recuperation of presence and energy for the female self. Whereas Eurydice is traditionally represented as a woman who can only live by virtue of her husband's art—Orpheus is, significantly, a masculine figure for poetry itself—H. D.'s poem wrests her into a resistant autonomy:

> At least I have the flowers of myself,
> and my thoughts, no god
> can take that;
> I have the fervour of myself for a presence

---

9. Campbell 166, Wharton 56.
10. Campbell 132, Wharton 85.
11. Campbell 112 and 138; Wharton 100 and 29, respectively.

and my own spirit for light . . .
(*Collected* 55).

H. D.'s response to Wharton's *Sappho* was therefore deconstructive as well as reconstructive. Her intertexuality resembles Emily Dickinson's, as described by Susan Howe: "Forcing, abbreviating, pushing, padding, subtracting, riddling, interrogating, re-writing, she pulled text from text" (29).

Mirroring

When we realize that Sappho's presence in the work of H. D. is no less significant than Homer's in the work of Ezra Pound, or Dante's in the work of T. S. Eliot, we are on the approach to a fresh understanding of her modernism. Likewise, the realization that Sappho is to H. D. what Ovid was to Shakespeare, invites us to view the tradition of English literature with fresh eyes. Adrienne Rich has commented that, "Re-vision—the act of looking back, of seeing with fresh eyes, of entering an old text from a new critical tradition—is for women more than a chapter in cultural history: it is an act of survival" (*On Lies, Secrets and Silence* 35). Such a radical revision cannot be attempted here, so I will conclude by indicating just two of the rhetorical tropes that characterize H. D.'s writing, and connect it with those of predecessors such as Sappho and Shakespeare.

We have already located what Gates calls a "discursive cross-roads" (*Signifying Monkey* 65) between H. D.'s Anglo-American poetics and African-American language rituals; this crossroads is also an axis connecting her work with that of ancient Greek lyrists and English Renaissance poets. Among their shared tropes is the *oxymoron*: Sappho's *bitter-sweet*, Shakespeare's *heavy lightness*. This is a form of double-talk that foregrounds ambivalence, expressing not merely paradox and contradiction, but the possibilities of "both and neither" (H. D., *Bid Me to Live* 176–77). Eve Sedgwick, discussing gay studies, uses the term "open-secret structure" and adds: "it's only by being shameless about risking the obvious that we happen into the vicinity of the transformative" (22).

Oxymoronic expressions such as "scented and stinging," "sweet and salt" (*Collected* 36) record the debt to Sappho in H. D.'s earliest published poetry. In the nineteen-twenties, the pattern is freer: love-gifts are "lovely, perilous," the highest rapture is of "speech unsaid" (128, 110). In the forties, it deepens and develops: at the visionary climax of "The Walls Do Not Fall" we—the "nameless initiates"

who "know our Name"—"were there or not-there" (521, 559). So
this mature work begins by confronting the semantic crisis inscribed
in the oxymoron, which is "that process of holding two opinions
simultaneously, 'knowing them to be contradictory and believing
in both of them' " (Preminger ed. 873). H. D.'s entire endeavour
was dedicated, in the Sapphic tradition, to a transformation of opposites that transcends paradox: "The *gloire* is both," she wrote in
Bid Me to Live (176). The project of reconciliation in her mature
poetry—between people of different races and genders, between
militarists and pacifists, material and spiritual values, in the great
Trilogy of the Second World War and, at the end of her life, in *Helen
in Egypt*—can be traced in the very rhetoric of her previous work.

The crucial figure in such a context (if a pun may be permitted)
is that of the *crossroads:* "we are at the cross-roads," we read in the
Trilogy, "the tide is turning" (H. D., *Collected* 524); later, a moment
of crisis in her childhood is remembered as "an image at the crossroads" and connected with the catastrophes of Greek tragedy (H. D.,
Tribute to Freud 29). H. D. knew that, in ancient Greece, Hermes
was not only the gods' go-between but also "master of shrines and
gateways / ... and the cross-road / and the street" (*Collected* 349).
Was not her first published poem "Hermes of the Ways"? As *numen*
of the crossroads, Hermes was represented by a phallic stone; but
not all manifestations of this god are masculine in form. In her
autobiography, Audre Lorde called her lover Afrekete, identifying
her with the "youngest daughter" of the "great mother" of African
religion (*Zami* 252). Presiding over thresholds and crossroads, the
divine Afrekete represents the intersection between natural and su-
pernatural forces. By invoking Afrekete, as "mischievous linguist,
trickster [and] best-beloved whom we must all become" (255), Lorde
positioned herself on a boundary that is simultaneously erotic, cultural, and linguistic. Her poetic sequence *Black Unicorn* featured
Afrekete's masculine counterpart, Eshu: Lorde identified this figure
as "the linguist who both transmits and interprets"(6). Henry Louis
Gates says of the same god: "linguistically Esu [sic] is the ultimate
copula, connecting truth with understanding, the sacred with the
profane, text with interpretation" (*Signifying Monkey* 6). This divinity of the African diaspora embodies the archetypical guardian of
crossroads and intermediary of the gods, the original of the trick-
ster-figure known in African-American fable and song as the "Signifying Monkey." Gates describes this figure's discourse as "double-
voiced," and his very name as an oxymoron:

The ironic reversal of a received racist image of the black as simi-
anlike, the Signifying Monkey—he who dwells at the margins of discourse, ever punning, ever troping, ever embodying the ambiguities
of language—is our trope for repetition and revision, indeed, is our
trope of chiasmus itself, repeating and simultaneously reversing in
one deft, discursive act.   ("The blackness of blackness" 285–86).

The origin of *chiasmus* is in the Greek verb meaning "to place
cross-wise" or "mark with a cross," the cross being the letter *chi*.
Thus X marks the locus of reversal and revision in thought, and
of structural transition in language. As rhetorical trope in modern
literature, chiasmus retains an iconic function; this "hybrid word-
image" (Nänny 51) represents a crossing or turning-point, like the
chorus *strophe*. Shakespeare compressed Richard II's indecision into
a pun: "Ay, no; no, ay: for I must nothingness be" (*Richard II*, IV.1),
while H. D.'s Helen resists a similar fate with "nothingness? no, not
nothingness" (*Helen in Egypt* 199). At any level of the text, chiasmus
involves inversion, symmetry, transformation, and repetition: of
sounds, words and phrases, semantic, thematic, and narrative patterns. Adrienne Rich uses chiasmus to reinforce meaning in "A
woman in the shape of a monster / a monster in the shape of a
woman" (*Fact of a Doorframe* 114). In both prose and poetry, H. D.
revelled in its potential. Like Sappho's depiction of lovers "face to
face," she presents a mirror-image of same-sex love in "Her is
Fayne. Fayne is Her" (*Her* 181). She finds another kind of reciprocity
in Shakespeare's twins: "Judith was Hamnet. Hamnet was Judith"
(*By Avon River* 36). In *Red Roses for Bronze*, functional chiasmus is
equally explicit:

> Yourself in myself,
> mirror for a star,
> star for a mirror . . .
> (H. D., *Collected* 247).

Chiastic patterning, in which the form imitates or represents the
meaning, may well be an inheritance from the structural mnemonics
of archaic Greek poets such as Sappho and Homer. Page duBois has
demonstrated its presence in the well-known fragment that refers
to "the highest apple,"[12] and sees it as an integral feature of Sappho's
sound-effects (42). For this reason, chiasmus has been described as
"intrinsic to oral creation" (Nänny 53). Traces of that epic inheritance can be found in the question-and-answer patterns of *Helen in*

12. Campbell 105(a), Wharton 93.

Egypt, which are typified by delayed chiasmus: *"The Dream? The Veil? . . . The veil? the dream?"* (107, 138). In English verse, however, chiasmus is a legacy of lyric as well as epic. The baroque lyrist George Herbert, whom H. D. celebrated in *By Avon River*, makes much use of this trope in the reversals of his relationship with the Lord: "Let me not love thee, if I love thee not" (43). His poem "Bitter-Sweet" signifies on Sappho, while in H. D.'s "Fragment Forty" (*"Love . . . bitter-sweet"*),[13] the same oxymoron is turned into a complex chiasmus:

> Ah, love is bitter and sweet,
> but which is more sweet,
> the sweetness
> or the bitterness?
> (*Collected* 174)

As we might expect, chiastic structures occur most frequently in H. D.'s variations on Sappho. In "Fragment Thirty-six" (*"I know not what to do: my mind is divided"*),[14] disjunctive repetition enacts the speaker's dilemma: *"my mind* waits / to grapple with *my mind"*(*Collected* 167). When the same speaker considers whether to "turn" from art to love, or from love to art, the possibilities of turning are represented rhetorically by a delayed chiasmus:

> is song's gift best?
> is love's gift loveliest?
> . . . .
> is love's gift best?
> nay, song's the loveliest:
> (H. D., *Collected* 165–6)

A similar mirroring calls attention to H. D.'s depiction of the goddess of love, in "Fragment Forty-one,"[15] as "shameless and radiant . . . radiant and shameless" (*Collected* 181–83). This envelope form of chiasmus recalls the "folded texts" and hidden meanings of the ancients, reminding us of the hinged tablets used to consult the oracle at Dodona and the continuing practices of cryptography. Writing itself is a form of signifying—more vivid in Sappho's semi-literate times than in our own—and chiastic patterning is a kind of picture-writing.

---

13. Campbell 130, Wharton 40.
14. Campbell 51, Wharton 36.
15. Campbell 131, Wharton 41.

In the long-lost stanzas of "Amaranth," H. D. posited a genealogy in which Sappho was the vital link between herself (a mortal poet) and the immortal Aphrodite. In doing so, she implicitly claimed—as Shakespeare had done in his Sonnets—that she would achieve immortality through her work. In Sappho's Ode to Aphrodite (the complete poem now placed at the head of her *oeuvre*),[16] the goddess demonstrates a close and protective relationship to the poet by addressing her directly with the words "Who wrongs you, Sappho?" (Campbell 55). In H. D.'s "Amaranth," once again, "the goddess speaks"; her speech is addressed to the man (whom Martz identifies with Richard Aldington), but marks out the woman (whom he identifies with H. D.) as a poet under her special protection: "*She too is of the deathless*," says Aphrodite, "*she too is my poet*" (H. D., *Collected* 315).

Works Cited

Benstock, Shari. "Expatriate Sapphic Modernism: Entering Literary History." In Jay, Karla, and Joanne Glasgow, eds. *Lesbian Texts and Contexts: Radical Revisions*. New York: New York UP, 1990:183–203.

Burnett, Gary. *H. D. Between Image and Epic: The Mysteries of Her Poetics*. Ann Arbor, U.M.I. Research Press, 1990.

Campbell, David A., ed. and trans. *Greek Lyric Volume 1: Sappho and Alcaeus*. Loeb Classical Library. Cambridge, MA: Harvard UP, 1982.

Carson, Anne. *Eros the Bittersweet: An Essay*. Princeton, NJ: Princeton UP, 1986.

Collecott, Diana. *H. D. and Sapphic Modernism, 1910–1950*. Cambridge: Cambridge UP, 1999.

duBois, Page. *Sappho is Burning*. Chicago: U of Chicago P, 1995.

DuPlessis, Rachel Blau. *H. D.: The Career of that Struggle*. Brighton: Harvester, 1986.

———. *Writing Beyond the Ending*. Bloomington: Indiana UP, 1985.

Friedman, Susan Stanford, and Rachel Blau DuPlessis, eds. *Signets: Reading H. D.* Madison: U of Wisconsin P, 1990.

Gates, Henry Louis, Jr. " 'The blackness of blackness': A Critique of the Sign and the Signifying Monkey." In *Black Literature and*

---

16. Campbell 1, Wharton 1.

Literary Theory. Ed. H. L. Gates Jr. New York: Methuen, 1984:285–321.

———. *The Signifying Monkey: A Theory of Afro-American Literary Criticism*. Oxford: Oxford UP, 1988.

Greer, Germaine. *Slip-shod Sybils: Recognition, Rejection and the Woman Poet*. Harmondsworth: Penguin Books, 1995.

Gregory, Eileen. *H. D. and Hellenism: Classic Lines*. New York: Cambridge UP, 1997.

———. "Rose Cut in Rock: Sappho and H. D.'s *Sea Garden*." *Contemporary Literature* 27 (1986): 525–52. Repr. in Friedman, Susan Stanford, and Rachel Blau DuPlessis, eds. *Signets: Reading H. D*. Madison: U of Wisconsin P, 1990:129–54.

Gubar, Susan. "Sapphistries." *Signs* 10.1 (1984): 43–62.

H. D. *Bid Me to Live*. 1960. London: Virago Press, 1984.

———. *By Avon River*. New York: Macmillan, 1949.

———. *Collected Poems, 1912–1944*. Ed. Louis L. Martz. New York: New Directions, 1983.

———. *Helen in Egypt*. 1961. New York: New Directions, 1974.

———. *Her*. 1981. London: Virago Press, 1984.

———. "A Note on Poetry" (Letter to Norman Pearson). *Agenda* 25. 3–4 (1987 / 8): 71–76.

———. *Notes on Thought and Vision & The Wise Sappho*. 1982. London: Peter Owen, 1988.

———. *Palimpsest*. 1926. Carbondale: Southern Illinois UP, 1968.

———. *Tribute to Freud*. 1974. New York: New Directions, 1984.

Herbert, George. *The Complete English Poems*. Ed. John Tobin. Harmondsworth: Penguin Books, 1991.

Howe, Susan. *My Emily Dickinson*. Berkeley, CA: North Atlantic Books, 1985.

Jay, Karla, and Joanne Glasgow, eds. *Lesbian Texts and Contexts: Radical Revisions*. New York: New York UP, 1990.

Jay, Peter, ed. *The Greek Anthology: A Selection in Modern Verse Translations*. London: Allen Lane, 1973.

Jay, Peter, and Caroline Lewis, eds. *Sappho Through English Poetry*. London: Anvil Press, 1996.

Lawrence, D. H. *The Complete Poems*. Ed. Vivian de Sola Pinto and Warren Roberts. Harmondsworth: Penguin Books, 1977.

Lobel, Edgar, and Denys Page, eds. *Sappho: Poetarum Lesbiorum Fragmenta*. Oxford: Oxford UP, 1955.

Lorde, Audre. *The Black Unicorn*. New York: Norton, 1978.

———. *Sister Outsider: Essays and Speeches*. Trumansburg, NY: Crossing Press, 1984.

——. *Zami: A New Telling of My Name*. Trumansburg, NY: Crossing Press, 1983.

Nänny, Max. "Chiasmus in Literature: Ornament or Function?" *Word & Image* 4 (1988): 51–59.

Pound, Ezra. *Selected Prose*. Ed. William Cookson. London: Faber, 1973.

Preminger, Alex, and T.V.F. Brogan, eds. *The New Princeton Encyclopedia of Poetry and Poetics*. Princeton, NJ: Princeton UP, 1993.

Rich, Adrienne. *The Fact of a Doorframe: Poems, Selected and New, 1950–1984*. New York: Norton, 1984.

——. *On Lies, Secrets and Silence: Selected Prose, 1966–1978*. London: Virago Press, 1980.

Sedgwick, Eve Kosofsky. *Epistemology of the Closet*. London: Harvester Wheatsheaf, 1990.

Snyder, Jane McIntosh. *Lesbian Desire in the Lyrics of Sappho*. New York: Columbia UP, 1997.

Swann, Thomas B. *The Classical World of H. D.* Lincoln: U of Nebraska P, 1962.

Wharton, Henry Thornton. *Sappho: Memoir, Text, Selected Renderings*. 4th edition, 1898. Repr. Amsterdam: Liberac, 1974.

Woolf, Virginia. *A Room of One's Own*. 1928. Harmondsworth: Penguin Books, 1945.

H. D.'s Heterodoxy: the Lyric as a Site of Resistance

Eileen Gregory

My intent here is to define a particular aspect of the lyric that may allow us to assess H. D.'s lyric project more clearly. I propose a way of reading her poetry that imagines the edges against which a poem plays and pushes—that may recognize a kind of dialectical struggle at work even in so-called escapist poems with Hellenic themes. This quality of the poems can best be traced out in recognizing the demands H. D. makes on a reader, the way in which she implicates the reader in a staged resistance to orthodoxy and compels participation in censorable desire. This line of thought will conclude in a brief reflection on the ironies of institutionalizing H. D.—of normalizing or naturalizing her essentially heterodox and radical posture.

I must begin by making large and sweeping claims about the lyric genre itself. I am aware of the dangers of making such statements, but I risk them anyway, with the hope of calling into focus a few things that may be true. My first claim: that lyric poetry is potentially the most radical and subversive of literary genres. This assertion goes against common wisdom: the lyric has consistently been described in critical terms that stress its divorce from the public sphere. The fictions we have of lyric, coming essentially from German romanticism—the lyric as solitary speech, overhead song—effectively consign it to the sphere of the irrelevant and marginal.

Nevertheless, it has a subversive potential. In literal terms, as serving political resistance, it can be consigned to memory, known by heart, so that it has the possibility of surviving organized political suppression, bringing solace and remembrance; and it has frequently served invisibly to sustain defeated peoples when almost everything else of a known world has been destroyed. But in more ordinary terms, the lyric is potentially subversive because it concerns dimensions of experience that make irrepressible claims, and those claims almost inevitably challenge a conventional, collective sense of order. For this reason, lyric poetry is basically heterodox, I would claim. Orthodoxy, in its root sense, is right opinion: heterodoxy, in its root sense, is the *other* opinion—the body of opinion other than the orthodox. Lyric exploration, in its fidelity to desire and sensuousness, to feeling, to the hiddenness of meaning, constantly plays against, tests, and resists orthodoxy, by which I mean, the received large explanations of what is desirable and valuable in human life, the formulas of received wisdom encoding how one ought to feel and think.

This argument was recently confirmed for me in an eloquent study by Stephen Owen, *Mi-Lou: Poetry and the Labyrinth of Desire*, who likewise finds lyric poetry to be in a radical position of resistance to the norms of the community:

> By words the community binds us, and poetry fights back with words: perfect words, double-edged words, weighted words, words made to rebel against the drudgery to which the community commonly puts them. . . . Perilous conditions may be taken for granted, and unreasonable enthusiasms may become, for a moment, our own. . . . Most of all, poetry may seduce us with a freedom of opposition that can hold all contradictory and unrealized possibilities together in one fierce countermotion. (3)

Owen takes as his original Western paradigm the first known Greek lyric poet, the soldier Archilochus, living in the seventh century B.C. In a famous poem he cheerfully admits having abandoned his shield in battle in order to save his life—for which "lyric truthtelling" he was later driven from outraged Sparta. I was first struck with a similar nonchalance in studying the poetry of Sappho—according to legend, by far the greatest lyric poet of all. Sappho, too, writes in the seventh century B.C., writes a couple of centuries after Homer, and her poetry constantly takes his epic language, which defines the Greek political and cosmic order, the public heroic life, and turns it around, using it in the argument for intimate erotic life.

One of the surviving fragments shows this reversal in a startling
way:

> Some say a cavalry corps,
> some infantry, some, again,
> will maintain that the swift oars
>
> of our fleet are the finest
> sight on dark earth; but I say
> that whatever one loves, is.
>
> This is easily proved: did
> not Helen—she who had scanned
> the flower of the world's manhood—
>
> choose as first among men one
> who laid Troy's honor in ruin?
> warped to his will, forgetting
>
> love due her own blood, her own
> child, she wandered far with him.
> So Anactoria, although you
>
> being far away forget us,
> the dear sound of your footstep
> and light glancing in your eyes
>
> would move me more than glitter
> of Lydian horse or armored
> tread of mainland infantry
> (trans. Mary Barnard, 41)

The claim here is radical: it deliberately decenters and wholly reori-
ents a conception of value. The finest, most moving, most valuable
sight on the dark earth is whatever one loves. This is the illicit stance
of much lyric poetry: *Some* say, but *I* say. Where is the authority
determining what is most beautiful?—the radical I. But the emphasis here is not simply on the subjective, but more basically on the
claims of desire, when these are put in a contest with accepted,
orthodox claims. The beauty of light glancing in Anactoria's eyes,
set against the golden glitter of armies. The most delicate and
ephemeral, set against the most massive. What is true of this poem
is true of other of Sappho's lyrics, from what we can tell from fragments. She was known for her writing of *epithalamia*, wedding
songs, in the context of festivals of marriage—the institution in

which the wife, in bearing and nurturing children, serves the preser-vation of a patriarchal order. But Sappho's songs in celebration of female homoerotic life—the life of beauty, grace, and desire culti-vated among girls and young women—employs all the diction and tropes of the marriage songs, so that homoerotic bonds, the ties of desire, affection, and friendship between women, are seen as sacred and binding to the soul. In both these instances, Sappho's appropria-tion of the language of orthodoxy in celebrations of the sphere of intimate life is a form of resistance and subversion.

I am suggesting in these examples that the lyric, in its fidelity to the claims of erotic, affective life, pushes against known boundaries, against the constraints of accepted descriptions of the valuable, the pious, the normal, the true. Without this kind of poetic resistance, those explanations given by culture—unreflective, proverbial, habit-ual, morally coercive—obliterate distinction, grace, and elegance, cancel as trivial what seems most precious and significant, falsify the feelings. In other words, the lyric may be understood not as isolated speech (overheard, solitary song), but as a collective site of resistance, serving to insist upon a certain kind of truthfulness not defined by rationality or social solidarity. For certain poets this kind of resistance is constant. Emily Dickinson's poems so frequently begin in rage at the pious cliché that is untrue to real suffering and joy: "They say that 'Time assuages' / Time never did assuage / An actual suffering strength / As sinews do, with age." And the poem is not only a site of resistance, but also potentially a site of conver-sion. The Greeks associated the lyric with the enchantment of magic spells, with incantation initiating daemonic possession, and with the melting power of divine persuasion (Segal). It persuades one to imagine the world from the vantage point of feeling and desire, and this is a dangerous thing, in that desire ruptures and overturns the known and proven. And this is the subversive dimension of the lyric, explaining why so little of Sappho and other Greek lyricists survives, why, in fact, manuscripts were at some points systemati-cally destroyed, but why almost all of authors like Pindar, Thucyd-ides, Plato survive—writers who substantiate the value of male, public, political order.

This lyric resistance to the orthodox is one of its essential ele-ments, existing in even the simplest of lyrics, and in simple ways: in the stretching and reversing of language, in the breaking of accepted forms to serve new necessities. It is to some extent a formal matter, because established poetry itself becomes part of an orthodoxy that a poet is compelled to resist, so that the poetic line and poetic cadences become fraught arenas. And in another complication, the position of a woman poet is a distinct one in terms of this argument, in that she must also resist the conscriptions of a male lyric tradition, male reflections of the nature of erotic life, feeling, reflection. That gendered resistance is, of course, central to many poets, certainly to Dickinson and H. D., so there are many kinds of resistance possibly at work in a poem at once.

If these ideas are tenable, then so might be this principle of reading: One might grasp what is really at stake in a poem by attempting to discern how it resists, and what it resists—understanding the implied or explicit dialectic of the poem. In terms of H. D.'s poetry, this is a matter of noting the presence of the censor. So much of her poetry counters a critical voice or voices more or less unspoken, articulating moral and aesthetic norms that stand for confinement and deathliness. Critics have long pointed out this tension in the poems of *Sea Garden*—clearly the elemental "sea garden" itself and its ascetic ecstasy is in opposition to "cities," and its wildness in opposition to the hothouse flowers of the "sheltered garden." And the passion and exhilaration of these poems, their insistence on a difficult and broken sense of beauty, are constantly distinguished from conventional senses of beauty: the marred and torn sea rose is "more precious / than a wet rose / single on a stem" (*Collected Poems* 5). Almost every poem in this collection draws a sharp edge of some kind. But I would argue that this dialectic is also present even in the more sensuous and classical poems of *Hymen*; the edge there is indeed their sometimes explicit eroticism and sensuality, which is deliberate, and firmly performed. This impurity or luxuriousness made her husband Richard Aldington uneasy, and caused T. S. Eliot to voice his aversion to their "morbid carnality" (Aldington 179; Eliot 488). And here perhaps we note another principle of reading in these terms: one knows what is at stake in a lyric poem, what it resists, by noting what aggravates and agitates the critics, what touches a nerve, impinging on orthodox order.

I would like to explore the complexity of H. D.'s play with the censor, while suggesting another dimension of her heterodoxy: the way in which she engages the reader so that he or she is compelled to judgment and choice, compelled to affiliation or rejection. H. D.'s poems are marked by a peculiarity that comes from their radical orientation to the obverse, that angle of vision "when my soul turned round, / perceiving the other-side of everything" ("Sigil,"

Collected Poems 412–13). What does it mean to see from "the other-
side"? H. D. makes remarkable demands upon the reader, and also
invites remarkable intimacy—within the context of a possible conversion of perspective.

I would like first to consider a poem entitled "Epitaph," which
appears on H. D.'s gravestone in Bethlehem, Pennsylvania. It was
published in *Red Roses for Bronze* (1931).

> So I may say,
> "I died of living,
> having lived one hour";
>
> so they may say,
> "she died soliciting
> illicit fervour";
>
> so you may say,
> "Greek flower, Greek ecstasy
> reclaims for ever
> one who died
> following
> intricate songs' lost measure."
>   (*Collected Poems* 299–300)

It is easy to mistake this poem as a slight, inconsequential thing, as
so much of H. D.'s poetry has been mistaken. Susan Friedman first
pointed out to me—as we were standing before H. D.'s gravestone
reading these lines on the centennial of her birthday—how very
strange and equivocal they are. The poem represents a somewhat
typical practice of hers: it teases, provokes, and confounds, and,
moreover, it has an edge. The poem disconcerts in its hypothetical,
conditional mode—I *may* say—because epitaphs usually are termi-
nal in utterance ("Here lies one . . .,"). And the poem disconcerts
in the offhand, casual way (so . . . so . . . so . . .) that it projects the
possible trajectories of a reputation, the ways of summing up the
life and career of the dead poet in future time. H. D. is perfectly
aware that reputations are unstable and subject to arbitrariness and
distortion. More than this, as so many of H. D.'s lyrics do, the poem
sets up a linguistic field of differing and even antithetical voices
that play against each other: "So I may say . . . So they may
say . . . so you may say." For me, the troubling aspect of the poem
is the way in which it covertly traps the reader within this triangle
of hypotheses.

The poem implicitly invites the question: Where, finally, would the reader position herself in the act of summing the poet up, were he or she called into account by an epitaph? Let's look at the turns of the poem. I would say that there are three fictions here of the poet's career, none of them entirely adequate. The first, "So I may say, / I died of living, / having lived one hour": the lyric I, speaking as subject, sums up the life in terms of singleness and intensity, indeed in keeping with the typical fiction of lyric subjectivity. Second, "They" say, speaking of the poet as other: "she died / soliciting illicit fervour." This judgment is a crucial one, at the center of this poem, and at the center of H. D.'s writing, because it does, in fact, represent predominant critical judgments of H. D.'s lyrics that the poetry solicits illicit fervour; that is, it summons from the gods, pleads for *in* the reader, a possession by feeling and emotion, an excitation and animation, that is "illicit"—a word that means illegitimate, not allowed, prohibited by law or custom, unauthorized. The word "soliciting," used in conjunction with "illicit," recalls "solicitation" in the criminal sense—the invitation to prostitution. I don't think I am pushing the implications of this position; critics who dislike H. D. dislike her intensely, and they imply moral grounds for their disdain. Moreover, H. D. is lucidly aware of her illicitness. It is no accident that major poems center around Helen of Troy and Mary Magdalen. H. D. likes illicitness, the posture of standing beyond the boundary of the sanctioned, daring one to step over, to step in.

So the position of "them" in this play of possibilities represents the dismissal of the career, coming out of an antipathy that is in some sense accurate in grasping something essential at stake. Then there is the third possibility, the most puzzling, what "you" may say: "Greek flower, Greek ecstasy / reclaims forever / one who died / following / intricate songs' lost measure." This third judgment objectifies the poet: *one* who is reclaimed by the dead, who has become her song, the impersonal "H. D.," and thereby gathered into the artifice of eternity (the timeless "Greek flower"). Is this "you" the reader—the intimate other to the poet, the one whom she trusts to accept her terms? Is this judgment the preferred one? It *seems* like a closure and a summing up, because it is lengthier and metrically more heavily weighted than the others; intricate songs' lost measure. On the other hand, the three positions are parallel in structure, and they belong to a single sentence. I suspect that at the time of writing this epitaph, around 1930, H. D. is ambivalent about this Greek persona, and above the audience that has insisted on it—the "you" who must have the crystalline poet, who will petrify her in this position (as indeed seems to be the case, since this stanza is engraved in stone in Bethlehem). So the "you" here (the reader) is not entirely trusted.

But for me something else happens in reading the last stanza. The reader does respond to the closure that it implies, to its sublime lift, its suggestion of finality. And I least resist it. "Greek flower, Greek ecstasy" seems to me like illicit solicitation: too much Greekness, "flower," and "ecstasy" together too much. She pushes me too far. H. D. frequently pushes even a sympathetic reader very far. So then, am I positioned with the censors in the second stanza? Perhaps so; either that, or I accept this poet as simply extravagant (a word which means, by the way, wandering outside the boundaries). H. D.'s "Epitaph" taken as a whole, I am arguing, sums up the career as a daring performance within a complex linguistic space. The reader is provocatively brought into this performance and made complicit in the multiple turns with regard to authoritative voice. In particular, the reader is made complicit in the gesture of censorship, forced, in a sense, either to reject or acknowledge affiliation with scandalous excess.

This reading—which may be oversubtle—comes from observing a certain point of consistency in H. D.'s writing: her awareness of edges against which her writing pushes, and her demands upon a reader to enter into alliance with her vision. She has an amazing ability to name accurately the terms in which her work is criticized and dismissed: the censor—whom she knows intimately—is everywhere a part of the dynamic of her writing. And the reader, as in this poem, is often implicated in that dynamic, called to judgment and choice. The better-known case takes place in *The Walls Do Not Fall*, when the poet is cataloguing the attributes of the "old self" that now seem inadequate in the context of a desire for transformation. This amazing catalogue of flaws in personal and artistic integrity—it goes on for three sections of the poem—includes, but goes far beyond what the most negative of H. D.'s critics have claimed about her writing. It concludes:

> . . . imagery
> done to death; perilous ascent,
> ridiculous descent; rhyme, jingle,
>
> overworked assonance, nonsense,
> juxtaposition of words for words' sake,
>
> without meaning, undefined; imposition,

deception, indecisive weather-vane;

disagreeable, inconsequent syllables,
too malleable, too brittle,

over-sensitive, under-definitive,
clash of opposites, fight of emotion

and sterile invention—
you find all this?
                              (*Collected Poems* 534–35)

For the detached reader to be turned upon and accused so suddenly is one of the most shocking moments in *Trilogy*. The reader
was perhaps imagining herself as benign and indulgent, but she has
nevertheless been secretly gratified at the poet's self-excoriation, at
the clarity of it, the unstoppable flood of it, and because, after all,
the reader *has* found all these flaws in the writing. It appears for
seventy lines that both the poet and the reader are engaging fully
in the perspective and the rhetoric of the censor; but suddenly the
poet withdraws again into her integrity or self-possession, and turns
her rage and irony outward. The reader sees that he or she has all
along been implicated with the censor—the one, as in "Epitaph,"
who wants to sum up the career in terms of its ungainly excess.
What happens in this remarkable passage, I think, is that the poet
paradoxically earns respect in the very catalogue of her failures,
and that the turn upon the reader, with fresh authority, serves to
provoke a crisis of affiliation. Is the reader to see as the critic sees, or
follow the extravagant turns of the poet in process? This aggressive
question—"you find all this?"—obliquely demands, "are you still
with me?"

These two poems represent a kind of entrapment of the reader in
a compact with the poet. Of course, one is always free to reject the
compact (and many do). But H. D. also typically engages the reader
in another way—in another linguistic space characterized by intimacy—startling and sometimes disconcerting intimacy, because the
reader finds herself here in another space, governed by strange necessities of desire. One of the most compelling of these is "Helmsman," from *Sea Garden*: "O be swift— / we have always known
you wanted us" (*Collected Poems* 5–7). The voice is a collective one,
in which "we" are included. But what is this desire that we have
always known, and who is that has *always* wanted us, and what is
this urgency that compels the whole poem, a desired connection

without which we are caught in random rhythms: "our boat
climbs—hesitates—drops— / climbs—hesitates—crawls back— /
climbs—hesitates / O be swift—we have always known you
wanted us." Whatever this power is that is solicited by us, it touches
the place where self-knowledge and desire are joined in an openness
to possession, abandonment of control (Helmsman—another steers).
This large gesture of the poem also defines its edge: it is a scandalous kind of self-surrender.

Another unnerving poem that takes the reader into intimate but
unknown relations is "Adonis" (*Collected Poems* 47–48):

I

Each of us like you
has died once,
each of us like you
has passed through drift of wood-leaves,
cracked and bent
and tortured and unbent
in the winter frost,
then burnt into gold points,
lighted afresh,
crisp amber, scales of gold-leaf,
gold turned and re-welded
in the sun-heat;

each of us like you
has died once,
each of us has crossed an old wood-path
and found the winter leaves
so golden in the sun-fire
that even the live wood-flowers
were dark.

II

Not the gold on the temple-front
where you stand,
is as gold as this,
not the gold that fastens your sandal,
nor the gold reft
through your chiselled locks
is as gold as this last year's leaf,
not all the gold hammered and wrought
and beaten
on your lover's face,
brow and bare breast
is as golden as this:
each of us like you

has died once,
each of us like you
stands apart, like you
fit to be worshipped.

It is difficult to articulate the impact of these disconcerting first lines: "Each of us like you / has died once." The "you" addressed in the poem, like the helmsman, is a presence, a dying body that each of us knows. *Each* of us: this not only includes "us" collectively, but individually, and the inclusion of the reader in these terms necessitates a complex kind of recollection. If indeed each of us has died once, how has this happened, how has each of us died? How have I died? I ask myself, and I *do*, strangely, wonder. We have died like Adonis: Adonis, the lover of Aphrodite, killed violently, mourned by the goddess: also a fertility god who dies and is reborn each year. So this death implicitly has to do with erotic suffering and annihilation; but it also entails a process of rebirth. What is the death of Adonis like, that each has suffered? It is like the transformation of fallen leaves within the distintegrative process of winter: leaves "cracked and bent / and tortured and unbent / in the winter frost, / then burnt into gold points, / and lighted afresh." The poem emphasizes not the new life of spring, but the dead and tortured leaves, latent in winter. This latency, hiddenness in death, is what is golden, precious, beautiful, more golden that the statues of the gods. Through this transforming loss and latency "[e]ach of us like you / has died once, / each of us like you / stands apart, like you / fit to be worshipped." These last lines too are disconcerting. How does each of us stand apart in this death, fit to be worshipped? Because, perhaps, this death, this erotic suffering, is what *makes* us *each*—distinct from others. But worshipped! The implications of this are shocking, because at this point we might begin to realize that the poet has been assuming that each of us is the body of the god. She has been compelling us imaginatively through the disintegration of the god's dying body, as if each of us underwent the mystery that the myth points to. The reader as divine body: this is heterodoxy, if ever there was.

These remarks on H. D.'s heterodoxy—her resistance to the confinements of right-opinion—lead me to ask another, general question, which struck me upon my very first encounter with this poetry, and that remains with me. How can H. D. be accommodated in the academy? Because the academy as an institution represents intellectually the most coercive kinds of orthodoxy. The reading of poetry right now takes place in an intellectual climate that sets up strict categories of what is acceptable and allowable. The climate of the academy, I would venture to say, has never been more censorious. H. D.'s writing really does challenge the very suppositions of this kind of institution, that are built to master and make intelligible and controllable the whole realm of feeling, of intimacy, that poetry opens up. Why *do* we read poetry in universities? What are we claiming to want to know, when to read it in this context encourages one to ignore its riskiness, its profound subversions and challenges? Robert Duncan's remarks in one of the early segments of *The H. D. Book* have struck me from the beginning as getting to the heart of H. D.'s heterodox challenge:

> The way the poet H. D. admitted, let-in, to her self through the poem, and then, in a double sense, admitted to the listener or reader, . . . let life use you this way—this was not shameful (as crying out, "*O Wind, rend open the heat,*" being intense about trivial things like pears, threatened the composure of household, gang, school and city or state, and was shamed, put down, as one must put away childish things), to propose the truth of what was felt, to articulate just the emotion that was most vulnerable and in need, took courage. (10)

The censors—not only in the other, but in each of us trained to tame the wildness of language—are very powerful. And in this context, reading H. D. risks shame, one of the most powerful and visceral of emotional tools of orthodoxy. H. D., of course, knew the censor too, and the devastation of shame, but consistently chose, throughout her career, to risk the boundaries, to risk shamelessness.

Works Cited

Aldington, Richard. *Richard Aldington and H. D.: The Early Years in Letters.* Ed. Caroline Zilboorg. Bloomington: Indiana UP, 1992.

Duncan, Robert. "Beginnings. Chapter 1 of the H. D. Book: Part I." *Coyote's Journal* 5–6 (1966): 8–31.

Eliot, T. S. *The Letters of T. S. Eliot. Volume 1: 1898–1922.* Ed. Valerie Eliot. New York: Harcourt, Brace, Jovanovich, 1988.

H. D. *Collected Poems 1912–1944.* Ed. Louis L. Martz. New York: New Directions, 1983.

Owen, Stephen. *Mi-Lou: Poetry and the Labyrinth of Desire.* Cambridge, MA: Harvard UP, 1989.

Sappho. *Sappho: A New Translation*. Trans. Mary Barnard. Berkeley
   and Los Angeles: U of California P, 1958.
Segal, Charles. "Eros and Incantation: Sappho and Oral Poetry."
   Arethusa 7.2 (1974): 139–60.

Between Painting and Writing: Figures of Identity in H. D.'s Early Poetry

Marina Camboni

> Every woman has that quality of being a
> virgin, of being the temptress-prostitute, of
> being the mother. I feel that these, more than
> anything, are the common life of all women.
> —Martha Graham, *Blood Memory*

Mary Magdalene or, of Chance and Necessity

Chance brought me to London on the last day of an exhibition at the Tate Gallery devoted to "The Age of Rossetti, Burne-Jones & Watts."[1] As I entered the first room, a painting drew my attention, Frederick Sandys's *Mary Magdalene* (circa 1859). It immediately reminded me of H. D.'s Mary of Magdala in the *Trilogy* and inspired the train of thought that is the starting point of this essay. When translating H. D.'s *Trilogy* I had examined a great number of paintings representing Mary of Magdala, trying to visualize the shape of

---

1. The full title and dates of the exhibition are: "The Age of Rossetti, Burne-Jones & Watts: Symbolism in Great Britain 1860–1910" (October 1997–January 1998).

the alabaster jar Mary wants to obtain from the Magus Kaspar, in order to select the Italian word capable of conveying its particularity. I knew how important figurative art, and Renaissance paintings in particular, had been for H. D. and her work. No painting, however, had given me the clue I needed. But when I saw Sandys's *Mary Magdalene* I knew his representation was related to H. D.'s Mary Magdala, even though she might not have had it in mind, or even have seen it, when she wrote *The Flowering of the Rod*. As a Pre-Raphaelite, Sandys shared aesthetic aims with others of the Brotherhood; these were expressed in a similar style and, to some extent, in what the art critic Erwin Panofsky called common intersubjective content (153).

Pre-Raphaelite arts and crafts had not only been central to H. D.'s apprenticeship and youthful imagination, as she acknowledges in *Asphodel* and in late autobiographical writings, but, at least until World War I, they were very much part of her everyday life in London where, for example, she regularly attended tea-parties at Violet Hunt's house, South Lodge.[2] There William Morris's wallpaper and chintzes were a visible presence of the recent past, actively contributing to the cultural atmosphere of the gatherings. In *Asphodel*, Hermione, one of H. D.'s alter egos, addressing her ostensibly insensitive friend Fayne Rabb, traces a direct line of descent from the painters of the Pre-Raphaelite Brotherhood and the Decadent writers: "We are legitimate children. We are children of the Rossettis, of Burne-Jones, of Swinburne. We were in the thoughts of Wilde," she insists, concluding soon after: "London repudiated the rhododendron beauty of those people. Or outgrew it" (53–54).

Walter Pater had anticipated that the following generations would be "renerved, modified by the ideas" (158) of this small but highly influential group of writers and critics. As Eileen Gregory has clearly demonstrated (*Hellenism* 75), Pater's criticism had provided the architectural framework connecting the Pre-Raphaelites and the Decadents. Even though H. D.'s modernist contemporaries in London had rejected Pater together with the Decadents, he formed a part of what might be called their cultural genetic material. Like Virginia Woolf, who knew that she had inherited "instincts already acquired by thousands of ancestresses in the past" (*Moments* 80), H. D. was well aware of both her ethnic and cultural imprinting,

---

2. Besides Barbara Guest's biography of H. D., *Herself Defined*, see Violet Hunt's *Flurried Years*, Brigit Patmore's *My Friends When Young*, and *Rebecca West: A Life*, by Victoria Glendinning.

and knew that her vision of herself as woman had been molded by Pre-Raphaelite images.

Yet, as an American and post-Victorian who had had access to higher education, she was also one of the New Women who could imagine themselves in roles different from those of mother and muse. Moreover, the city where H. D. had lived ever since 1911, where her autobiographical narratives are set, where her Imagist group and related artists gathered—among them women actively involved in the feminist cause, like May Sinclair, Violet Hunt, and Brigit Patmore—was also the London where the Suffragist militants demonstrated in the streets to obtain the vote, in whose prisons women were force-fed, where the "woman's cause" (Rowbotham 13) was as much a part of everyday life and discourse as the Decadent and "modern" aesthetic was a part of artistic discourse.

There were other attitudes H. D. may have felt she shared with the Decadents: their criticism of Victorian mores and morality, and their social marginality. As the editors of *The Freewoman* phrased it, the situation of contemporary women was such that they were "compelled . . . to recognise the disorder of living according to the law, the immorality of being moral, and the monstrousness of the social code" ("New Morality" 61).[3] As an aspiring writer, she may also have subscribed to Oscar Wilde's idea that "all Art" was "to a certain degree a mode of acting, an attempt to realise one's own personality on some imaginative plane" (49).

In *Asphodel*, Hermione defines herself as a literary and cultural subject through an intersubjective confrontation with Fayne, her lover and specular self.[4] In this way, however, while acknowledging her debt to the Pre-Raphaelites and the Decadents, Hermione also

---

3. In 1911, Dora Marsden, a suffragist and former member of the WSPU, in joint editorship with Mary Gawthorpe, launched *The Freewoman*, a journal devoted to the construction of a feminist sense of self. It later became *The New Freewoman* and, from 1914 to 1919, *The Egoist*, the journal which published Pound and the other Imagists. H. D. was its literary coeditor, together with her husband Richard Aldington in 1916 and early 1917, before T. S. Eliot took over. Dora Marsden may well have been the model for the feminist organizer in H. D.'s narrative sketch "The Suffragette," as Susan Stanford Friedman has pointed out (*Penelope's Web* 7). On H. D. and Dora Marsden see also Collecott, chapter 5, and Camboni, "Dora Marsden, Ezra Pound H. D. and 'The Art of the future.' "

4. See also the instances of intersubjective confrontation in *Trilogy* analysed by Marina Sbisà in the present volume.

admits that she is divided between her own acceptance and the widespread criticism, from both literary and feminist avant-gardes, of all types of symbolism.

In the 1940s, H. D. devoted two as yet unpublished novels to the Pre-Raphaelite circle: *The Sword Went Out to Sea* (*Synthesis of a Dream*) (1946–47) and *White Rose and the Red* (1947?—48).[5] And in a late autobiographical piece, tracing a line of development in her art, she explains that she knows "more about them or sometimes seem[s] to know more about the Rossetti-Morris circle" than she does about her own contemporaries, that there is a "sense of continuity" that "inspires me" ("H. D. by Delia Alton" 194–95). Considering herself their soul daughter, she stresses the spiritual rather than the genetic links that tie her to these men of the past, the key figure of this spiritual genealogy being William Morris, whose little tea table—a prophetic tripod—she had bought and used, in the Second World War years, for her séances.

If, in the quotation from *Asphodel*, Hermione represents herself deterministically as a genetic result of the Decadents, in the second instance the writer H. D. herself manifestly spins the spiritual and imaginary thread that led her back to the nineteenth-century artists. Although they look very similar, nothing could be more different than the two statements, the first one asserting a necessity, the second a free choice. Between them stretch not only time and H. D.'s personal, social, and cultural history, but also the authorial, thematic, formal, and mythical changes in her poetry.

In her book-length essay *H. D. and the Victorian Fin de Siècle*, Cassandra Laity has devoted an articulate and groundbreaking analysis to the relationship between H. D. and the Decadent writers. And Eileen Gregory's *H. D. and Hellenism*, while sharing Laity's conclusions, further investigates the impact that Paterian and Decadent models of Hellenism had on H. D.'s writing. Gregory rightly points out how H. D.'s Hellenism and her visionary and oracular projections of self are part of her search for a spiritual integrity and an authentic and autonomous poetic expression as a woman; nevertheless, she does not connect them to contemporary feminist representations of both social change and construction of identity. Moreover, though emphasizing the influence of Paterian statuary on H. D.'s writing, she overlooks the way H. D. also associates writing and

---

5. The manuscripts are in the Collection of American Literature, Beinecke Rare Book and Manuscript Library, Yale University. For dates of composition see Friedman and Duplessis 457.

painting, which she sees as parallel ways of rendering inner experiences.

What follows is an analysis of figures of identity in H. D.'s poetry, starting with their relation to and difference from Pre-Raphaelite and Decadent images of women. I shall consider the personal, political, philosophical, aesthetic, and ethical aspects of H. D.'s poems and point out ways in which differences in her early and later poetic works correspond to her increasing sense of authority as a poet and her growing belief in the social significance of poetry.

Figures

Through Hermione's naming, one after the other, Pre-Raphaelite painters and Decadent writers, H. D. reveals her conception of poetry and painting as distinct artistic concretizations of the same perceptual and emotional content. She makes it even clearer through the first of her fictional alter-egos, Midget of *Paint It Today*, who feels she can choose to tell "a story or set a scene of a blue world" (25), where the color blue stands for her friend-lover Josepha, whose eyes reflect the blue of a painting by Monet. The opening paragraph of *Paint It Today* introduces Midget's questioning mind: "A portrait, a painting? Do not paint it of yesterday's rapt and rigid formula nor of yesterday's day-after-tomorrow's criss-cross—jagged, geometric, prismatic. Do not paint yesterday's day-after-tomorrow destructiveness nor yesterday's fair convention. But how and as you will—*paint it today*" (3).

What is relevant here is not so much the reference to the portrait as a genre, as the emphasis on the present, with the narrator positioning herself in the middle of a line whose opposed extremities are past and future styles. By opting for "today," she criticizes the more conventional styles of the past and the geometric-futuristic style that she sees as being the result of past destructive attitudes rather than representing the new in art.

But her present has two temporal dimensions. As the present of experience, bound to the moment, it is always a "today," a presence immediately to be transformed into its mnemic image that, as time passes, will be stored in the mind and, "hung with the affections of the past," will become a weight and a tyrant (*Paint* 10). This presentational and static "today" (living) is in manifest contrast with the mobile present of "another state of emotional life or being, a life of being that contain(s) the past and the future" (being) (12). H. D.'s work as an artist was from the start also a search for a connection between the two states of *living* and *being*, where *being* rather than *living* is dynamic and in process.

In her poetry, figures animate the dialectics of *being* and *living*.

The word "figure," while suggesting a spatial form, spans the visual and verbal art mediums, in that it can refer to pure creations of the mind, represented fictional or historical beings, conscious elaborations and figures in the unconscious, as well as rhetorical expressions. Erwin Panofsky sees in the figure in a painting a unit visually molded (182), and stresses its structural function. André Chastel, on the other hand, calls attention to the subjective and referential power of figures and also points out the human tendency to gather all knowledge within them, or to endow the intelligible with a personality (28), a tendency to be found in a variety of art forms. In literature, while figures as visual images, characters, or symbols belong to fictional invention, as figures of speech they belong to *elocution*, the word, and contribute to convey the overall sense of a writer's work.

Figures may become material objects within whose form stories can be contained or symbolically condensed. They can also be the carriers of inner drives and identifying projections, of passions and desires—Dante's first movers of the world and of actions. They are what I call "figures of identity."[6] They are the basis of this essay, as they appear in H. D.'s work, in their different concretizations, whether connected to canonical representations in verbal and visual art, or evocative of natural or mythical characters, subjects of will and action, or as figures of speech.

Such figures can be defined as the poet's "subjective correlatives."

Paintable

It is precisely the contrast between *being* and *living*, rendered as an opposition between symbolic and classical or imagistic art, that H. D. brings to the fore through Hermione's "Morgan le Fay" identity when in *Asphodel* she writes:

> Paintable. Things seen in perspective become things to be grappled with. Art. Isn't art just re-adjusting nature to some intellectual focus?

---

6. What I call "figures of identity" are images of a complex psychic reality. Like Freud's parental figures, they are projections or constructions that are necessary for the development of the individual.

The things are there all the time, but art, a Chinese bowl, a Chinese idol, a brass candle-stick make a focus, a sense of proportion like turning the little wheel of an opera glass, getting a great mass of inchoate colour and form into focus, focussing on one small aspect of life though really it is only a tiny circle, a tiny circle. You get life into a tiny circle by art and that was where Morgan le Fay was wrong with her craft for she would say all art is man's mere imagining and see, the shell by the shore, the one petal of a water-lily is a sort of crystal glass, a bright surface and you yourself staring at it, may make things in the air, pictures, images, things beyond beauty beautiful.

(175)

Setting what can be called realism in art against a more symbolic, imaginative, and aesthetic form, Hermione first traces a line from Renaissance perspective to Cézanne's focal point, which, like an opera glass, delimits but also organizes the compositional space.[7] Hermione next opposes the perspectival tradition of painting to symbolic art in which figures, charged with emotions, are means of self-expression for the artist as well as *loci* of beauty, and things are spiritually connected. In this case, the work of art is a suggestive symbol, not a sign representing natural reality: it stirs emotions rather than produce sensations. The dynamic pull between a present and a symbolic time where past and future unite is clearly expressed in this passage.

The name, the anchor in language to which stories and mythical constructions are bound,[8] is the place where Hermione's figure for her magician self and Sandys's *Morgan le Fay* (1862–63) meet, only to lead to different symbolic meanings. In Sandys's painting, the Queen of Avalon, a witch who casts spells against her brother King Arthur, exemplifies the mendacious and predatory character of patriarchal representations of such mythical figures as Lilith, Cassandra, Salome, Medusa, and Medea, who also loom large in Pre-Raphaelite paintings and the works of Decadent writers, an indication of the artist's sexual anxiety.

As Morgan le Fay, Hermione identifies herself, like Midget in *Paint It Today*, with society's outcasts, who include "we magicians,

---

7. According to Herbert Read, this line can be extended to include what he calls "the imagist." "It has been claimed that the capacity for realizing and retaining the image in a state of perceptive vividness is the quality that distinguishes the artist from other men, but in fact it is the distinguishing quality of one type of artist—the imagist" (24).

8. On the linguistic and symbolic meaning of names see my "Hilda Doolittle, la donna che divenne il suo nome," especially pp. 7–17.

we failures, we ourselves, our very selves, poets and lovers," and especially lesbian lovers "excrementitious . . . projected forth, crystallized out, orient pearls"(*Paint* 23, 18). Morgan Le Fay is a figure of identity of the poet as gender-identified and marginal woman, who creates beauty (a pearl) out of her body as if out of material waste.

Together with the name, Sandys's and H. D.'s versions of Morgan Le Fay share the attribute of psychic power: a female power that male Decadent writers believed was dangerous to them, but was considered by many women to be a positive force, associated with intuition. The words of the editors of *The Freewoman* help us to understand H. D.'s use of Morgan le Fay as one of her figures of identity:

> Seeking the realization of the will of others . . . women have almost lost the instinct for self-realization . . . but they have gained something which . . . is the highest manifestation of spiritual intimacy known to the world . . . women's intuitive faculty, a sixth sense for the cognition of psychic phenomena. Through this sense, women will make their greatest revelations of life-manifestation to the world. By means of it, they will push open the door of the super-world. . . . We can now proceed to state that the faculty has been bought at a high price, so high indeed as to annul its entire virtue.
>
> Women have the intuitive faculty, without the experience upon which to practice it. ("The New Morality" 62)

This psychic and spiritual potential was not really a power, but the only legacy women had left to other women. Though resulting from a forced renunciation of intelligence, soul, and self, it could become a stepping-stone for women who wanted to explore the material, intellectual, and spiritual potential of life.

Both early and late in life, H. D. explicitly connected her spiritual potential to her gift of poetry, which was also her gift of vision. This awareness enabled her to identify with figures associated with magic, mysterious powers, or community with the godhead, like Joan of Arc, Cassandra, and Mary of Magdala. Especially in her earliest poetry, however, (see "The Gift," *Collected* 338–39), this gift was represented as divisive, dispersing her deeper identity in two opposite directions, one leading to the rock-hard truths of eternal life, the other to the consuming pleasures of the senses.

Sandys's *Mary Magdalene* makes its appeal to the senses. She belongs to the host of fallen women and femmes fatales who spin a magical web that entraps men. Victorian viewers would have seen it as the representation of a prostitute, because prostitutes were often spoken of as Magdalenes. The prototype of the repentant sinner in Christian art, especially after the Counter-Reformation, she carries an ointment jar, her identifying attribute, which she may hold in her hands or have at her feet, while her long loose hair, suggestive of her past life as a whore or courtesan, is also a sign of repentance.

In Sandys's painting, Mary's head and bust are shown against a background of dark green wallpaper with a pattern of paler leaves, reminiscent of a Morris design. Her hair worn loose, flowing like molten metal across her shoulders and over a shawl with a floral print, reminds one of Dante Gabriel Rossetti's Lilith, whose "enchanted hair" is "the first gold" ("Body's Beauty" 1.4), and of the bride through whose hair "sudden serpents" seem to hiss in Swinburne's "Laus Veneris" (14, II. 115–16). Mary Magdalene, like Rossetti's Lilith, is "subtly of herself contemplative," and in this attitude can draw "men to watch the bright web she can weave, / Till heart and body and life are in its hold" ("Body's Beauty" II.6–8).[9] Holding the ointment jar fast at her neck in a gesture that marks her claim to the precious possession, she emphasizes a passion already embodied by this object. She looks into outer space, as if unaware of any observer, with a soft and intensely mystical contemplative gaze. Indifferent to whatever may happen around her, she is enveloped in a sensuous silence, her parted lips ready for a kiss rather than for speech. Wrested from her story in the gospels, she is "in state" (Bairati 49), a static symbol reenacting the fixed role she is assigned in Victorian, indeed in Christian tradition, reinforcing both cultural and artistic codes.

Mary is most notably alone; she is there for the painter to contemplate and portray, like the figure in *The Little White Girl: Symphony in White No. 2* (1864), by James McNeil Whistler, a transplanted American who was a friend of Swinburne and the Rossettis. In this painting a young woman dressed in white is shown standing beside a fireplace and holding a Japanese fan. Like Sandys's Magdalene, she gazes with unseeing eyes, apparently lost in thought. The reflected image of her head and face is seen in the mirror. The girl, young and graceful as she stands before the looking glass, seems careworn in her mirrored reflection.

---

9. A description of his painting *Lady Lilith* (1864–68), the poem was originally entitled "Lilith."

Swinburne composed "Before the Mirror" as an interpretation of this painting. In the poem the girl is imagined as thinking of "old loves that drifted, / she knew not why." The poet provides yet another example of the sad story and decay characterizing a woman's life, and leaves on her face the ambiguous grace and deep mystery he suggests is so appealing to men.[10]

But "Before the Mirror" is also a Swinburne poem that H. D. quotes in her novel *Hermione*, suggesting, as Cassandra Laity has pointed out, a "spiritual twinning between the girl and her ghostly sister image" (*H. D. and Victorian Fin de Siècle* 37). Through Swinburne's words Hermione can represent and understand her spiritual, erotic, and poetic powers. The "twin-self sister," the image in the mirror (who in the novel is her female friend and lover Fayne Rabb),[11] does not reflect a life of failure but rather Hermione's anticipation of future fulfillment. The reflected image may also be Hermione's soul, the spiritual essence inherent in the female body.

Isolated from other women, from society itself, the women represented in both Sandys's and Whistler's paintings, as well as in the poem, are different images of the same idealized woman.[12] As Christina Rossetti unequivocally put it in her poem "In an Artist's Studio": "One face looks out from all his canvases, . . . Not as she is, but as she fills his dreams" (ll. 1, 14). Thus, while portraying women who may have played an important part in the painter's or in the writer's life, these figures convey their creator's desires, anguish, uncertainties, and aspirations, whether worldly or mystical.

Dante Gabriel Rossetti was quite frank about it. In his Neoplatonic story "Hand and Soul," the medieval painter Chiaro, in a moment of crisis, is visited by a mysterious lady who tells him she is his soul. By painting her with "eyes which seek out labour, and with a faith, not learned, yet jealous of prayer," he will have his "soul stand by (him) always" (Dorra 21). The women represented in Rossetti's paintings are not separate individuals, but figures of his desire for spiritual achievement through art. Just like Sandys's Mary

---

10. On the relationship of Swinburne's poems to Rossetti's and Whistler's paintings see Christopher Newall and Andrew Wilton. On images of women in Pre-Raphaelite paintings and texts see Griselda Pollock and Lynne Pearce. H. D. mentions Whistler's famous "Ten O'Clock" lecture in *End to Torment* (23), when writing of young Ezra Pound reading to her Morris's poems and other nineteenth-century texts.
11. See Laity "H. D. and A. C. Swinburne" 475–76.
12. See Lewis Johnson and Griselda Pollock.

Magdalene, eternally holding the jar with the ointment of resurrection, his figures stand for feminine souls that form, with the artist, an androgynous unity.

Pre-Raphaelite paintings offered to women like H. D.—alienated from their mothers and the ideal of domesticity as well as from the disparaged subculture of "feminine" writers—myths and forms that could be used as molds to be filled with new contents, expressive of their desire to develop spiritually and intellectually beyond the gender limits imposed on them, identifying woman with matter, matrix, and emotion.

H. D. may have felt distinct from the women who were fighting for more material benefits. As the "new feminist" Dora Marsden posited in *The Freewoman*, she wished to become "self-conscious and introspective" ("Notes of the Week" 3), finding herself reflected in the mirror of her poetry; thus she would finally and fully realize her spiritual separateness from man.

The Garden and the Sea

In *Villa by the Sea* (1877) by the Swiss painter Arnold Böcklin, a painting also known as *Iphigenia in Tauris*, a distressed female figure in black, almost hidden within cavelike ruins in the garden of a villa by the sea, watches the waves break against the rocks. The painting, as the critic William Ritter wrote in 1895, conveys a sense of eternal waiting, of death and the passage of time: "Iphigenia is always there, always contemplative, her feet and veils lapped by the plaintive sea" (Dorra 74).

The painted scene, and Ritter's words, bring to mind the closing lines of William Morris's poem "A Garden by the Sea" (1867, 1891), in which a man is remembering a little garden "Anigh the murmuring sea." In the first line the man's voice introduces us to a "garden-close" he knows, "set thick with lily and rose," where he would desire to wander if only his beloved, now dead, "could return." Through his words we envision the absent garden where no tree, house, or bird speaks of usefulness, but instead lilies and roses, associated with beauty and the gratuitousness of aesthetic pleasure, suggest the ornamental role of the dead woman, whose domesticated sexuality fills the place, appealing to the speaker with its colourful presence and seductive perfume.

Whereas the first two stanzas concentrate on the garden, in the third and fourth the scene moves to the "dark shore." Just as in

Böcklin's painting, here too the sea is tormented and tormenting, but the woman, who is physically absent, is only evoked, synecdochically, through parts of her body which are also love fetishes: "Her feet" in the second stanza, and her "unforgotten face" in the last one.[13] Reduced to a ghost, she inhabits the dark cave of death that her lover is willing to enter, like Orpheus, to recover his Eurydice. By the end of the poem her whole figure is suggested by her face, "Once seen, once kissed, once reft from me / Anigh the murmuring of the sea."

After introducing the reader to the closed but luscious and paradisal garden, the author leaves us facing the sea of death and eternal loss. At this point we become aware of the underlying existential story conveyed by the speaker's words. Within this narrative the woman is nothing less than Everyman, and her garden is life itself, much too short for any man born of woman, and too soon lost to death. Moreover, as a ghost who haunts the mental and textual scene, she is reminiscent of the ghostly presences in Swinburne's "Forsaken Garden," where time and the elements take over after the lovers and their passions, the garden flowers and all other signs of human life have disappeared.

The unquiet and disquieting sea of Böcklin's and Morris's gardens becomes in H. D. the sea of poetic achievement, exploration of life and multiple possibilities; like her flowers, it stands for the tenacious woman artist.

The similarity between the title of Morris's poem and *Sea Garden* (1916) leads us to H. D.'s first published collection of poems, and helps to highlight the differences. Whereas Morris's title has a clearly descriptive quality, H. D.'s takes us directly to an imaginary place where boundaries disappear, together with the spatial preposition "by." In *Sea Garden* the subject of experience has no recognisable identity in a world divested of all geographic coordinates, while past and present mix to form a timeless whole. We are left with a disembodied voice that leads us through emotions elicited by the sensual apprehension of a rose or a pear tree, and by its pursuit of hidden gods or lovers: in each instance we are forced to relive the speaker's epiphany. The trees and the rocks, the sea and hard stubborn flowers, the wind and the sand are figures that stand for the speaker as subjective correlatives.

---

13. On the dissociation of the female body into fetishised parts in Victorian iconography see Nina Auerbach.

Two figures dominate the scene in H. D.'s garden, though in a variety of shapes and colors: the hard flower and the blowing wind, objectified projections of a subject that perceives itself as at once static and dynamic. A third element could be called "pursuit" (which is also the title of one of H. D.'s poems): the subject's search for something hidden, be it god or spirit, lover or emotion. It represents the work of the imaginative mind in its "Hellenic, avid . . . naked kind of thinking" (*Palimpsest* 275, 297), in which Hellenism and spirituality are one with the young H. D.'s American Puritan ethical sense.

Whether it be flower, garden or tree, divine or human, every object in *Sea Garden* is represented in the perfection of its form and its essential nature. It has the hardness of crystal that Pater calls for in a work of art, but neither its transparency nor its refractive ability. It is instead laden with the weight and opacity of the earth's rocks and the earth's colors. The "Sea Rose," with which the collection opens is, like Gertrude Stein's "rose is a rose is a rose," shorn of the whole body of traditional cultural and sexual associations: it sheds all the feminine connotations of "a wet rose / single on a stem—" (*Sea Garden* 1). While the "wet rose" is isolated and immobile, the sea rose is borne away by the wind, as if it were a grain of sand. Vexed by the elements, it develops a form of resistance that allows it to survive and acquire "an acrid fragrance / hardened in a leaf," a fragrance that is also the unique perfume that in H. D.'s major poetic sequences becomes a symbol of spirituality and the work of art, the essence of eternal life and resurrection.[14]

Nowhere does the aesthetic and symbolically positive meaning of H. D.'s "sea garden" so stand out as when it is contrasted to the negatively connoted "Sheltered garden," where "every way ends, every road, / every foot-path leads at last / to the hill-crest—" where flowers are beautiful but of a "beauty without strength." This suffocating enclosure is as oppressive as the heat that immobilizes the pear ("Pear Tree"). It is to this kind of garden that the lover in Morris's "Garden by the Sea" would have liked his beloved to return. From this enclosure H. D.'s speaker, here betraying her gendered identity, wants to escape, as if from a prison, fleeing for her life rather than disappearing in death. Outside this garden is the shore, "where sea-grass tangles with / shore-grass" ("Hermes

---

14. For Diana Collecott, H. D.'s use of the word "fragrant in her early poems" connotes "the sensual delicacy of Sapphic sensibility, even the physical immediacy of her own 'Greek World' "(*Sapphic Modernism* 11).

of the Ways"), and where the wind creates a movement that symbolizes change and process. The herm, which in "Hermes of the Ways" looks in three directions, is a key symbol of this process, since it stands for an exile: someone who, having given up or lost both identity and place of origin, is open to more than one option, more than one direction in life. And the wind that moves the flowers here and there is the transforming process itself, the essence of life: interior daemon and universal Spirit.[15]

Transformations

The hard, stony quality of H. D.'s poetic flowers, the cutting edges of their forms and of her verse, and the statuesque figure of the beloved in "The Contest" can be thought of as the poet's debt to Pater's Hellenic ideal of artistic perfection. Yet H. D. seems to reverse the hierarchical order Pater assigns to sculpture and poetry. For her, poetry is clearly the highest expression of intellectual light, of visionary and emotional power. And the use of color in her poetry, the poet's palette, contributes emotion and sensual pleasure, indeed the involvement of the whole body in the intellectual apprehension of reality.

Sculpture and painting are the two arts whose distinct languages H. D. attempted to combine and incorporate in her poetry. In so doing, she did not so much translate painting and sculpture into poetry as use them as formal and symbolic starting points for her own figures.[16] A comparative reading of two poems by H. D. and Morris's "Pygmalion and the Image," in relation to the sequence of four paintings Edward Burne-Jones devoted to Morris's poem, will illustrate her transformation of theme, artistic matter, and figures.

---

15. For a more detailed analysis of the poems in *Sea Garden*, see my "Scolpire l'emozione."
16. I am indebted to Jurij M. Lotman's interpretation of the relationship between the different semiotic languages of a culture (*Semiosfera*). In one of his most important essays, "Rhetoric as a Mechanism for Meaning-generation", he writes that "there are two different ways of reflecting the world and working out new information ... the one operates as a discrete system of coding and forms texts. ... In the second, the text is primary." These systems are mutually untranslatable. To establish a relationship of adequacy between the two, semantic tropes are created (pages 37–38).

The two poems by H. D., "Pygmalion" and "Eurydice," first published in *The Egoist*[17] and then in the *Collected Poems* of 1925, are also early instances of her revisionary work.

"Pygmalion and the Image," based on one of the stories in Ovid's *Metamorphoses*, is a narrative poem that William Morris included in his *Earthly Paradise* (1868–70). In the first few lines the narrator's voice introduces us to Pygmalion, a misogynous sculptor who, weary of life, sets to work on a block of marble in which he detects "A woman's form now imaged doubtfully." Addressing Venus, he promises to make the "block of stone . . . thy maid." But the statue shaped by his artistic hands is so beautiful that "A strange and strong desire he could not name" rises in his breast, and in a very short time he burns with so fierce a passion that he removes the statue to his own bedroom, to have the stone woman always in sight.

At this point, the narrator introduces the artist's own perspective, and we see the statue through the sculptor's eyes. His words evoke images in Sandys's, Whistler's, and Rossetti's paintings:

> Naked it was, *its unbound locks were laid*
> Over the lovely shoulders; with one hand
> Reached out, as to a lover, did it stand,
>
> The other held a fair rose over-blown;
> *No smile was on the parted lips, the eyes*
> *Seemed as even now great love had shown*
> *Unto them, something of its sweet surprise,*
> *Yet saddened them with half-seen mysteries,*
> And still midst passion maiden-like she seemed;
> As though of love unchanged for aye, she dreamed.
> (italics added, 166)

Under the auspices of Venus, the statue eventually turns into a woman. Breaking her inanimate silence, she also finally speaks and offers him her soul. Her words, however, do not initiate a dialogue

---

17. They were both printed when H. D. was substituting for Aldington as literary editor. I quote from this first version of the texts where small differences in the selection of words, in the organization of the stanzas and, most particularly, in the use of dashes and other punctuation, support the reading of the poems as dramatic (or lyric) monologues and emphasize their visual construction on the page. The last published version, on the other hand, is more attuned to an interior monologic flow of words.

with her creator-husband. Instead, they tell of her subjection as his devoted lover and wife. This is even clearer in Burne-Jones's paintings, particularly the 1875–78 series. The second painting of the series, *The Hand Refrains*, illustrates the painter's balanced creation of an aesthetic ideal (the statue) pitted against the reality of physical passion (Victorian artist-dreamer). Burne-Jones measures himself with the supremacy of sculpture as an art form and plays with shades of white to create the movement from marble to body, from ideal to real. In the fourth painting, *The Soul Attains*, while Galatea's naked body retains the frozen mobility of the statue, the red color on her closed, silent lips, and her blue eyes, lost in meditation, emphasize both her sexuality and her passivity in accepting her lover-sculptor's devotion. On the floor, a single cut rose stands for woman as well as for sexual fulfillment. As in the paintings discussed above, there is no interaction between the two figures in the scene. Galatea embodies and realizes the man-artist's desire, both aesthetically and sexually.

"Pygmalion" by H. D. focuses on the artist and his questioning mind, rather than on the object of his art and desire. The first stanza summarizes the part of Morris's poem where Pygmalion, weary of life, goes back to work on the piece of marble. While alluding to this antecedent, however, H. D. moves to different territory:

> Shall I let myself be caught
> in my own light,
> shall I let myself be broken
> in my own heat,
> or shall I cleft the rock as of old
> and break my own fire
> with its surface?

Pygmalion feels divided between action and reflection. On the one hand, the light of intellect, the heat of spiritual and artistic energy, are so strong in him as to induce complete stasis, thus becoming destructive forces. On the other hand, he is not sure whether his shaping the rock into a statue, while appeasing his creative urge, will result in a work of art.

The problem is the distinction between artist and the work of art, as the first few lines in the second section reveal: "Which am I, / the stone or the power / that lifts the rock from the earth? / Am I the master of the fire, / is this fire my own strength?" The artist experiences a sense of self, of power and authority that differs from what he used to feel when he deemed himself a god, and the gods were images he had created. Now he is possessed by the fire of a

divine passion that calls into question his former opposition between subject and object of art, creator and creature. He perceives
in the rock, in matter itself, which should be inert, a will of its own.

The allusion in these lines to the part of Morris's text in which
the block of marble seems to reveal the shape of a woman serves
to emphasize a change in perspective. H. D.'s focus is not on the
narrative plot of male desire,[18] anticipated by the artist's foreglimpse
of a female shape in the marble, but on the subjectively experienced
relation between the artist's creative power and the divine energy
hidden in the matter. In this way H. D. gives prominence to the
artist's self-reflexive act and blocks narrative development in her
text, all the while keeping the cultural tradition of classical, and
Victorian, co-texts in the background.

The artist, who in the third section admits that "fire has shaken"
his hand, in the fifth acknowledges that the gods he created in the
past "have melted into the light / ... / they have gone / ... / Each
from his marble base / has stepped into the light" and his "work
is for naught." Statues, even the most perfect ones, which represent
the principle of pure intellectual light and the Paterian Greek ideal,
have cut all connection with their maker. What is left is the fire of
artistic creation. If light belongs to the gods, in fact, fire belongs to
the artist. In the poem light and fire are the two extremes of a scale
on which fire is the bodily and light the mental or ideal extreme.
The concluding question of the poem, although it offers no definite
solution, does seem to suggest the artist's choice. In the sixth and
last section, the question in the first stanza, "or *shall* I cleft the rock
as of old / and *break my own fire / with its surface*?" (my italics),
receives a fuller sense and a possible answer:

> Now am I the power
> that has made this fire
> as of old I made the gods
> start from the rocks—
> *am I the god*
> *or does this fire carve me*
> *for its use?*
>   (my italics)

The last two lines of the poem are structured as a *permutatio* of the
three lines in the first stanza, where fire stands for the creative force

---

18. The quintessential story has been described as spurred by the subject's
    lack or loss and ending with the acquisition of the desired object. On

guiding the artist's hand and shaping the work of art. Commuting
subject and object, the rhetorical figure in the last stanza presents
the image of the fire that carves the artist for its own use. The final
question leaves us with the artist's suspicion that he himself and
his art are the involuntary carriers of the gods' fire.

The chiasmus guides us to the center of the poem, in stanza IV,
where the artist says: "over my head, fire stands," and the Pentecostal reference signals God's gift of spirit and tongues.[19] While the
burning recalls Walter Pater's "to burn always with this hard, gemlike flame" (*Renaissance* 152), the Pentecostal fire over the artist's
head displays H. D.'s distance from the Paterian "ecstasy" and "suc-
cess in life," for this burning is part of an inspirational and esoteric
rather than a pagan classical tradition. H. D. is much closer here to
May Sinclair's treatment of the theme. In Sinclair's *The Divine Fire*
the protagonist genius-poet reads the following lines from Iambli-
chus's *De Mysteriis Egyptiorum*:

> If, then, the presence of the divine fire and the unspeakable form of
> the divine light descend upon a man, wholly filling and dominating
> him, and encompassing him on every side, so that he can in no way
> carry on his own affairs, what sense or understanding, or perception
> of ordinary matters should he have who has received the divine fire?
>
> (174)

Sinclair's divine fire changes the young man's perception of "ordinary matters." In H. D.'s poem fire, not petrified into form like
Pater's "gemlike flame," is a live force and a molding agent. It
shapes the artist as well as "ordinary matter," which eventually
will become a work of art. There is neither separation nor opposition
between the two, but instead specularity, rendered in the poem by
chiasmus. This rhetorical figure reveals the woman artist hidden in
the character of Pygmalion. It also shows how well aware the author
was of the double position, as creator and object-muse, occupied in
her own time by the woman artist, and her refusal to accept the
hierarchical implications of this position.

In the poem, fire stands for an inner spirit that burns like desire
and gives direction to the author's will. H. D.'s implicit poetic stance
seems at this point to be that there is no single creative act which,
with a *fiat*, transforms nonbeing into being. The artist is not the God

---

the connection between male desire and narrativity see *Alice Doesn't.
Feminism, Semiotics, Cinema* by Teresa De Lauretis, chapter 5.

19. On H. D.'s uses of chiamus see Diana Collecott's essay in this volume.

of Genesis, who uses language to create the universe as a hierarchy of separate parts. Instead, creation seems to be a process, leading not only to the created object, but also to further definition of the creator-artist. Rooted in an inchoate spiritual energy, such a creation exceeds both subject and object, and accounts for the mysterious power of words, reaching well beyond the craft of the artist.

While the same Pygmalion evokes a mythical figure and a culturally transmitted story revived by constant repetition, H. D.'s version, which centers on the artist's reflection on art as a molding force, also involves the reader in the text.[20] Thus she places herself in the American poetic tradition of Emerson, Whitman, and Dickinson.

The poem that follows "Pygmalion" in the section of her first *Collected Poems* called "The God" is "Eurydice," a poem that can also be read intertextually with Morris's "Garden by the Sea." Although it is based on the well-known myth of Orpheus and Eurydice, by concentrating on Eurydice's point of view and voice, the poem opens up a new narrative path. Once again, H. D. singles out and builds on a key moment in the story: Orpheus' disobedience, which results in Eurydice's return to the underworld. As Diana Collecott writes, the poem is "an extended speech act" (*Sapphic* 170) that takes the form of an apostrophe Eurydice addresses to an Orpheus who is more her enemy than her lover. It is his "arrogance" and "ruthlessness" that have "swept" her "back / where dead lichens drip / dead cinders upon moss of ash."[21] In the second section of the poem, Eurydice, alluding to the fatal moment, asks:

> Why did you turn,
> why did you glance back—
> why did you hesitate for that moment,
> why did you bend your face
> caught with the flame of the upper earth,
> above my face?

While emphasizing Eurydice's frustration and anger, this unrelenting, repetitive sequence of questions brings into focus and amplifies, like a cinematic slow motion, Orpheus' fatal *turning towards* her,

---

20. On the involvement of the reader in the text see Gregory's essay in this volume.

21. In May Sinclair's words, " 'Eurydice' is the challenge of the self-delivered, defiant soul sent up out of hell to Orpheus, the arrogant and ruthless, the white, would-be deliverer—her challenge to death and hell" ("Poems" 462).

which has become a *turning against* her. But it is the following stanza
that is strikingly revealing:

> What was it that crossed my face
> with the light from yours
> and your glance?
> What was it you saw in my face—
> the light of your own face,
> the fire of your own presence?

Eurydice might well be one of the female figures in the Pre-Raphaelite paintings discussed above, expressing her awareness of being
used as a man's mirror.[22] Speaking from the object position she has
been made to occupy, she rebels against it. Becoming subject of
speech and creator of her world, she fights her prescribed destiny
of deathly love nourishing the male's ego.

In sections four and five, Eurydice expands on the experience of
living on the earth again. The images of flowers of different colors,
accumulating line after line, build up the feeling of a richly sensual
and full life, only to heighten the sense of loss: of her lover, of her
sentient body.

> So for your arrogance
> and your ruthlessness
> I have lost the earth
> and the flowers of the earth,
> and the live souls above the earth,
> . . .
> you who have your own light,
> who are to yourself a presence,
> who need no presence.
>
> Yet for all your arrogance
> and your glance,

---

22. In *A Room of One's Own* (1928) Virginia Woolf pointed out male artists'
use of women as mirrors to reflect and enlarge their own images. See
also Collecott's essay in this volume. In the year 2000, not much can
have changed if in a letter-poem by Kathleen Fraser, Echo still writes
to Narcissus: "Echo is She who watches Narcissus look for himself
and returns him to himself, slightly altered, by her very attentiveness"
(*Translating the Unspeakable* 5). Although Echo's words are ironic and
she finally writes "So I divest myself of the disembodied me," the
problem of women's authority in language and literature is still very
much alive.

I tell you this—

such loss is no loss,
. . .
such terror—
is no loss.

The questions of the previous stanzas have turned into sheer accusation. From her darkness Eurydice sees Orpheus' light better than ever. But, stepped in light, like the gods Pygmalion made, Orpheus can also dissolve into light and disappear from her life. On the basis of this last loss, as if resting on a void—in the final stanza of the poem—Eurydice finally constructs her possession of herself:

At least I have the flowers of myself
and my thoughts—no god
can take that:
I have the fervour of myself for a presence
and my own spirit for light.

And my spirit with its loss
knows this;
though small against the black,
small against the formless rocks,
hell must break before I am lost.

Before I am lost,
hell must open like a red rose
for the dead to pass.
(my italics)

Again, words like "fervour" and "spirit," here antithetical to "light," take us back to the molding fire of "Pygmalion." This time "fire" is the saving energy Eurydice finds in herself, giving her the power to talk her way out of death's colorless silence. The repetition in "hell must break," "hell must open" emphasizes the force of Eurydice's will, that can bring her back to life and sexuality. The two statements, in their chiastic form, add the figure of specularity to the doubling already present in the repetition. Once again, in this last stanza H. D. uses chiasmus: through an act of reflection Eurydice finds in herself a means of salvation.

Eurydice is reminiscent of the woman in Whistler's above-cited painting, whose reflected image sums up her woman's destiny of love and death. In H. D.'s case, however, Eurydice stands for the woman who is also an artist, and her mirror image reflects her will to change that destiny. As a woman, by focusing on herself she can speak in a female voice. Yet, she must do so from the deathly object position she has been made to inhabit. Revolting against man and his world order, she constructs her own antagonistic discourse and world.

Through Eurydice the writer H. D. acknowledges also that the authorial quest—for a story and an identity distinct from those projected on her by Orpheus—must originate in a state of loss, that is, of the lack of this separate identity. This, together with her destiny of love, death, and silence, is the deep black hole of hell a woman artist must climb out of in order to start her search.

H. D.'s narratives of the 1920s and 1930s tell of such a loss. Though apparently following the usual pattern of Western narrativity, her female heroines' quest is a search not for an object, but for a subject of desire. Her women start and end their quest in the only place they need but also feel free to explore: their own minds, bodies, and life experiences.

This pattern of narration as reflection, however, left H. D. where she had started. By the 1930s she was well aware of this repetitiveness.

In the 1940s, war broke this repetitive pattern and, just like Julia in *Bid Me To Live (A Madrigal)*, H. D. became "centralized," "found a focus" (106). With the poems that were to become her war *Trilogy*, H. D. set out on a new personal and authorial quest, beautifully expressed in a few lines of section 43 of *The Walls Do Not Fall: "we are voyagers, discoverers / of the not-known, the unrecorded; / we have no map; / possibly we will reach haven, / heaven."*

Responding to a new call, H. D. believes that her poetic work *must* open a path out of the hellish valley of destruction war had plunged contemporary Europe into. As Eurydice in the early poem *must break open* the hell that entrapped her as a woman, so in *Trilogy* the poet-speaker believes her word and her work are needed to break the pattern of warfare that structures and perpetuates the self-destructiveness of human relations, and to discover new paths to personal and collective salvation. Thus the figure of the writer in her works now starts a quest toward a more complex authorial identity.

The new social role H. D. envisaged for the poet was a renewed link with the Pre-Raphaelites and particularly with William Morris, with his ideal of a world of social justice where arts and crafts would blend high and low culture, engaging spirit, mind, and body, and exercizing a cohesive force on society.

H. D. outlined past and present authorial stances in *Bid Me To Live*, a late *roman à clef* set in the First World War years, but first published in 1960. Once again the Eurydice-Orpheus myth is central to understanding her self-representation as a writer. In the novel, Rico (the D. H. Lawrence character) questions, in a letter, Julia Ashton's—H. D.'s alter ego—ability to create an Orpheus. The letter is co-textualized in such a way as to become a pretext and the vehicle for the age-old antagonism of man and woman (writer):

> I don't like the second half of the Orpheus sequence as well as the first. Stick to the woman speaking. How can you know what Orpheus feels? It's your part to be woman, the woman vibration, Eurydice should be enough. You can't deal with both.   (51)

In the subsequent lines we learn that Julia sees in Rico an incarnation of Orpheus. If we interpret this episode as autobiographical information, we can infer that H. D.'s published poem "Eurydice" is only part of a longer poetic sequence in which Eurydice's monologue is followed by Orpheus' words. It also reveals a story of censorship, and the author's clear denunciation of the external and internal limitations applied to female writers. Thus the first narrative works of H. D. should be read as dealing with prohibition as well as loss.[23]

Pertinent as it may be, this would be a naïve and reductive reading of what is, after all, not an autobiography but a novel, and must be understood as such. In the novel, Rico's letter is the first part of a narrative whose second part moves in a different direction. Julia's voice is now that of the mature H. D., who finally claims the authority of speaking for men as well as for women. In her maturity, H. D., having built on loss, rebels against prohibition. This is what Rico's letter has prepared the ground for. His words are at once the antecedent, the context and the starting point of Julia's new stance as author:

> for women, any woman, there was a biological catch and taken at any angle, danger. . . . There was one loophole, one might be an artist. Then the danger met the danger, the woman was man-woman, the man was woman-man. But Frederico, for all his acceptance of her verses, had shouted his man-is-man, his woman-is-woman at her. . . . He was willing to die for what he believed, would die probably. But that was his problem. It was a man's problem, the man-artist. There

---

23. On this aspect see Rachel Blau DuPlessis's illuminating essay, "Family, Sexes, Psyche. An Essay on H. D. and the Muse of the Woman Writer" in *The Pink Guitar*.

was also the woman, not only the great mother-goddess that he worshipped, but the woman gifted as the man, with the same, with other problems. Each two people, making four people.   (136)

Julia claims a universality to be gained, not through impersonality, but—as with the color white, which in her *Trilogy* is the sum of all colors—by a composition of the sexes in a complex whole. In this way she also acknowledges that there is no spiritual or superior understanding that is not rooted in the body. An artist can reach universality only if she takes on both male and female experiences, and imagines being one, the other, and both. This is part and parcel of her poetics of "spiritual realism." Julia voices the author's revisionist dialogue with the texts of patriarchal culture. The novel contextualizes its author's new Dantean progress from hell to heaven. In *Trilogy*, Pater's gemlike flame yields to the blue flame of transformation in the alchemical alembic, where the art object is a pearl, symbol of resurrection through and in a woman's body and a woman's art.[24]

Mary of Magdala, or the Figure of Dialogue and Resurrection

H. D.'s new poetics of dialogue and transformation is first given artistic form in her *Trilogy*, particularly in the sequence in the third book, *The Flowering of the Rod*, devoted to Mary of Magdala, which has a narrative and cinematic quality. Mary is the incarnation of a number of Marys: the woman sinner as well as Mary of Bethany, but also Mary, the mother of Christ and the classical and biblical *matres lacrimosae*. Her long, mysteriously radiant hair associates her with mermaids and magic and with a long line of antagonistic women going back to Lilith and to some religious myths of origins. Mary is neither alone nor silent and, in contradiction to Sandys's painting, she has no jar. The jar is what she desires and must obtain from the magus, or Arab merchant, Kaspar.

In sections 13–15 we see Mary paying a visit to Kaspar's booth in the market, in an effort to buy his precious myrrh. He refuses to acknowledge her request, but "the un-maidenly" woman does not take the "hint," does not sidle "gracefully / at a gesture of implied dismissal." Instead, standing up to rejection, Mary engages him in

---

24. See section 4 of *The Walls Do Not Fall*, the first book of H. D.'s *Trilogy*.

a dialogue: "She said, I have heard of you; / he bowed ironically and ironically murmured / I have not had the pleasure, / his eyes now fixed on the half-open door" (15). Refusing to leave his booth, she closes the door behind her, forcing him to look at her. What he sees, however, is not the actual woman, the person who wants to buy his myrrh, but a figure outside of her prescribed place in the world: "it was her hair—un-maidenly— / It was hardly decent of her to stand there, / unveiled, in the house of a stranger."

It is Mary's irony, her resolute behavior, her wilful association of her self, her name and myrrh: "I am Mary, she said, . . . / . . . I shall be Mary-myrrh" (sec. 16), that wins Kaspar. By means of word-play she associates the incense symbolic of resurrection with her own name, thus shaping a rhetorical and symbolic figure that includes male (Christ-myrrh) and female (Myrrha, Mary) identities. If Kaspar *has* the myrrh, she *is* Myrrh.

Mary of Magdala and Kaspar are the two characters through whom H. D. presents the conflict and the meeting between what the two sexes want, know, and are. Only when Kaspar, shedding his rational mind, opens up to vision and intuition, does he finally see her as a separate subject speaking for the different identities she has assumed within and outside the accepted canon of Western tradition. Only then can he understand the origin of things and be admitted to the Nativity scene. In the last section of the third book of *Trilogy*, Kaspar, looking at Mary, discovers that what she holds in her arms is not the baby Jesus, but a bundle of myrrh. The myrrh is the child; Myrrh is also Mary. Thus the boy child is also a girl child: they are one in resurrection.

The final birth scene in *Trilogy* represents a solution of male-female antagonism. It also stands for the salvific authorial mind, in which the two sexes are joined, giving birth to the male-female child, the pearl, the work of art.

Though it is the woman-author herself who demands awareness from the culturally hegemonic male subject, dialogue is for H. D. the necessary first step toward salvation in history and spirit.

Works Cited

Auerbach, Nina. *Woman and Demon: The Life of Victorian Myth.* Cambridge, MA: Cambridge UP, 1982.

Bairati, Eleonora. *Salomé. Immagini di un mito.* Nuoro: Ilisso, 1998.

Camboni, Marina. "Scolpire l'emozione. La dinamica classicità di H. D. Imagista." In *H(ilda) D(oolittle) e il suo mondo.* Ed. Marina Camboni. Palermo: Annali della Facoltà di Lettere e Filosofia, Studi e Ricerche 22, 1995:27–38.

———. "Hilda Doolittle, la donna che divenne il suo nome." *VS. Quaderni di studi semiotici* 76 (1997): 7–29.

———. "Dora Marsden, Ezra Pound, H. D., and 'The Art of the future' ": Part II. *HOW* 2 4 (September 2000). http: / / www.departments.edu / stadler_center / how2 /.

Chastel, André. *Favole Forme Figure.* Torino: Einaudi, 1988. Italian trans. of *Fables Formes Figures.* Paris: Flammarion, 1978.

Collecott, Diana. *H. D. & Sapphic Modernism.* Cambridge: Cambridge UP, 1999.

De Lauretis Teresa. *Alice Doesn't. Feminism, Semiotics, Cinema.* Bloomington: Indiana UP, 1984.

Dorra, Henry, ed. *Symbolist Art Theories: A Critical Anthology.* Berkeley: U of California P, 1994.

DuPlessis, Rachel Blau. *The Pink Guitar: Writing as Feminist Practice.* New York and London: Routledge, 1990.

Fraser, Kathleen. *Translating the Unspeakable: Poetry and the Innovative Necessity.* Tuscaloosa and London: U of Alabama P, 2000.

Friedman, Susan Stanford. *Penelope's Web: Gender, Modernity, H. D.'s Fiction.* New York: Cambridge UP, 1990.

———. and Rachel Blau DuPlessis, eds. *Signets: Reading H. D.* Madison: U of Wisconsin P, 1990.

Glendinning, Victoria. *Rebecca West: A Life.* London: Weidenfeld and Nicholson, 1987.

Gregory, Eileen. *H. D. and Hellenism: Classic Lines.* Cambridge: Cambridge UP, 1997.

Guest, Barbara. *Herself Defined: The Poet H. D. and Her World.* New York: Quill, 1984.

H. D. *Asphodel.* Ed. Robert Spoo, Durham and London: Duke UP, 1992.

———. *Bid Me to Live (A Madrigal).* Redding Ridge, CT: Black Swan Books, 1983.

———. *Collected Poems 1912–1944.* Ed. Louis L. Martz. New York: New Directions, 1983.

———. *End to Torment: A Memoir of Ezra Pound.* Norman Holmes Pearson, and Michael King, eds. New York: New Directions, 1979.

———. "Eurydice." *The Egoist* 4.4 (May 1917): 54–55.

―――. "H. D. by Delia Alton." *H. D. Centennial Issue. The Iowa Review* 16. 3 (1986): 174–221.

―――. *Palimpsest.* 1926. Carbondale: Illinois UP, 1968.

―――. *Pygmalion. The Egoist* 4.2 (February 1917): 21.

―――. *Notes on Thought and Vision & The Wise Sappho.* San Francisco: City Lights Books, 1982.

―――. *Paint It Today.* Ed. Cassandra Laity. New York: Houghton Mifflin Company, 1917.

―――. *Sea Garden.* Boston: Houghton Mifflin, 1917.

―――. *Trilogy: The Walls Do Not Fall, Tribute to the Angels, The Flowering of the Rod.* New York: New Directions, 1973.

Hunt, Violet. *I Have This To Say: The Story of My Flurried Years.* New York: Boni and Liveright, 1926.

Johnson, Lewis, "Pre-Raphaelitism, Personification, Literature." In Marcia Pointon, *Pre-Raphaelites Reviewed.* Manchester: Manchester UP, 1989.

Laity, Cassandra. "H. D. and A. C. Swinburne: Decadence and Modernist Women's Writing." *Feminist Studies* 15 (Fall 1989): 461–84.

―――. *H. D. and the Victorian Fin de Siècle.* Cambridge: Cambridge UP, 1996.

Lotman, Jurij M. *La semiosfera.* Ed. Simonetta Salvestroni. Venezia: Marsilio, 1985.

Lotman, Yuri M. "Rhetoric as a Mechanism for Meaning-Generation." *Universe of the Mind: A Semiotic Theory of Culture.* Trans. Ann Shukman. Intr. Umberto Eco. Bloomington, IN: Indiana UP, 1990: 36–53.

Lowell, Amy. *Tendencies in Modern Poetry.* New York: Macmillan, 1917.

Marsden, Dora. "Notes of the Week." *The Freewoman* 1.1 (23 Nov. 1911): 3–4.

―――. "Views and Comments." *The New Freewoman* 1.1 (June 1913): 3–5.

―――. and Mary Gawthorpe. "The New Morality." *The Freewoman* 1.4 (14 Dec. 1911): 61–62.

Morris, William. *Earthly Paradise. A Poem.* 1868–70. New York: Longmans, Green, and Co., 1903.

Newall, Christopher. "Themes of Love and Death in Aesthetic Painting of the 1860s." *The Age of Rossetti, Burne-Jones & Watts: Symbolism in Great Britain 1860–1910.* Ed. Andrew Wilton and Robert Upstone. London: Tate Gallery Publishing, 1998:35–46.

O'Brien, Kevin J. *Saying Yes at Lightning: Threat and the Provisional Image in Post-Romantic Poetry.* New York: Peter Lang, 2002.

Panofsky, Erwin. *La prospettiva come "forma simbolica."* Ed. Guido D. Neri. Milano: Feltrinelli, 1997. Italian trans. of "Die Perspektive als 'Symbolische Form'." 1927; "Das Problem Des Stils in Der Blindenken Kunst." 1915.

Pater, Walter. *The Renaissance.* Ed. Adam Phillips. Oxford: Oxford UP, 1986.

Patmore, Brigit. *My Friends When Young.* London: Heinemann, 1968.

Pearce, Lynne. *Woman, Image, Text: Readings in Pre-Raphaelite Art and Literature.* Toronto: U of Toronto P, 1991.

Pollock, Griselda, ed. *Vision and Difference: Femininity, Feminism & Histories of Art.* London and New York: Routledge, 1988.

Read, Herbert. *The Philosophy of Modern Art.* 1964. London: Faber and Faber, 1975.

Rossetti, Christina, "In an Artist Studio." *The Complete Poems of Christina Rossetti.* vol. III. Ed. R. W. Crump. Baton Rouge and London: Louisiana State UP, 1990.

Rossetti, Dante Gabriel. "Body's Beauty." *Collected Writings.* Ed. Jan Marsh. Chicago: Ivan R. Dee Publisher, 1999.

Rowbotham, Sheila. *A Century of Women: The History of Women in Britain and the United States.* Penguin Books, 1999.

Sinclair, May. *The Divine Fire.* 1904. New York: Henry Holt, 1905.

———. "The Poems of H. D." *Fortnightly Review* (March 1927): 329–45. Reprinted in Bonnie Klime Scott, ed. *The Gender of Modernism.* Bloomington: Indiana UP, 1990:453–67.

Swinburne, Algernon C. *Poems.* Philadelphia: David McKay Publishers, n.d.

Wilde, Oscar. "The Portrait of Mr. W. H." *Complete Short Fiction.* Ed. Ian Small. Harmondsworth: Penguin Books, 1994.

Wilton, Andrew. "Symbolism in Britain." In *The Age of Rossetti, Burne-Jones & Watts: Symbolism in Great Britain 1860–1910.* Ed. Andrew Wilton and Robert Upstone. London: Tate Gallery Publishing, 1998:11–33.

Woolf, Virginia. *A Room of One's Own.* 1928. Harmondsworth: Penguin Books, 1945.

———. *Moments of Being.* Ed. Jeanne Schulkind. St. Albans: Triad, 1981.

Beyond One and Two:
The Palimpsest as Hieroglyph of
Multiplicity and Relation

Paola Zaccaria

> There were things under things,
> as well as things inside things
> —H. D., *Writing on the Wall*

In *Writing on the Wall*, the memoir of her analysis with Freud, printed in serial form in *Life and Letters Today* (1945–46) and later published, together with *Advent*—a journal of her first period of analysis with the Austrian analyst—in *Tribute to Freud* (1956), H. D. writes about the discovery, made by her brother and herself when they were very little, of the "underworld": namely, holes like "open graves," hidden under a log from a pear tree where strange little creatures lived—ants and white repulsive slugs. A few lines above she had mentioned the homophony between pears and pairs (of children). Of the little underground tombs she writes that they resemble "Aztec or Egyptian burial chambers" (*Writing* 20). The "things under things," the "sepulchral cells" of these early recollections are psychospatial childhood configurations that would forever mark her future perceptions and her future semantic areas.

On the following page she speaks of her father's study as a kind of temple: "The study was not flat on the ground but set on a series of square stone pillar-like foundations" (*Writing* 21). The memory of her father descending the stairs resurfaces as an image reminiscent of "Bible illustrations or . . . reproductions of, say, the early nineteenth-century French painter, David . . . its prototype can be found engraved on Graeco-Roman medallions . . . or black background of jars or amphorae of the classic Greek period" (*Writing* 22). Besides witnessing the psychological and discursive intertwinings of the "superimposition,"[1] we have here one of the innumerable examples of the inscription of a peculiar kind of thought / vision / writing. This works on the association principle and has to be read not only from a psychological perspective and by means of psychoanalysis, but must also be interpreted with the aid of the tools of a sentient imagination, of entropathic thought. Nor can we disregard the parallels between the Freudian "dream-work" and the poetics of Modernism, which is structured, just like the dream-work, on indirection, concealment, displacement and condensation.

The past comes back in the present of the act of writing, in the writing present. H. D. refers to "The actuality of the present, its bearing on the past, their bearing on the future" (*Writing* 23). Past, present, and future are not enough; she adds: "there is another time-element, popularly called fourth-dimensional." (*Writing* 23).

So we have several elements: the discovery of the underworld, made by a pair; her father as a Greek or Biblical figure descending the stairs of a temple; the mingling or overlapping of times. In my subjective progress toward a sentient-sensitive understanding of H. D.'s complex, multilayered discourse, some elements are particularly suggestive. First, there are two children, male and female, who discover and become fascinated by the underworld; then there is the child who became the female poet, H. D., long estranged from the domestic pear tree, who looks back on that experience. In the process of writing, what she has seen-touched-felt-known between infancy and adulthood, superimposes, intersperses the childhood image-discoveries with the associated cultural images she has become familiar with in the meanwhile—Egyptian and Aztec burial cells. The discovery made as a pair—male and female child—is still present in the singular-subjective transcription of the experience as

---

1. For Diana Collecott "superimposition" is a mental operation that implies the reading of one thing in relation to another; also called "superposition," it is defined as "the Placing of one image on top of another" (170).

seen from a here-now standpoint, which does not discard the there-then perception.

She goes on for many more pages about the structure of two, of pairs: brother and sister, pairs, "matches" (24). Matches, forbidden to children, in this episode are replaced by a magnifying glass molded in the form of the ankh, the Egyptian symbol of life, which is also the hieroglyph of the planet Venus, as well as a male-female symbol: it is represented as a circle over a handle in the form of a cross. Everything can become something else, can have another face, another meaning, like the conscious and the unconscious. This takes us back to pairs-matches:

> There were two's and two's and two's in my life. There were the two actual brothers (the three of us were born within four years). There were the two half-brothers; there were the two tiny graves of the two sisters (one of those was a half-sister but there were the two or twin-graves). There were the two houses. . . . There were the two Biblical towns in Pennsylvania, Bethlehem where I was born, and Philadelphia, where we moved when I was eight. There were for a time in consciousness two fathers and two mothers, for we thought that Papalie and Mamalie (our mother's parents) were our own 'other' father and mother. . . . There were two of everybody . . . there were the two maids . . . there were my two parents. . . . My father had married two times; so again, there were two wives, though one was dead.
> Then in later life, there were two countries, America and England as it happened, separated by a wide gap in consciousness . . . nevertheless there is a duality, the English-speaking peoples are related, brothers, twins even, but they are not one. So in me, two distinct racial or biological or psychological entities tend to grow nearer or to blend, even, as time heals old breaks in consciousness.
>
> (*Writing* 31–32)

Everyone comes from the pair, from two (father-mother), and everything in life seems a repetition-reperformance of that pair, as if H. D. were driven by the need to introject the couple, by a compulsion to (re)construct matches, pairs: the couple, father and mother.

Sigmund Freud, whom she came to know in 1933–34 when he was an elderly man, is the double who "makes a pair" with her father; but he is also a repetition-likeness of God, of Dionysus. This man, the very doctor who is analyzing her, becomes, on the basis of the remembrance-revision-dream work-transference, related to her, to her work, to her—to her father and to her mother. Everyone is one and two and still more; everyone moves out of one, of two; moves out of the double gaze, the double pace, and approaches a multiple identity. Freud is the doctor, the father, the (old) lover,

God, the prophet, and much more. When seen as "a figure," when "transcribed" and turned into a symbol, Freud the Father, Freud the God, and so forth, becomes, in the consciousness of the writer and in her "signs," intermingled with (1) her own "race," because, like her mother's father, Freud—and she herself—were the children of the culture of Mitteleuropa; (2) God-father figures: his "configuration" is notably Dionysian, especially because of his prophetic gifts; (3) her own father, on whose desk there were fabulous sacred objects (although in the form of modern office tools), on whose office walls there was a single painting: she is not sure if it was a reproduction of Rembrandt's "Lesson in Anatomy," but she remembers that it was "about doctors" (*Writing* 35). Fabulous ancient objects were also on Freud's desktop: "It is only now as I write this that I see how my father possessed sacred symbols, how he, like the Professor, had old, old sacred objects on his study table" (*Writing* 25).[2]

Why is it necessary that the doctor of the soul, the prophet who prophesies that she will be a poet, should be intimately related to her? Putting aside psychological answers and associations, what astounds me in the writing of this poet is the beating and rebeating of the idea-representation of the multilayering of an idea-thing-meaning-vision-memory. Things, human beings, visions, images, are all "real" to her. Everything—physical and ideational alike—has its own dimensions: "length, breadth, thickness, the shape, the scent, the feel of things" (*Writing* 23). Everything is meaningful because all things are related (in)to her consciousness.

We shall analyze two poems that are closely linked with the ideas, contents, and experience that led to *Writing on the Wall*: "The Dancer" and "The Master." Both poems were written soon after her therapy with Freud, although "The Master," a poem about Freud, was revised many times and never published during her lifetime. Both poems create a central goddess-like figure, Rhodocleia, "the dancer," who in some ways originated in H. D.'s relationship with Freud and her (critical) love-response to him, but also, most probably, as Dagny Boebel suggests, on the "two American modern dance innovators," Loie Fuller and Isadora Duncan, "who had died only a few years before the poem was written" (16). This dancer represents the body-mind-sensuality of a never-still woman-deity, a kind of Gradiva-like figure reminiscent of various layers of Gradiva's

2. Diana Collecott has kindly pointed out that this has also to do with H. D.'s interest in hand practice of photomontage and collage.

traditional iconology,[3] but she is also a double and indeed the very essence of the poet herself. Consider the opening lines of "The Dancer":

> I came far,
> you came far,
> both from strange cities,
> I from the west,
> you from the east;
>
> but distance can not mar
> nor deter
> meeting, when fire meets
> ice or ice
> fire;
>
> which is which?
> either is either;
> you are a witch,
> you rise out of nowhere,
> the boards you tread on,
> are transferred
> to Asia Minor;
>
> you come from some walled town,
> you bring its sorcery with you;
> I am a priestess,
> I am a priest;
> you are a priest,
> you are a priestess;
> I am a devote of Hecate,
> crouched by a deep jar
> that contains herb,
> pulse and white-bean,
> red-bean and unknown small leek-stalk and grass blade;
>
> I worship nature
> you are nature.
>   (*Collected* 440)

---

3. H. D. may have been thinking of Freud's study on Gradiva (the name given to a Greek bas-relief representing a walking-dancing young woman) entitled "Delirium and Dream in 'Gradiva' by W. Jensen" (1907). Freud's essay was inspired by Wilhelm Jensen's story "Gradiva—ein pompejanisches Phantasiestuck" (1903).

What comes into the foreground is the play on "I" and "you": both pronominal figures are introduced from the start, although we do not yet know who the "I" and "you" may be. The I-you play continues, suggesting oneness and duality, similarity and difference through the reiteration of terms (far . . . far; meeting . . . meets; ice . . . ice; which (is) which; either (is) either; you . . . you; I . . . priestess . . . priestess; priest . . . priest; bean . . . bean; nature . . . nature), and the mirroring of their contrast (I / you; west / east; fire / ice; ice / fire; priestess / priest; white-bean / red-bean), and also the use of terms that emphasize similarity and communitas, such as "both," "either." Even redoubling reflexivity can be turned into contrast, as happens with the nominal compounds "red-bean" and "white-bean," which are similar in that they are both legumes, but different in color; or with the word-play on "which" and "witch" whose sound is similar, but whose meanings are different (so that to the question "which?" the answer could be "a witch"). And then there is the explicit reference to a sexual doubling, a bisexuality, in the "I" and the "you": both priest and priestess, male and female, ministers of sorcery, of underworld rites (and here the "things under things," the "sepulchral cells" of *Tribute to Freud* come to mind).

Both the still unknown-unnamed "I" and "you," moreover, come from "far"; both from "strange cities." Strange is semantically connected to "stranger," although one comes from the West and the other from the East. A stranger she felt, even when she was a child, at home. A stranger she was because although born in the West, her mother's father came from Central Europe, just as Freud himself did.

In the second verse of this first part, the spatial word distribution that she has chosen ("fire meets / ice or ice / fire") brings together, on the same line, "ice . . . ice," although the opposite meaning hinted at by the "or" connecting-separating the reiteration is amplified by the vertical reading, where ice is opposed to fire; at the same time, the verb she uses, "meets," suggests not so much an opposition as an encounter. If we think of the result of fire meeting ice or ice meeting fire—the melting of solid water into liquid water, which most probably will extinguish the fire—we realize how Janus-like meanings become; west and east, I and you can either be annihilated in this encounter and become one and the same thing—ashes—or, if fire survives ice, who can tell "which (was) which"? When such a meeting takes place, nobody can tell: "either is either." Either: both; one and two; reciprocity. The repetition of "either," which means one or the other of two, and which contains in itself the idea of reiteration and interchangeability, is a magnifying of the idea of reciprocity.

The thirteen sections of the poem are composed of stanzas of different lengths, all very short; sometimes a single line contains only one word, but never more than ten: the page is left with a great amount of marginal blank space on both sides of the printed lines. The story, the written poem, is central, it directs the reader's eye right (in)to the middle of the page. The blank spaces on the right and left, almost two thirds of the whole space, speak of silence, of what has been erased of the previous layers of the palimpsest.[4] This story, this poem, this wor(l)d, is H. D.'s hieroglyph; it is what remains, in the poet's consciousness, of older myths-histories. And in this space the "I" who worships art, who has "come from afar," tries to capture "the poem, / writ in the air" (44–42) by the dancing of someone whom we later identify as the "you."

> Fair,
> fair,
> fair,
> do we deserve beauty?
> pure,
> pure
> fire,
> do we dare
> follow desire
> where you show
> perfection?

Defined first through adjectives (fair, pure, loveliest, strong) then by nouns referring to hot-cold elements (ice, snow, ember, fire, flame, the sun) and the flowers (red-rose, rhododendron) and colors, and finally defined as "a miracle" in the third section, where nonetheless she is never referred to as "you," "you" reappears in the

---

4. The palimpsest is, to quote Susan Stanford Friedman, "H. D.'s own scribal trope, her prose oeuvre is a palimpsest"; it is made of repetitive layers, of writings "erased to make room for another" (*Penelope's Web* 91). Palimpsest is also the name of a story sequence she wrote around 1923. The palimpsest is, together with the hieroglyph, one of the key figures of H. D.'s writing. In it she condenses psychic, historical, literary, mythological, cultural, temporal, and spatial layers: conscious and unconscious dynamics, the cycles of history, artistic innovation interplaying with tradition, erasures and revision, past and present, here and there. It has, of course, also to do with intertextuality and infratextuality; with photomontage and collage; with cinema and painting.

fourth section, where "I" has disappeared, only to be incorporated
in a wider community (which includes the reader as well), referred
to as the "we" who follow "your flame, / O woman." We have to
wait until the fifth section for this "woman" to be openly addressed
as "you" and called "wind in a stark tree, / . . . the stark tree unbent," "box," "arrow," "butterfly," "moon-flower." Having become "the dancer," in the sixth section the "you" is finally invoked
as Rhodocleia and described as a female figure at once both strong
and frail who, as she runs, awakens the rhododendrons with her
dancing feet and is herself a flower; she is at the same time the
chaste and ecstatic Aphrodite. This running body, this flashing spirit
reappears in "The Master":

> She is a woman
> yet beyond woman,
> yet in woman.
> (*Collected* 455)

"She" is the source, the subject—and not the cause or the object—of
the "dart and pulse of the male, / hands, feet, thighs, / herself perfect" (*Collected* 456).[5]

The nomination-representation of this dancing body, of this body
in the process of love-making, of this disclosing flower, is matched
by visions of ancient magical signs that have to be deciphered, by
words-hieroglyphs whose significance-rhythm is as yet undisclosed.
Here H. D. constructs a rhythm that follows the rhythm of breathing
and depicts the running rhythm of the body of a woman in love.
This fleeting figure has already been painted on prehistoric graffiti,
Egyptian hieroglyphs, Greek artefacts, and so on, but its mystery is
still unfathomed. This dancer is the Gradiva who enchanted Freud
with her ineffable, unattainable grace. The desire fueling this figure's dancing is the same as that which fuels the poetry making of
the poet who seeks to answer Freud's dictum, in *Tribute to Freud*,
that woman is perfect, but she has no spear. The poet's ongoing
desire records woman's perfection by embodying her consummate

---

5. The three following pages are a further development of some parts of
two earlier essays on H. D., written in Italian. They are respectively
entitled: "L'operazione di triangolazione del soggetto in desiderio di
comparare: con-, tra- Frida Kahlo e H.(ilda) D.(oolittle)," in Liana Borghi; "Oltre il materno, il palimpsesto. La mitopoiesi generativa di Frida
Kahlo e H.(ilda) D.(oolittle)," in Carla Locatelli.

accomplishment in the rhododendron, in the young woman named Rhodocleia: "O heart of the sun / rhododendron, / Rhodocleia."

It is Boebel's opinion that in "The Dancer" H. D. makes possible "a woman's liberation from Apollonian choreography"—the feet and arm movements of the dancer are reminiscent of Isadora Duncan's and Loie Fuller's "Dyonisian" dancing, but they also palimpsestically hark back to ancient popular Greek dancing (Boebel 28).[6]

H. D. had already made use of eroticized flower imagery in *Sea Garden* (1916), where in wild landscapes not fit for the cultivation of flowers, various vigorous plants and flowers (the sea rose, the sea poppy, the lily, the iris, etc.) grow. The reiteration of floral images which are reminiscent of female sexual organs

> the rhododendrons
> wake
> there is purple flower
> between her marble, her birch-tree white
> thighs,
> or there is a red flower,
> there is a rose flower
> parted wide,
> as her limbs fling wide in dance
> ecstatic
> Aphrodite
> (*Collected* 456)

endows this hyperdetermined, incessantly reproposed imagery, with a semantic cypher oozing associations with the sexual-erotic field. In "The Dancer" and "The Master"—the texts that stage this female figure who is body, poetry, earthy vulva flower, priestess and witch, meteor and flame, poet and, as such, immortal having something of the divine, numinously able to transcribe the rhythmic writing of the yearning body, the body in the throes of desire—Rhodocleia is a female subject in whom physiology, feelings, spirit, and art are not split. Here the male principle, Freud-Dionysus, is present as the sun-god but not as the Muse: he is the wise old man who acknowledges her as a poet ("You are a poet," he says in "The Master"), accompanying her toward the realization of her poetical-prophetical powers.

---

6. Isadora Duncan's and Loie Fuller's leaps and rhythms had already broken the rules of the ballet, which according to Duncan, deformed the female body: she wanted her free dance to express freedom and absence of hierarchy (Boebel 19).

H. D., letting herself be inspired by graffiti and hieroglyphs, creates Rhodocleia to draw-represent the rhythm of the yearning female body as a dancing, love-making, poetry-making body. And at the very moment when the words give birth to the body-flower, the poetical "I," the "I" in the process of poetry-making, lets herself be carried on by the rhythm of the created pulsating body and goes on to represent this sensual body through a rhythmic sensual language that relies on tropes of echoing and reiterative circles. Here we witness an extraordinary aesthetic performance, of momentous significance in the establishment of a female path to poetry: the poetical figure, the figure born of the poet's sensuous sensitive thought, feeds its own creator and impels her to go on with the creative act:

> Rhodocleia,
> rhododendron,
> sway, pause, turn again;
>
> rhododendron,
> O wide rose,
> open, quiver, pause
> and close;
>
> rhododendron,
> O strong tree,
> sway and bend
> and speak to me;
>
> utter words
> that I may
> take
> wax
> and cut upon tablets
>
> words to make men pause
> and cry
> rhododendron
> to the sky;
>
> words that men may pause
> and kneel,
> broken
> to this pulse we feel;
>
> rhododendron,
> laurel-tree,

sway, pause,
answer me;
    ("The Dancer," *Collected* 448–49)

The vocative appellation ("Rhodocleia,"[7] "rhododendron," "O wide rose," "O strong tree") speaks of the subjectivity of the poetical-priestly "I" as an I in the act of adoring-writing the "you," the celebrated-created subject who is, like the celebrant, priest-priestess. It would be difficult to distinguish the cells of textual subjectivity—the goddesslike figure—from the creating subjectivity ("which is which? / either is either"). The poet, the woman stranger coming from the west, meets her creature, coming from the east, who is an idea, and the transcribing of it. She is a real girl and a symbolic rendering of female youth; she is both the witch and the priestess, the priest and the priestess—the male and the female. She is art and nature ("I worship nature / you are nature," 440–41), fire and ice, divine beauty—"chaste Aphrodite" ("The Dancer" 446). She is both "the sun / born in a woman" ("The Dancer" 443) and human woman ("O woman," 443) the "wind in the stark tree" and the stark tree, bow and arrow, bird and mer-maid (444), butterfly and flower. She is the inspiring woman and poetry itself, the muse and the poem. She is called "sister," "singing-sister" (447).

In "The Master," Rhodocleia "is a woman / yet beyond woman, / yet in woman" (455), a "flower / that in itself . . . / [is] perfect" (456). Rhodocleia, woman in "controlled vibrance," is called by her father "stylus," "arrow." Her form is the poetry itself, which the singing "I" is in the process of composing now, with the hand hurrying to capture all that the visual-ideative emotion is in the process of transmitting. In a trancelike state—as if spell-bound—the poet repeats, like magic formulae, many expressions (e.g., "fair / fair / fair"). At the same time, hers is a state of complete consciousness—note the accurate details, the precise information, the circumstantiated invocations throughout both poems—the

---

7. Dagny Boebel, who, like me, has looked in Walker's book of symbols for the meanings of "rose," has also made the important suggestion that "Cleia" in "Rhodocleia" may be "a reference to Cleia, or Cleis, the name of the mother and the daughter of Sappho" (27), thus reinforcing the possibility of reading this figure as a way the poet chose of escaping phallic representation and phallic order through the sapphic, sister-like bonding between the poet and the dancer, who is also called "singing sister."

I in the process of writing is endowed with the attributes of the eye-
hand of a subject in the process of painting and with the eye-camera
of the film director who simultaneously shoots and gives instruc-
tions. It is as if the sister arts—cinema, photography, and painting—helped her not to fix her visions in still, "sculptured" figures,
notwithstanding her ideative indebtedness to classical art. Rhodocleia is the nymph bathing in the waters of the contemporary
age, revived essentially thanks to the electric twentieth-century mobility of the feeling gaze that perceives the dancing body, the body
that dances itself into poetry. Moreover, this very inextricability,
intertwining of the creating subject—the poet plunged by her own
vision into the linguistic dance, and the created figure, Rhodocleia—moves the reader to question the "ownership" of the
poem: who is the proprietor of the artistic production? Does it belong to the one who writes-depicts, or is the poem born of a partaken
desire: the poet writes only because she or he activates the presence
of the other, of an-other in the text. This is why the woman from
the West invokes the other within herself—the woman from the
East. This is why the western woman poet asks for help from the
eastern tradition: so that her vision can be more intricate and intriguing; this is why the woman from modern cities longs to meet the
woman from ancient cities ("walled town," "The Dancer" 440) who
has preserved magical gifts ("sorcery"), the combined forces of desire and art capable of generating ever-new images, ever-new words
and rhythms that nonetheless retain shades of ancient words and
rhythms, challenging the poet to sing on and on, multiplying sense
and significance.

And besides, is it not true that poetry—that art in general—is a
common good, a communal property, given the fact that no artist,
no poet can create or write all by himself-herself, without relating
to others, because language, any aesthetic language, nourishes itself
and is able to grow by means of the need for relation? Just as the
need for relation is the force that moves the interpreter to cross the
threshold of the text, to enter into the poet's space so as to construct
a hermeneutic dialogue with the subject who created the text, setting
up relational hermeneutic modalities.

Rhodocleia—the dancer: incarnation. Incarnate body of poetry.
Incarnate discourse of desire, of woman desiring (an)other woman
and letting herself be carried along by the rhythm of a body desiring
poetry. Rhodocleia is desire made (poetical) discourse, which allows
for the incessant flow between the physical and the symbolic, between the pure, naked center of the female body and the "ecstatic
Aphrodite" who teaches men that "woman is perfect":

O God, what is it,
this flower
that in itself has power over the whole earth?
for she needs no man,
herself
is that dart and pulse of the male,
hands, feet, thighs,
herself perfect.
("The Master," *Collected* 456)

It is the desire for fluidity, contiguity, continuity, connection that drives H. D. to "assemble" images of different ages and cultures; to "merge" reality and dreams; to "re-envision" old myths and scriptures and "envision" new discourses-figures-wor(l)ds where "each word was separate / yet each word led to another word, / and the whole made a rhythm / in the air, / till now unguessed at, / unknown" (454).

It was the consciousness of being a stranger everywhere and yet a poet / priest / prophet which brought H. D. to create a "female divine genealogy" (Iragaray 1985) for women poets: Rhodocleia, the "heart of the sun," "Lord become woman" (*Collected* 461), the flower "that in itself had power over the whole earth" (*Collected* 456).

Not wanting to be separated from her mother, resenting her mother's special fondness for her brother ("she likes my brother better." *Writing* 33), H. D. learns the lesson: "If I stay with my brother, become part almost of my brother, perhaps I can get nearer to her" (33). But, she adds, except when she was sick, she never succeeded in being very close to her mother, whose name was Helen. She will go away from her mother-motherland and seek another side of Helen—(Helen) in Egypt, where, in reactivating her desire for her mother, she who gave her life and the word, H. D. revives the wor(l)d and, at the same time, revives her psychic life, which activates a revision of reality. Intertwining bios and graphos, actuality and memory, H. D. saves both body and writing, creating an intertexture that shows the existing interconnections. The generative sign cannot exist in the absence of corporality, and likewise, it is impossible for the body to inscribe itself in the absence of signs that speak of the body and of what belongs to it.

A stranger wherever she went because she was without a mother (land), H. D. would always yearn to decipher ancient heretical signs, hieroglyphs, palimpsests—to look for the sign under the sign. She transferred this need-yearning for closeness, for being in relation, to the ethical-aesthetical act of relating different writings and strata: different spaces, times, sexes. Rhodocleia is the palimpsest of everything that in H. D.'s consciousness is related both to womanhood and to poetry. As I sought to establish in a previous study entitled "Beyond the maternal, the palimpsest: the generative mythopoiesis of Frida Kahlo and H.D," the palimpsest is the inscription of duality (under the one, under the first stratum, there is the two, another stratum, a second text-language-vision), of multiplicity (when some of the text is scraped down, the reader can find evidence of three, four, and even more layers-texts). Moreover, the act of she-he who discovers-interprets the palimpsest is not simply meant to recover the first, original text, but is also an attempt to reconstruct the history of all the layers, to relate the different texts that exist in the same space, so as to recover the history of time. She-he who unveils the palimpsest puts herself-himself in a location I like to call "the third-between-two" or "the one among more than two." She-he is the one who opens up channels between different textualities to see how they differ and what they have in common, in order to set up a dialogue amongst them. This is what H. D. accomplished while reading-contemplating the figures of her mind (now) as moulded in the figures of classical, pre-Colombian, Egyptian signs; this is what the "I," the poetical voice-interpreter, accomplishes while reading the figure of Rhodocleia, created by H. D. out of a dialogue between different fields of discourse (literary, psychoanalytical, mythological, alchemical, and artistic, but also experiential). Rhodocleia is also touched by the "cyphers" of many transformation figures and, in addition to having the capacity of naming-representing female eroticism and artistry, she is endowed with a deeper, more subjective meaning, the personal meaning H. D. attributes to that figure-symbol. And then there are also the personal meanings I, the critical narrator, attribute to her because of the culture(s) in which my subjectivity is grounded: the interrelatedness of the threads that compose H. D.'s and my personal "cultural body" gave birth to this very text you are in the process of reading right now.

Literally, "palimpsest" means "rubbed smooth again" and refers to a parchment or tablet on which various layers of signs have been superimposed, or as H. D. herself says in the epigraph to *Palimpsest*, "a parchment from which one writing has been erased to make room for another." In the palimpsest the temporal category (successive writings) is added to the categories of erasure and contemporary regeneration: if it is true that a text is erased, other signs are rewritten, regenerated (*palin* means "again"). The palimpsest, as the place of "erasures" and of new inscriptions, can be figured as a "textual body" in that it partakes, like the biological body, of the phases of birth and death, but also of repeated regeneration—of life, of texts. In electing the palimpsest as an emblem to indicate the plurality of subject and text, H. D. has sought a way out of monologism. At the same time, in electing a multiple origin, she has subtracted herself from the monotony to which the patriarchal tradition would have condemned her. Beyond one, beyond binarism, trying to weave within the text mother-tongue, mother-land, mother-matter, real mother, and symbolical mothers, H. D. uncovers the multiple roots that give life to the gendered body-textual body that both (either is either) take the form of a palimpsest. As the space of the junction of different times and writings, the palimpsest is par excellence the space of dialogue, a figure of the unceasing dialogue of voices through different ages, but also a figure that designates the interpreter as the third-in-between, whose goal is to create a dialogical interaction between texts.

The palimpsest is, for H. D., the way of representing the complexity of the self. It is a figure that also refers to hybridity and translation as generative weaving between different textualities.

Such contemporary scholars as Witte ("Recension," "Archeological"), Edmunds, and Miller have rightly taken into account both the historical context, especially the fact that the 1920s and 1930s were a period of archeological interest in King Tutankhamen's reign (H. D. herself undertook, together with her mother and Bryher, a voyage to Luxor in 1923) and the influence, on modernist literary practices, of archeological and mythological studies of African, Egyptian, Mexican, and Chinese, that is, non-Western cultures.

Apart from the philological interest that reconstructing the archeological and mythological "dictionary" of the poet's writings can provide, these insights strikingly suggest that H. D.'s prose and poetry are the result of her archeological, mythological, and psychoanalytical interests, and that she chose the form of the palimpsest and the figure of the hieroglyph because of her drive toward connectedness, which she applies as well to ideas, knowledge, creativity. Because of this drive, her own being becomes the site where past and present, historical memory and personal remembrance, archeology and neology, Greek and Egyptian afterworld legends, the Orphic mythologies and the Osiris-Isis cycles, archeological excavation and cultural and personal excavation of the psyche, mythology, and personal history are brought together.

For more than a decade, Pound and Eliot had actively sought "to resuscitate the dead art / Of poetry" in Mauberley's and Prufrock's London waste land. Their shoring of historical scraps and archeological fragments against the ruins of Western mythological and biblical traditions bespoke of general artistic impulse to excavate the deeper layers of culture, to cull from non-Western sources what Freud called the dream of the race and Pound the tale of the tribe (Witte, "Archeological" 64).

In this act of excavation, modernist writers recalled ancient myths or found new inspiration in the patterns offered by ancient art, just like those contemporary artists who, to fuel their avant-garde experiments, took inspiration from Egyptian geometric designs. According to Meredith Miller, "H. D.'s insistence on the maternal, preoedipal nature of Egypt is . . . in part a response to a masculinist strand of early modernism associating Egypt's geometrical figures with virile, hard-lined art, a way out of the softness of Greek art" (78–79).

What is peculiar about H. D.'s experiments with writing after she had developed a way of her own beyond Imagism, both in her lyric prose and in her finely wrought free verse, is what Wenthe defines as "the problem of how, in practicing the modernist free verse, to avoid mere contemporaneity—to give her verse a sense of antiquity" and at the same time how to merge her poetical preoccupations with her interest in the unconscious (114), that is, how to conjoin discourse and the unconscious through prosodic sound effects, that is rhythm. Seen in this light, the palimpsest can be viewed as the model she devised to achieve what can be roughly defined as a double goal. Through the very act of bringing together different myths, times, cultures, and languages, and layering her own text with them in keeping with the teaching of the palimpsest, everything new and old can be reseen, reread, reperceived, and rewritten simply by seeing, reading, reperceiving one myth, a past epoch, a different culture, another language from the point of view of another time, myth, and so on, thanks to the centrality accorded in her vision to the work of the unconscious (and to Freud's studies of the unconscious, although she questioned, de-montaged, dis-assembled his procedures), which can be retraced through the exhumation and analysis of fragments of lost memories. H. D. weaves her palimpsestic textures so that they can undoubtedly be read as the hieroglyph of her own unconscious racial psyche, which, because of her palimpsestic drive toward connectedness, she equates with the cultural archeological collective memory of humankind.

The palimpsest, then, is a figure that bespeaks temporal, cultural, and psychosexual transformations; it is a way to excavate the sedimentation and go back, layer after layer, to the "original voice," which may be less permeated with masculine symbols and signifiers, and may be closer to the "hieroglyph of the unconscious." The palimpsest is a space she creates for herself between the different writings, beyond the different times, so that she can speak both without and within the heteroglossia of different languages and discourses, while at the same time being the locus of the intertwining of different languages and discourses.

As I have said elsewhere, the texture created out of interweaving is the exact reverse of the linearity present in arts and discourses constructed according to an aesthetic order that presupposes hierarchies and authority. Feeling that she was a palimpsest of different races, ages, cultures, texts, she must have always felt like a stranger, without a fatherland, moving from expatriation, through everchanging "homes," toward a diasporic polyglot subjectivity and literature. She repeatedly shows, in the poems from "The Master" and "The Dancer" on, how West and East, past and present merge in her and create a "continuum space" that is the direct descendant of her fascination with palimpsestic figurations, and vice versa.

In this regard, I would like to stress two points. First, the older Hilda Doolittle gets, the more open she becomes to experience and thought; it is evident from the Second World War onwards that instead of becoming more rigid or resistant to new experiences-experiments, as often happens with age, she becomes more and more a desiring body, the voice of desire, a desire that drives her toward everchanging reperceptions, reinscripturations.[8] Second, the poems themselves are linguistic, mythological palimpsests in that they incarnate her own "palimpsestic" identity. Unable for some

---

8. Michael Kaufman discusses the paradoxical relationship between H. D. and the "canonical critics." In her so-called imagist period, with a few exceptions (Kaufmann names Aldington and Monro), none of the critics acknowledged that her poems provided poetic examples of the precepts of imagism, while Pound and Hulme quarrelled over the "ownership" of the idea without being able to embody it poetically. Later, when she decided to free herself from the "crystallization" and "frozenness" the label "imagist poet" had given to her work, the same critics who had dismissed imagism, dismissed her decision "to move away from the earlier imagist style that they had declared so limited and narrow" (67).

reason to identify with either her mother or her father (see Friedman, *Penelope's Web*), unwilling to interiorize a single stable sexual identity, she transforms her earlier uneasiness about her conflictual sexual drives into a source of further richness. In addition, such stylistic figures as anagrams, associations, cryptograms, puns, and neologisms, with their weight of connections and superimpositions, speak of a language and subjectivity that reject a monovocal meaning, rejecting the ordered catalogue in favor of multivocality, ambivalence, the playful, and the ever-changing never-the-same: figures of the palimpsest (what is an anagram if not a word that contains another word?) and (bi)sexual desire.

What is a rose, which is also a tree, which is also a cup, a suggestion of eroticism, a name for a woman, a name for a goddess, a name for a dancer, a name for the loved one, a name for herself, for any woman who aspires to be different, to be differently represented? Who and what is Rhodocleia, Rhododendron, rose, rosebud, rose-bush, rose-tree? Why these expansions, this compounding of names—multileafed name of a multipetalled flower—if not for a staging, performing of the palimpsest of the rose as herself and as the other, all the roses of all different times, cultures, languages, myths?

The dancer is the visual incarnation of music, a song, a poem, the very prosody she is in the process of creating, born of her lyrical self. It is the flesh and pulsating heart of her poetical score, which is born while she is in the process of creating through the connection of conscious and unconscious, past and present, the everyday and the aesthetic. The dancer is herself a palimpsest, encompassing poet and poem; she is the woman in the process of writing (now) and the woman who has been sung (in the passing of time). She is the "Greek flower, Greek ecstasy" H. D. speaks of in "Epitaph" (*Red Roses for Bronze, Collected* 299): flower and ecstasy of ancient aesthetics that are born anew in the flower and the ecstasy of the American aesthete who lives in exile and "who died / following / intricate songs' lost measure" (300). The very term "ecstasy" has intricate implications: it suggests that one has been transported, both physically and aesthetically out of oneself, elsewhere, has distanced oneself from oneself. "To be beside oneself" can make the ecstatic subject easily and closely approachable by the other; it allows the ecstatic subject to be both subject and object, lover and loved one, desiring body and desired body. The ecstatic mode can set the poet free to create that other figure, the dancer, who is portrayed as body and as spirit, hieratic and sensual.

The dancer is memory and is palimpsest. She is born of the prosodic alchemy that sets up short circuits between past and present,
between cultures distant in space and time, between different epis-
temologies—such as psychoanalysis, classical studies, history, literature—which are palimpsestically brought together in the textual
act-word-dance. The dancer-flower-poem acquires "a larger, hieratic significance," as Wenthe would say (118), behind the here and
now, transcending time and space, since she is the incarnation of
poetry.

What power moves H. D. to expand, delve into, and deepen in
such a way a simple name, the name of a flower, a name for a
woman? The reading of the poem gives the sensation of a kind of
revelling in the pleasure of driving the simple name further and
further on, undoing its meanings only to recreate new ones from
the old ones, and-or return to the original meaning by means of the
new ones. The flower, and the rose in particular, is traditionally a
feminine symbol. In the rose we can retrace ancient legends of female divinity and sexuality, but we can also retrieve the Christian
symbology of femininity (the rose is associated with both Mary and
Saint Rita). The very name "rose" is a parchment of meanings
fraught with traces of female mythologies and divinities, female
language and sexuality that, through the mythologem of the rose,
have managed to survive and that H. D. incorporates in this new
body-myth-symbol, Rhodocleia, which is at the same time a palimpsest bearing traces of previous stories, and also the hieroglyph of
the new—the new woman as well as the new poetry.

Audre Lorde would certainly call this impulse to diffuse and fuse
words and meanings an expression of the erotic force. Certainly,
the fact that this power comes from a bisexual woman allows it to
determine both the infinitude of meanings and associations, and the
palimpsestic structure of her poetic writing. There are no boundaries set here for the poetic voice who conjoins her unconscious
with the "unconscious of the race" within the act of versification,
which, being so close to her psychical state, can follow the pulse of
her in-breathing poetry. Her metrical feet can follow the dancing
feet of her muse, who is at the same time the rhythm of poetry.
Neither are there boundaries set for the reading subject who, in the
process of rejoicing in such a liberated and liberating, unfettering,
ongoing dancing language, learns step by step the liberty of creation
and H. D.'s not-so-secret thought. The unconscious is "a mode of
reality, affiliated with the body, and with divinity" (Wenthe 131),
and the poem is the locus where it can most nearly be approached

through rhythm. But even when language is governed by associative relations (assonance, word-play, parallelism, and similarity) and is thus, in a sense, closer to the unconscious and freed of the laws of versification, the model of the palimpsest presents itself as the mould within which the poem is formed. This is because association, parallelism (and its implicit co-trope, difference), similarity (and its negative, dissimilarity) imply placing one thing next to-against the other, coupling, connecting, and ultimately relating multiplicity. An example of what I mean can be found in the last stanza of section III of "The Master" where, once again, "the dancer" becomes the palimpsest of poetry-dance-perfection-divinity, the embodiment of woman's perfection that Freud had denied in their meetings:

> how could he have known
> how each gesture of this dancer
> would be hieratic?
> words were scrawled on papyrus
> words were written most carefully,
> each word was separate
> yet each word led to another word,
> and the whole made a rhythm
> in the air,
> till now unguessed at,
> unknown.

Here we have sound-repetition ([h], [w]); word-repetition (how, word(s), were, each); apparently oppositional meanings (known, unknown, "word . . . separate / . . . each word led to another word") brought together by the conjunction "yet": a cadenced prosody that is the result of the associative power of sounds. In the image of separate words that yet lead to other words she brings together the associative process of psychoanalysis, the poetical process of word-construction, the temporal-spatial processes of intertextuality. The following line, "and the whole made a rhythm," stresses, through the all-inclusive word "whole," the palimpsestic act drawn out of the connective, associative wording; the shape of that act, "a rhythm in the air," is the dance. The specification "till now unguessed at, unknown" makes it explicit that the result of this connection between words on the associative level has given form to a figure, a dance, which is completely new, never seen-heard before: Rhodocleia, the hieratic dancer who, at the same time, embodies female difference (unguessed at, unknown) and bisexual difference, but also to a rhythmical, prosodic difference in the ongoing modernist poetical quest. The rhythmically stressed, hieratic cadence of the concluding stanzas of "The Dancer" (see section X

above; section XI reinvokes "Rhododendron, / O wild-
wood, . . . rhododendron, / O white snow . . . / rhododendron,
swear to me . . .") and "The Master" ("madly, / madly, / we were
together, / we were one; / / we were together / we were one; . . . /
Rhodocleia; / Rhodocleia, / . . . Rhodocleia") not only show how
these poems are central to H.D.'s development toward a poetical
writing practice, wherein prosody and the unconscious work together in the service of poetry. Their ritual mnemonic rhythms are
also reminiscent of spiralling, palimpsestic works that connect the
newly created figure of Rhodocleia to drowned or silenced or forever lost divine, yet human female figures from ancient stories,
ancient portraitures, ancient sculptures, such as the Athena with
(out) the spear that Freud showed her in his studio.

As I conclude my critical narratives of H. D.'s experiments with
poetry during the period of her analysis with Freud and during
World War II, I must admit that the words used to speak of H.
D.'s performances with words—palimpsest, hieroglyph, myth—are
terms oozing with what we feminist thinkers used to call some years
ago "phallologocentrism." Palimpsest, myth, hieroglyph refer to
constructions that originated in men's minds and are suggestive of
a male symbolic order. As a reader of H. D.'s words, I am always
suspicious of being entrapped in the very system she (and I too)
wanted to dismantle; I am concerned about her profound descent
into patriarchal ideologems. I can sense a lot of "dangerous" signs
on my way to her and on her way inside-beyond patriarchal palimpsests, mythologies, hieroglyphs. She is always at work possessing,
revising, rereading, reworking language as a system of signs and
meanings, disrupting and reassembling, connecting and superim-
posing or disassembling. So much work, so much pain, so much
solitude on her way make me feel sorry for her, but also uneasy,
because I fear that constant reiteration of her tie to her mother and
father, as well as to what is primeval, primitive, mythical, may, in
the end, reconfigure patriarchy, and that there may be shades of a
colonialistic attitude, or at least exoticism, in her perpetual projec-
tion of nostalgia for the mother somewhere else—another space,
another time. What did she fear? Why did she not yet dare to throw
away certain things, laboring instead to assemble material, as Joyce
did, comparing as many mental and cultural constructions as she
could and working "on the margins," through the spaces opened
up by the multiplicity of existing versions of one and the same
myth, or "searching for traces of the feminine in language and mythologies, the spaces wherein the traces would be strongest and

most concentrated would be in the past, or in the jars and pyramids which envelope the past" (Hardin 158)? She, Hardin shows, "overwrites" the poem and

> forces the reader to expand the text to include . . . also the words not written but similar to the written ones in meaning, composition, letters, or sounds . . . the poem itself becomes palimpsest, mirroring the myths which to her are palimpsests of language and identity.
>
> (Hardin 153)

Why this anxiety of revision, this unremitting reworking of myths, albeit "through the margins" of them? As Ann Louise Keating warns, if the revision of myths simply aims at a feminization of humanistic beliefs, at a substitution of "god the father" with "god the mother," the result of this replacing will not challenge existing ontological and epistemological systems—will not imply change. H. D.'s retrieving of mythologies other than Eurocentric, and her linking of different cultures from different times, add a political valence to her constructions: myth is a political and aesthetic tool that lets her drive down to origins and then resurface to the present, having been modified during the journey, her search for the maternal is a way of inscribing her mother while relating her to herself, to future female readers, and also to the male world. Moreover, we feel that it is her devotion to myths, her incapacity to discard them, that impels her to work palimpsestically. Even her insistence on hieroglyphs, her ceaseless renaming of herself (see the list in Silverstein) trying to fix her identity in a cryptogram—a hieroglyph—speaks of a compulsion to embody herself in a sign; but the never-ending shifting of names also implies an identity-name in constant flux.

This is the puzzling question posed by H. D.'s mature work. On the one hand she works inside patriarchal culture, striving to know it as much as possible, and then, working "through the margins" of it, she reinvents a(nother) story, a different story, not simply a female story, but a complex bivocal bisexual story. It was hard to discard the whole (old) story all by herself, notwithstanding the undoubted support of Bryher and other female friends. She had a profoundly rooted, strong devotion to fathers, brothers, male friends and lovers, "masters." There was a never fully achieved, only-female identity that, on the one hand did not allow her to simply move into an all-female world, and on the other left her with a feeling of inescapable bonding to man's world as well. This may explain her being until the end bilingual, bisexual, binocular, faithful and unfaithful to both sexes, to father and mother, to man and woman, to America and Europe, to Freud and Bryher, to the cinema and literature, to prose and poetry, to history and imagination, to past and present, to daughter and lover, to art and thought, to Western and Eastern cultures, to the Bible and to the Egyptian Book of the Dead, to Greece and Egypt, and, finally, to Hindu and Buddhist thought.[9]

The list could go on, showing over and over again her palimpsestic cultural and spiritual "passages," which I do not consider, as Tarlo does, "syncretistic," because her desire is not to unify Greece and Egypt, or as Tarlo says, with reference to *Helen in Egypt*, to "unify Greek reason, associated with Theseus, with the intuition and transcendence associated with Egypt and the East" (177). I do not see H. D.'s mature creative works as simply syncretic. Just as hybridization is not a flattening syncretism, which implies "unifying" or "melting" different cultures, works such as the *Trilogy* or *Helen in Egypt*, or single poems written from the war years on, do not aim at unifying and merging the different cultural and spiritual palimpsests that inhabit her, that are her textuality. Her work takes shape from the palimpsest model, makes use of a palimpsestic methodology, aims at a palimpsest design that, for all the reasons discussed above, is not at all an act of syncretism, but an act of excavation and regaining, scratching and patching, digging deep down and bringing up to the forefront. Without claiming to be original, she works either through acts of selection, restoration, connection of fragments (on the sources of *Helen in Egypt* and the palimpsestic nature of the Helen figure, for example, see Gregory 86–87), from the locus of palimpsestic re-petitions (the Latin word *petere* means "to ask," "to try to reach"), or, by paying attention to what has been left out, unseen, unread, she performs acts of reading-writing "through the margins." It is an act of grace, of love, a wishful act of connection.

What is most striking when we look at her (self)representations as they are offered to us in her photographs as well as in her poetry and prose, particularly in her later years, is the multiplicity of signs life inscribed on her face, which, in some way, becomes the palimpsest of what she has gone through. Her (palimpsestic) face is the page on which she has tried to inscribe as many lines as possible,

---

9. See Tarlo on H. D.'s "library" of Eastern philosophy as a search for origins.

as many layers of meaning as possible, as if she had tried to live
through all previous cultures, constantly going further down into
the past to resurrect herself, not in the present, but in a future
passionately envisioned as different, where nothing is lost, but nothing remains as it was: everything is palimpsestically brought together in the hieroglyph of her successive meanings. And yet, I find
it difficult to ignore the question: do revisionistic reading-writings-
acts, the "Penelopean endlessness of (re)interpretation and inscription" (Friedman, *Penelope's Web*), really succeed in transforming the
symbolic order? At the same time, it is painfully difficult not to
appreciate the generosity of this dream, the need for connectedness
and communitas and interlinguisticity and intertextuality that her
writing-face-page springs from.

Works Cited

Baccolini, Raffaella. *Tradition Identity Desire. Revisionist Strategies in
H. D.'s Late Poetry*. Bologna: Patron, 1995.
Boebel, Danny. "The Sun Born in Woman: H. D.'s Transformation of
a Masculinist Icon in 'The Dancer.' " In *Unmanning Modernism.
Gendered Re-Readings*. Ed. E. J. Harrison and S. Peterson. Knox-
ville: The U of Tennessee P, 1997:14–29.
Borghi, Liana, ed. *Passaggi. Letterature comparate al femminile*. Urbino:
Quattro Venti, 2001.
Camboni, Marina, ed. *H(ilda) D(oolittle) e il suo mondo*. Palermo: An-
nali della Facoltà di Lettere e Filosofia, Studi e Ricerche 22,
1995.
Collecott, Diana. "Images at the Crossroads: The 'H. D. Scrapbook'."
In *Signets: Reading H. D.* Ed. Susan Stanford Friedman and
Rachel Blau DuPlessis. Madison: U of Wisconsin P,
1990:155–81.
D(oolittle), H(ilda). *Palimpsest*. New York: Houghton Mifflin, 1926.
Carbondale: Southern Illinois UP, 1968.
———. *Collected Poems 1912–44*. New York: New Directions, 1983.
———. *End to Torment: A Memoir of Ezra Pound*. Pearson, Norman
Holmes and Michael King, eds. New York: New Directions,
1979.
———. *Red Roses for Bronze*. London, Chatto & Windus, 1931.
———. *Trilogia*. Ed. Marina Camboni, Caltanissetta: Sciascia, 1993.

————. *Tribute to Freud: Writing on the Wall. Advent* (1956). New York: New Directions, 1984.

Edmunds, Susan. *Out of Line: History, Psychoanalysis, & Montage in H. D.'s Long Poems.* Stanford, CA: Stanford UP, 1994.

Friedman, Susan Stanford. *Psyche Reborn: The Emergence of H. D.* Bloomington: Indiana UP, 1987.

————. *Penelope's Web. Gender, Modernity, H. D.'s Fiction.* New York: Cambridge UP, 1990.

Genette, Gérard. *Palimpsestes.* Paris: Éditions du Seuil, 1982.

Gregory, Eileen. "Euripides and H. D.'s Working Notebook for *Helen in Egypt.*" *Sagetrieb* 14. 1&2 (Spring and Fall 1995): 83–88.

Harrison, E. J. and S. Peterson, eds. *Unmanning Modernism. Gendered Re-Readings.* Knoxville: The U of Tennessee P, 1997.

Hardin, Michael. "H. D.'s *Triology:* Speaking through the Margins," *Sagetrieb* 15. 1&2 (Spring and Fall 1996): 151–60.

Irigaray, Luce. *Sessi e genealogie.* Milano: La Tartaruga, 1985.

Kaufmann, Michael. "Gendering Modernism: H. D., Imagism, and Masculinist Aesthetics." In *Unmanning Modernism. Gendered Re-Readings.* Ed. E. J. Harrison and S. Peterson. Knoxville: The U of Tennessee P, 1997: 59–72.

Keating, Ann Louise. *Women Reading Women Writing.* Philadelphia: Temple UP, 1996.

Locatelli, Carla ed. *Co(n)texts: Implicazioni testuali.* Trento: "I Labirinti," Dipartimento di Scienze Filologiche e Storiche, Università degli Studi di Trento, 2000.

Miller, Meredith. "Enslaved to Both These Others: Gender and Inheritance in H. D.'s 'Secret Name: Excavator's Egypt.' " *Tulsa Studies in Women's Literature.* 16.1 (1997): 77–104.

Silverstein, Louis. "Nicknames and Acronyms Used by H. D. and Her Circle." *H. D. Newsletter* 1.1 (Winter 1987): 4–5.

Tarlo, Harriet. "The Underworld of H. D.'s *Helen in Egypt.*" *Sagetrieb* 15.1&2 (Spring & Fall 1996): 173–202.

Walker, Barbara. *The Woman's Encyclopedia of Myths and Secrets.* San Francisco: Martin & Row, 1983.

Wenthe, William. " 'The Hieratic Dance': Prosody and the Unconscious in H. D.'s Poetry." *Sagetrieb* 14.1&2 (Spring & Fall 1995): 113–40.

Witte, Sarah, E. "H. D.'s Recension of the Egyptian Book of the Dead in *Palimpsest.*" *Sagetrieb* 8. 1 / 2 (Fall 1989): 121–47.

————. "The Archeological Context of H. D.'s 'Secret Name' and 'Hesperia.' " *Sagetrieb* 15.1&2 (Spring & Fall 1996): 51–68.

Zaccaria, Paola. "Oltre il materno, il palimpsesto. La mitopoiesi generativa di Frida Kahlo e H.(ilda) D.(oolittle)." In *Co(n)texts: Implicazioni testuali*. Ed. Carla Locatelli. Trento: "I Labirinti" del Dip. di Scienze Filologiche e Storiche, 2000: 267–88.

————. "L'operazione di triangolazione del soggetto in desiderio di comparare: con-, tra- Frida Kahlo e H.(ilda) D.(oolittle)," in Borghi, Liana, ed. *Passaggi. Letterature comparate al femminile*. Urbino: Quattro Venti, 2001: 337–51.

PART II

"Write, write or die": The Late Poetic Sequences

Subject and Gender in H. D.'s *Trilogy*

Marina Sbisà

In Pursuit of a Woman-Author

As a philosopher of language and a feminist I am interested in the theoretical problems of feminine subjectivity. Thus, one of my concerns in reading H. D.'s *Trilogy*, the work of a woman poet, has been to understand the kind of subjectivity expressed in it.

I do not assume that a woman automatically speaks as a woman just because she "is" a woman (whatever this may mean). Many women accept external representations of themselves; that is, they agree to think of themselves according to guidelines established by the dominant culture or tradition, and, ultimately, by the male gaze, that is, by the interests and desires of men. Women who conceive of themselves in these ways may speak and act as subjects, but with a serious limitation: their self-consciousness is indirect, so to speak, because it is based on their acceptance of how they are seen by others, particularly by men. Moreover, many women still agree to express restricted forms of enunciating subjectivity, limiting themselves mainly to those speech acts that constitute reactions to other actions or events and do not presuppose any specific competence in the subject, apart from its being endowed with subjectivity. Such women may, for example, find it acceptable merely to protest or

complain, instead of criticizing or levelling accusations, or merely
to express opinions and feelings instead of making assertions or
assessments. This may be an aspect of the relation-centered cultural
attitude that has been deemed characteristic of women, in contrast
to the competitive cultural attitude of men (Tannen). But still, it is
a limitation to the feminine subject's autonomy.

I am not sure whether women who accept external representations of themselves or practise a limited enunciating subjectivity are
really "expressing themselves as women" when they speak, or even
when they write. Hence, I find it sensible, when considering the
literary work of a woman, to raise such questions as: Does the author express herself as a woman? And if so, how does she manage
it? For the same reason, I think that if we want to answer these
questions, we should not try to detect the influence of the actual
feminine individuality of the author on her work, but should instead
consider the text and the way in which it relates to matters of gender
and to the author's subjectivity. In particular, we should take into
account: (1) the kind of subjectivity built into the text; (2) the ways
in which the text represents, if at all, the feminine and masculine
genders and their relationship.

In this essay, I do not tackle the general question of whether an
author can express herself as a woman. I take it for granted that
this is possible. I want to analyze H. D.'s *Trilogy* as a case in which
that has been possible and focus on the ways in which we can
describe and understand the author's efforts in that direction.

Some tools for textual analysis

In my analysis I use some technical instruments of a semiotic nature.
I rely on the semiotics of enunciation outlined by Benveniste (*Problems, L'appareil*) and Ducrot, enriched by suggestions drawn from
speech act theory (Austin; cf. Sbisà *Speech*) and from Greimas's narrative semiotics (Greimas and Courtés; Greimas). I believe that these
instruments allow for highly individualized descriptions of the
enunciating subject, which, however, is not a single entity (to be
identified with a psychophysical individual) but an articulated construction involving various levels of subjectivity. As to the representations of gender conveyed by the text, these can be captured by
means of an analysis that is attentive to cohesion phenomena and
implicit meaning, relying on the framework of linguistic pragmatics
(Levinson, *Pragmatics*).

In the theoretical framework of the semiotics of enunciation, the subject or subjects expressed by a particular work are not to be sought outside the text (in the historical circumstances of its production), but within it, insofar as they are manifested or indicated linguistically. The linguistic manifestations of subjectivity are mainly connected with the use of deictic terms or the morphology of tense. But in order to single out a subject, we can also consider his or her acts, since where there is an act, there is also a subject. By "act" I mean, in accordance with the definition adopted by Greimas and Courtés (5), any doing that brings a state into existence or confirms it in its existence. In a text, there are two ways in which "acts" so conceived are present. They can be found at the level of the enunciated content of the text, as narrated or represented acts, and at the level of the enunciation, as acts of enunciation or speech acts. When a change is presented as brought about by a doing, it depends on *someone*'s doing: behind the doing, there is its subject. This subject, moreover, is to be considered as "competent" with respect to his or her act, since competence (intending or wanting to do something, being able to do it, and so on) is the necessary condition of performance. The same holds true in the case of speech acts. If an utterance counts as a speech act, there must be a subject behind it, who has to be taken as endowed with linguistic competence, communicative intentions, and any rights, obligations, and pieces of knowledge that make it possible for him to perform the speech act (Austin; Sbisà *Illocutionary; Linguaggio*).

I would like to distinguish three different levels at which subjectivity manifests itself in literary texts. First, to the whole of a literary work there corresponds an implicit "authorial subject" who is responsible for it (both from the point of view of content and from that of formal and stylistic choices). The authorial subject is the subject who has chosen to present us with a certain content, to entertain a certain communicative relationship with us, and to select certain codes or styles and certain intertextual references. He or she is identified by us on the basis of these choices, as the one who is responsible for them.

Second, when some linguistic markers of an enunciating subject show up in the text, we can identify a "linguistically indicated subject." Deictic terms—which include temporal and spatial adverbs, demonstratives, personal pronouns, and possessives—allow us to locate the enunciating subject with respect to the objects and events talked about in the text (Benveniste *L'appareil*; Levinson; Mühlhäusler and Harré). First-person pronouns and possessives signal the enunciating subject directly, while second-person ones locate him or her indirectly as the partner of his or her addressee. The enunciating subject is further characterized by modal verbs or adverbs that assign modal properties to him or her, or express his or her attitude toward the contents of the text, and by other lexical or syntactic devices (for example, mood) that function as speech act indicators. The linguistically indicated enunciating subject may coincide with the authorial subject or remain distinct from him or her. For example, the use of quotes or italics signals that the enunciating subject of the quoted fragment must not be identified with the authorial subject.

Third, the text itself may represent or stage further acting or enunciating subjects. These actors—characters, or figures—depend on the authorial subject's choices as to what they are, do, or say, and therefore occupy a subordinated position with respect to him or her. They may be staged as if they were independent from the authorial subject, when he or she narrates their performances and comments on them from the outside, without participating in the narrated events. But they may also mirror opinions and attitudes of the authorial subject, and even speak in his or her place.

The Subject(s) in *Trilogy*

In H. D.'s *Trilogy* there is a complex interplay among the three levels of subjectivity outlined above. In my analysis of the subject(s) in that poem, I focus on the second, intermediate level: that of linguistically indicated enunciating subjects. It will be on the basis of an analysis of this level that I occasionally refer to the other two. We shall thus see that in her poem, H. D. builds up her own enunciating subjectivity, not as dependent on other socially recognized ones, but in dialogic interaction with them.

First-person subjects

Throughout *Trilogy*, we often find first-person pronouns or possessives. In many cases, the enunciating subject thus signalled is aligned with the authorial subject and acts as a facet of the author's own enunciating subjectivity. If in these cases a second person pronoun is also present, it points to an ideal interlocutor. But there are other cases too: sometimes the subject who says "I" is a character, a subordinate actor:

I am Mary, she said, of a tower-town,
or once it must have been towered

for Magdala is a tower;
(*FR*:16)

or again, it is the author's interlocutor who uses first-person deixis, speaking in a simulated dialogue (while second-person deixis points to the interlocutor's interlocutor, that is, an enunciating subject aligned with the author):

This is a symbol of beauty (you continue),
she is Our Lady universally,

I see her as you project her,
not out of place

flanked by Corinthian capitals,
or in a Coptic nave,
(*TA*:37)

Even when there is no recognizable reported speech or simulated dialogue, it may be incorrect to identify the enunciating subject, who is linguistically indicated at a certain point of the poem, with the authorial subject of the whole poem. In that subject, it would be more appropriate to detect a facet or moment of the route along which the authorial subject develops, which is subordinate to the authorial subject and is endowed with specific or partial meanings. This is apparent, for example, when purposes are expressed, often by means of self-exhortation, as in:

Let us measure defeat
in terms of bread and meat,
(*WDNF*:33)

or in:

now having given all, let us leave all;
above all, let us leave pity

and mount higher
to love—resurrection.
(*FR*:1)

These purposes are clearly shared by the authorial subject, and therefore the subject who enunciates them can be considered as

aligned with her; but the expressed attitude marks only one step in
the development of the implicit, overall authorial subject. This kind
of gap between the linguistically indicated enunciating subject and
the authorial subject can be detected even when the author stages
herself as a character and uses first-person pronouns in narrating
her experiences or visions.

There are interesting half-way cases between the author's staging
of herself as a linguistically indicated enunciator and her reporting
a character's speech. One is the following:

> I sense my own limit,
> my shell-jaws snap shut
>
> at invasion of the limitless,
> ocean-weight.
> (*WDNF*:4)

Here the enunciating subject who says "I" is a shell (described in
the third person in the first part of the same section), which may
lead us to conclude that the "I" here occurs in the reported speech
of a character. But in the final lines of the section, the interlocutors
to whom the shell addresses itself turn out to coincide with the
addressees of the authorial subject:

> be firm in your own small, static, limited
>
> orbit and the shark-jaws
> of outer circumstance
>
> will spit you forth:
> be indigestible, hard, ungiving,
>
> so that, living within,
> you beget, self-out-of-self,
>
> selfless,
> that pearl-of-great-price.
> (*WDNF*:4)

It can therefore be argued that here the linguistically indicated enunciating subject is aligned with the authorial subject and gives voice
to some features of the author's poetics, becoming a metaphorical
representative of the authorial subject herself.

It should also be noted that the use of singular first-person deictics
("I," "me," "my") alternates with that of plural first-person deictics

("we," "us," "our"). The former emphasize personal experience, choices, judgments; the latter either replace standard singular first-person deixis with a poetic *maiestatis* plural, or refer to some collectivity that is presented as sharing experience or projects with the subject indicated by singular first-person deictics. First-person deixis in general is more frequent in the first and second books of *Trilogy* (*The Walls Do Not Fall* and *Tribute to the Angels*) than in the third (*The Flowering of the Rod*). In the first and second books it is plural first-person deixis that prevails, in the third it is the singular first-person deixis, pointing to a subject aligned with the author in the first thirteen sections and occurring within the reported speech of staged characters in the rest of the book. This suggests that subjectivity develops throughout the poem from forms in which dialogue, intersubjective confrontation, and reference to a community are essential to forms in which the authorial subject firmly expresses what she wants to express, either directly or through the staging of subordinated enunciators. This development corresponds to the progression of the authorial subject toward a full legitimation of herself, her poetic competence with regard to the sacred, and her mastery of words.

Qualifications of the enunciating subjects

The identification of the linguistically indicated enunciating subjects should be accompanied by a consideration of the ways in which such subjects qualify themselves. In connection with each of their speech acts, they are assigned (i) the related presupposed competence, without which they would not be able to perform the act, and (ii) some attitude that is implied or expressed by the performance of the act. Presupposed competence and expressed attitudes contribute to the reconstruction of the qualitative development of these subjects within the text and, insofar as they are aligned with the authorial subject, to the understanding of the overall architecture of *Trilogy*.

In the first book, *Walls Do Not Fall*, the enunciating subject aligned with the authorial subject attempts to announce her inspired message, but manifestly feels the need to justify her competence and make it acceptable to her addressees. A few passages concern the author's poetics and set out to legitimize her function as a poet, sometimes in contrast with other conceptions of poetry. The same attitude is expressed by the formal characteristics already noted (high frequency of first-person subjects aligned with the authorial subject and staging of simulated dialogues), as well as by the reference to polemic targets by means of the third-person deictic "they."

Many dialogic situations have an exhortative character that is expressed by the imperative mood (in the second person, or in the "let us" form). Such speech acts already presuppose some authoritativeness in the enunciating subject as a basis for suggesting or proposing the adoption of certain attitudes or kinds of behavior. Interrogative sentences are frequent too, and appear, curiously enough, mainly outside simulated dialogues: their presence indicates that the author is still in quest of her proper role, seeking the right way to express her inspiration.

It should be noted that the legitimation of the author's competence, as it is attempted in *Walls Do Not Fall*, is grounded in the attribution to the authorial subject (through enunciating subjects aligned with her) of a kind of knowledge closely linked to sensibility. Sensing or feeling something is not contrasted with knowing, but treated as its very basis. In *WDNF*:4 it is what the shellfish senses ("I sense my own limit") that enables it to know ("so I in my own way know / that the whale / can not digest me"). In *WDNF*:39 the link between knowing and feeling is exhibited by the enunciating subject with respect to an area of her competence crucial for the author as a poet ("I know, I feel / the meaning that words hide").

In the second book, *Tribute to the Angels*, the author's competence is no longer dealt with as in need of legitimation. Those linguistically indicated enunciating subjects that are aligned with the author are engaged primarily in asserting or arguing.

Affirmations are issued directly; the addressee is not urged to accept them, but is just faced with how things are (the repetition of the deictic assertion "this is" in *TA*:7, 23, 43, is emblematic of this expository style). There are fewer exhortative speech acts and more speech acts of explanation than in *Walls Do Not Fall*. Explanations presuppose authoritativeness in the enunciating subject and here this authoritativeness is not simply generic, but specifically regards knowledge. Although, particularly in the first part of the book, interrogative sentences indicate that the author is still involved in her quest, the space left for uncertainty shrinks remarkably: indeed, most questions are either leading or rhetorical, practically equivalent to affirmations as to their pragmatic function. Whereas in *Walls Do Not Fall* some invocations (to Osiris, *WDNF*:42; to Christ, *WDNF*:29) are cast in the interrogative form, in *Tribute to the Angels* the frequent invocations to the angels are cast in forms that presuppose an enunciating subject with some knowledge of the invoked entities (at times the invocation gives the author an opportunity to insert argumentatively organized explanations of their identities and attributes). Moreover, the reality of the experience for which thanks are given ("that we rise again from death and live") is itself presupposed. On the whole, we may say that the speech acts in *Tribute to the Angels* presuppose an enunciating subject endowed with knowledge and the acceptance of such knowledge by the addressees. It is perhaps interesting to add that in some sections of this book, the knowledge attributed to the subject is presented as grounded in visual experience, and in particular, as a purely ostensive, nonverbal knowledge coexisting, at times, with the refusal to denominate (as in the case of *TA*:13–14, where the linguistically indicated enunciating subject watches a mysterious jewel, but refuses to give it a name).

The argumentative aspect of *Tribute to the Angels* is apparent in some problematic and polemic sections. In *TA*:3 the author makes Revelation play against itself by recombining two quotations from it through the use of a "but," which evokes a remarkable argumentative potential:

> *I John saw. I testify;*
> *if any man shall add*
>
> *God shall add unto him the plagues,*
> *but he that sat upon the throne* said,
>
> *I make all things new.*[1]

The first three lines come from Revelation, 22:8 and 18, the fourth and fifth from 21:5; what is at stake in their contrast is whether H. D.'s own reelaboration of St. John's vision of the Heavenly Jerusalem in *TA*:2 violates a divine prohibition.

In *TA*:36–37, an "I" and a "you" argue about the interpretation of the vision of the White Lady, which has just been reported in the first person by an enunciating subject aligned with the author (*TA*:25—32). While the dialogues in *Walls Do Not Fall* question the

---

1. In the fourth line quoted, the word "said" belongs to the quotation from the Book of Revelation, while the word "but" doesn't. This suggests that the text contains a misprint ("said" should have been italicized, "but" shouldn't).

social legitimacy of the author's poetic discourse, this dialogue is concerned with its substantial content.

The third book, *The Flowering of the Rod*, begins with a series of sections rich in affirmations made by the enunciating subject (aligned with the author) about herself. For example:

> I am so happy,
> I am the first or the last
>
> of a flock or a swarm;
> I am *full of new wine;*
> (*FR*:8)

There are dialogic passages too, concerned primarily with the interpretation of imagery used in the poem, but they no longer have an argumentative style: the author's perspective is not argued for, but merely exhibited or exemplified. The authorial subject goes so far as to declare her intention not to argue, since argumentative discourse would be inadequate to what she wants to express:

> In resurrection, there is confusion
> if we start to argue; if we stand and stare,
>
> we do not know where to go;
> in resurrection, there is simple affirmation.
> (*FR*:3)

From section twelve on, the authorial subject changes her strategy. She reaches her highest degree of authoritativeness with respect to her text by acting as a narrator and a commentator. In sections twelve and thirteen, two characters, both endowed with subjectivity, are introduced. Kaspar and Mary, and as soon as they occupy the stage, the incidence of linguistically indicated enunciating subjects to be considered as aligned with the author decreases, indeed nearly disappears (as if such subjects had completed their task in the text of *Trilogy*). In fact, the act of narrating does not require a linguistically indicated enunciating subject and can be attributed directly to the authorial subject. First- and second-person deictics reappear in some of the short comments the author appends to her narrative ("not a beautiful woman really—would you say?", *FR*:13; "all we know is," *FR*:35). The very act of making comments also presupposes a subject endowed with some kind of both power and knowledge.

It is interesting to note, however, that the authorial subject chooses not to operate as an omniscient narrator, Kaspar and Mary depend on the author for the definition of their own identities and attributes, but this definition is left problematic. The identities of Mary and Kaspar are remodeled locally again and again and never achieve a full, stable definition. So the authorial subject herself appears as myopic, proceeding one step at a time within an incompletely defined horizon. The commenting subject is also far from being omniscient, because the required authoritativeness concerns values and not facts, and the comments made, however authoritative, count merely as expressing a point of view.

The limitations of the author's knowledge in *Flowering of the Rod* are paradoxical, but certainly not haphazard. The kind of knowledge relevant to the authorial subject's competence in this part of the poem is collocated along the limits of what can be known and said: it evokes these limits and admits of gaps. Thus, not only does the author herself refrain from exercising narrative omniscience, but also her character Kaspar (who is a wise man, a "Magus," possessing initiatory knowledge) is sometimes described as failing to know:

> no one would know exactly

> how it happened,
> least of all Kaspar.
> (*FR*:40)

Whereas in *Walls Do Not Fall* and *Tribute to the Angels* the author's knowledge is based on sensing, here a contrast can be detected between "sensing," which is placed in the foreground, and "knowing," at least insofar as this is seen as attaining linguistically expressible knowledge. But it should be noted that poetic knowledge is still at work (or even, more than ever): the implicit meanings of poetry go beyond the limits of what can be conveyed in words. And the author's competence, which makes this possible, is once again grounded in the dimension of "sensing," and particularly in memory, which is viewed as an internalized sensing and seeing. Memory is what drives the migrating geese toward Atlantis (*FR*:5); memory guides Kaspar from the encounter with Mary to the vision of the original Eden (*FR*:27, 33); and correspondingly, the authorial subject too proceeds backwards from the banquet at Bethany, just before Christ's Passion (*FR*:21–23), to the visit of the three Magi to Bethlehem (*FR*:42–43).

An interplay of voices

I now consider a specific strategy employed by the authorial subject to construct her subjectivity: the dialogue with, and appropriation of, the Word of God in the Bible. This strategy exploits quotation, marked by the use of italics.

Italics are a graphic device that can serve various purposes: they can mark emphasis, the fact that a certain word belongs to a language other than the main language of the text, or a quotation. All of these functions are somewhat analogic: the presence of different characters constitutes a change in the substance of expression and thus signals in writing what in oral speech would be achieved by the intrusion of a different speaking voice (an altered tone of voice, a switch to another linguistic code, a change of speaker). A quotation indicated by the use of italics is different from both direct and indirect reported speech. Its enunciator need not be mentioned (reported speech is usually accompanied by formulas such as "x says" or "x says that," which explicitly mention the enunciator), but is individuated merely on the basis of the quoted text. Therefore, he or she need not be an actual interlocutor or a fully developed character, but may remain a bare voice, distinguished from that of the authorial subject only by its different substance of expression.

Italics are often used in *Trilogy*. Words or sentences in italics appear in seventeen sections (out of forty-three) of *Walls Do Not Fall*, sixteen of *Tribute to the Angels*, and twenty-two of *Flowering of the Rod*. Most of these occurrences are quotations. Few (five in the entire poem) express emphasis, and some do not indicate quotations from preexisting texts, but voices imagined by the author as distinct from the voices of the authorial subject herself, her interlocutor, and her characters. (In *Flowering of the Rod*, for example, there is a voice expressing memory). I am concerned here only with italics indicating quotations, and particularly with those (the most numerous) drawn from the Bible. These quotations establish a close relationship, not easy to interpret, between the discourse of the authorial subject and the Word of God. The author cannot avoid confronting herself with the discourse of the patriarchal divinity of the Jewish and Christian traditions, but her aim is to draw from the Word of God inspirations that can transcend patriarchy.

H. D. inserts italicized fragments of the Bible in her text in various ways. Sometimes, authorial disclosure and quotation are separated by the use of parentheses or dashes; in other cases, a formula containing a verb of saying is used, often impersonal ("it is said") or passive ("we are told"). But in most cases the italicized fragments are inserted in the authorial discourse without any further indication that a change in the enunciating subject is taking place: either they are juxtaposed with the authorial discourse by means of punctuation (semicolon, comma) or they form mixed syntactic unities with elements of it. When the italicized fragments are juxtaposed with the authorial discourse (or with the discourse of a linguistically indicated enunciating subject), the relationship between the two discourses depends solely on the relationship between their contents. Thus, it is because of a contrast in content that the italicized fragment in *WDNF*:37

> *Thou shalt have none other gods but me;*
> not on the sea

> shall we entreat Triton or Dolphin,

sounds like an authoritative utterance, problematically opposed by the authorial discourse. In a similar way, we understand that the italicized fragment in *FR*:3

> seeking what we once knew,
> we know ultimately we will find

> happiness; *to-day shalt thou be*
> *with me in Paradise.*

exemplifies and justifies what has just been said by the author (or more precisely, by an enunciating subject aligned with her).

When the italicized fragments mix with elements in the authorial discourse to form new syntactic unities, the result is often somewhat different from the original syntagm or sentence in the source text. This suggests that the authorial subject is attempting to appropriate the message conveyed by the quoted fragment by re-enunciating it. In fact, the author sometimes alters the punctuations and omits or adds words, adapting the quoted fragment, first of all, to the structure of her text and the rhythm of its verse. For example, a sentence from the Song of Solomon, "Many waters cannot quench love," becomes the verse "for *many waters can not quench love's fire*" (*FR*:6). And from a longer and syntactically more complex passage from the Gospels, few italicized words are drawn:

> explicitly, we are told,

it contains

for every scribe
which is instructed,

things new
and old.
                    (*WDNF*:36; cfr. Matthew 13, 52)

By definition, the authorial subject is responsible for her textual strategies, and hence for her choice of quotations and the way in which she inserts them in the text. Thus it is legitimate to ask what the authorial subject is attempting to convey by the quotations she makes. In fact, there is a two-fold interference between the authorial subject and the quoted enunciating subject. On the one hand, the quoted speech is not deprived of its original meaning, but enriched by further meanings derived from its new contextualization; on the other hand, the image of the authorial subject is modified by the very fact that she is quoting, and sometimes even appropriating, the Word of God.

An intriguing example of recontextualization, involving the introduction of a new addressee, is provided by the following passage from a section where the contrast between arts and weapons is at issue:

... remember, O Sword,
you are the younger brother, the latter-born,

your Triumph, however exultant,
must one day be over,

in the beginning
was the Word.
                    (*WDNF*:10)

Here the enunciating subject, who is aligned with the authorial subject and manifests a polemic attitude toward the addressee, the Sword, addresses the latter a warning concerning the original superiority of the Word by means of a quotation from St. John's Gospel. The use of the quotation may seem merely instrumental, aimed at conferring solemnity to the thesis to which the authorial subject subscribes. But the Sword is surely on the side of what St. John calls "this world," and a warning concerning the original superiority of the Word is not inconsistent with the contrast between the word and the world typical of St. John's Gospel. The further meanings conveyed by the quotation—involving the author's desire to legitimize poetic wisdom on the basis of its creative use of language and its closeness to the dimension of the sacred (Camboni *Liberare*)—do not depend on the quoted text itself, but on the author's choice to quote it in that particular context.

Concluding then, the interplay of voices that the authorial subject puts on stage in all these different ways places her in a network of meaningful relationships and contributes toward strengthening her as a subject. Her enunciating subjectivity turns out to be remarkably dialogic: it is through continuous dialogic confrontations (not least those with the Word of God) that she attains higher levels of authority in her enunciation.

The Authorial Subject's Treatment of Gender

We now consider how the feminine and masculine genders and their relationship are represented in *Trilogy*. To this end we must leave what we can call, with Jakobson (*Shifters*) "the scene of enunciation" and focus on what could be called "the scene of enunciated discourse." Obviously, it is still the authorial subject, whose complex constitution has been discussed, who is responsible for the scene of enunciated discourse; hence, our consideration of that scene indirectly bears on the characterization of the authorial subject again.

In *Trilogy*, figures rich in gender connotations are evoked and used as poetic material. Among these, we find old Egyptian divinities such as Amon, Isis, and Osiris; other mythological characters such as Venus or Astarte; and Christ, Mary, Mary Magdalene, Abraham, the Magi. Among the images used by the author, many bear gender connotations (insofar as they are metaphorically associated with sexual stereotypes or, perhaps, archetypes): mysterious little boxes and butterflies, layers of snow and flowers, sea and brine, jars and perfumes, shells and migratory birds. Of course, the simple presence of these characters and images does not determine their use. Not surprisingly, the ways in which these ingredients are combined in the text suggest an unorthodox view of the genders.

It is not easy to make this view explicit, or to explain how and where it is suggested. As a poem, *Trilogy* draws on the implicit dimension of meaning, activated by the ways in which the text is structured. Among the most frequently used textual strategies for conveying implicit meaning, there is the juxtaposition of words or expressions, or their symmetrical contrasting. If standard expectations with regard to textual cohesion are assumed to be respected, the reader is led to consider such words or expressions as equivalent in some way (often, with respect to their referential function, in which case they identify either one and the same entity, or parallel properties of different entities). This amounts to implicitly proposing identifications or assimilations between entities or properties, and to shifting attributes from one entity to another. Such textual strategies are also employed to confer fluidity to gender attributes.

Gender issues are also implicitly tackled in the treatment of the theme of feminine autonomy in both the description and narration about female characters.

Equivalences, identifications, shifts

My first illustrations of textual strategies based on equivalence are unrelated to gender. When two referential expressions are juxtaposed so that the second is to be understood as in apposition to the first, it is implicitly conveyed that the two expressions are coreferential: that is, they refer, albeit in different ways, to the same entity. Thus, in

> Ra, Osiris, *Amen* appeared
> in a spacious, bare meeting-house;
>
> he is the world-father
> (*WDNF*:16)

the names of two Egyptian divinities and the name Amen (Truth), used in Revelation to refer to Christ, are treated as coreferential (as is further indicated by the anaphoric use of the pronoun "he"). And in the following passage, the stars are invoked also as little jars, precious boxes, and jewels:

> O stars, little jars of that indisputable
>
> and absolute Healer, Apothecary,
> wrought, faceted, jewelled
>
> boxes, very precious, to hold further
> unguent, myrrh, incense:
>
> jasper, beryl, sapphire
> (*WDNF*:24)

The coreference here has an obviously metaphorical value, but is effective nevertheless: it introduces into the text the equivalence between the figure of the star and those of the jewel and of the perfume container, which plays an important role in later parts of *Trilogy*. In this same section, moreover, predicates that appear to be pertinent to the stars and to the jars or boxes respectively are treated as parallel:

> that, as we draw them nearer
> . . . .
>
> will reveal their individual fragrance,
> personal magnetic influence,
>
> become, as they once were,
> personified messengers.
>   (*WDNF*:24)

This associates the figure of perfume to the notions of individuality and of mystic revelation, an association that recurs throughout the poem.

The assimilation of two referents by means of the parallel predicates applied to them sometimes has the effect of shifting one of these predicates from one referent to the other. Thus, both Hermes Trismegistus and Saint Michael fight against the darkness of ignorance and against the Devil:

> . . . Hermes Trismegistus
>
> spears, with Saint Michael,
> the darkness of ignorance,
>
> casts the Old Dragon
> into the abyss.
>   (*TA*:33)

While the spear is the traditional attribute of Saint Michael, here it is said to be used by Hermes. Of course, the Devil and ignorance are assimilated too.

These identifications and assimilations are not reductive. The point of the textual strategy employed is not to reduce a series of linguistically and culturally differentiated figures to references to a single entity, dismissing their differences as irrelevant, but to enrich the poetic approach to "spiritual realities" by highlighting their particular representations or individual modes and the ways in which they are interconnected (see *WDNF*:38). By exploiting coreferences, other equivalences, and shifts, the author is able to emphasize the availability of individual paths to poetic and sacred knowledge. This appreciation of individuality, by the way, is clearly related to H. D.'s own collocation within the Jewish and Christian tradition, which envisages resurrection (a transfigured state in which individuality persists, and a key word in *The Flowering of the Rod*), rather than the dissolution of the self in the infinite.

How do these textual strategies work with respect to gender? For example, "Love," used as the name of a divinity, is specified as being feminine by anaphora (*WDNF*:34: "Love, the Creator / her chariot and white doves"). The divinity referred to is recognizable as Aphrodite because of her attributes (the chariot and white doves), but is at the same time identified with the power that created the world by the (coreferential) apposition "the Creator." Here coreference and shift of attributes are both at work. In *Walls Do Not Fall*, Amen, who is explicitly characterized as masculine and Father and identified by means of coreferences with Ra and Aries, unexpectedly receives feminine features (albeit metaphorical): he says to his human interlocutor, "be Lamb, mothered again" (*WDNF*:21) and is addressed the entreaty "let your teeth devour me, let me be warm in your belly" (*WDNF*:22).

The description of the White Lady—the mysterious lady in white clothes whose apparition the enunciating subject describes and comments on in *Tribute to the Angels*—involves a shift of attributes, which implies an assimilation. She (a female character) receives the attributes of a male character (Jesus), to whom she is thus implicitly assimilated or compared (although, of course, she is not identified with him). Her description draws on the episode of Christ's transfiguration in the Gospel of Mark (9:3) and on the apparition of Christ after his resurrection in Revelation (1:13).

> For I can say truthfully,
> her veils were *white as snow,*
>
> *so as no fuller on earth*
> *can white them;* I can say
>
> she looked beautiful, she looked lovely,
> she was *clothed with a garment*

> *down to the foot,* but it was not
> *girt about with a golden girdle.*
> (*TA*:32)

By a shifting procedure typical of the author, the original reference of the quoted phrases to a male character is replaced by reference to a female character. Since the quoted phrases are recast in a new syntactic unit, they now apply to the lady referred to by "she" and indicated by the possessive "her" in "her veils." This conveys meaning at various levels. As soon as the original referents are identified, the status the author wants to assign to the White Lady is clarified too. She is dressed as Christ was when, still alive, he was transfigured, and lacks the golden girdle he wears after resurrection; therefore, she is no goddess, but a transfigured woman, in whom a future state of women, or perhaps of mankind, manifests itself. The shift of attributes from one gender to the other is also significant: the light of transfiguration, now coming from a female being, overcomes the traditional association of the masculine with light and the feminine with night and darkness. Moreover, since transfiguration heralds future glory, there is a clear implication that a new appreciation of the feminine is required and expected. The facts that there is no Child with the Lady and that she carries a book ("the unwritten volume of the new") indicate the direction in which the envisaged transformation is to go.

Thus *Trilogy* does not propose a search for the androgynous as a fusional totality of the sexes: in accordance with her appreciation of individual ways, and therefore of differences, the author is respectful of sexual difference. What she does instead is subvert gender expectations by assigning traditionally feminine attributes to male characters and traditionally masculine attributes to female ones.

The value of feminine autonomy

Dressed like a bride but without a bridegroom, the White Lady is also an expression of feminine autonomy. This theme is more widely developed, in a narrative form, in the third book of *Trilogy*, *The Flowering of the Rod*.

In *The Flowering of the Rod*, H. D. presents two characters (also subordinate enunciating subjects), Kaspar and Mary, and depicts their encounter. The narrated facts are very few: Mary receives a jar of precious ointment from Kaspar, which she will use to anoint

Christ's feet during a banquet just before his passion. The jar belongs to a set of two; the other had been taken to Bethlehem by Kaspar himself as one of the Magi. During the encounter with Mary, Kaspar has a vision that evokes the Islands of the Blest and the beginnings of mankind. These facts are enacted with a considerable richness of alternative facets, which leaves wide margins of indeterminacy, beginning with the problematic identities of the two characters. Kaspar is identified mainly, but not uniquely, as the magus who brought the myrrh to the Infant Jesus. Mary is identified as the woman who anointed Christ's feet in Bethany, but also as Mary Magdalene, and through her own words, Mara (a name that means "bitter"), Myrrh (mother of Adonis), and the plant and balm both called myrrh. Moreover, an equivalence is established in Kaspar's memory between this complex character and Mary the Virgin (Camboni, *Alchimie* 278), in spite of their distinct spheres of action (Bethany versus Bethlehem).

Surprisingly enough, the perspective of the narration is not Mary's: the author chooses Kaspar's perspective. Mary is a full-fledged subject, and an enunciator of discourse, but she is not seen from inside; she is, so to say, opaque. Kaspar is transparent; his states of mind, perceptions, beliefs and memories are represented directly. In the description of their encounter, Mary is represented as she appears to him. The author's alignment with Kaspar is further underscored by the qualifications they share as bearers of sacred or secret wisdom. (See *The Flowering of the Rod:* 29 for Kaspar, and the foregoing analysis of the qualification of the enunciating subject in *Walls Do Not Fall*, for the author). This violates gender expectations once again. Why is the author aligning herself with the perspective of a male character? Does she accept her poetic wisdom to be "neutral" (and therefore covertly masculine)?

I do not think that the author is doing something so trivial. I think, instead, that simply by bringing a male subject to meet a female character who is not constituted by her difference as an object, but rather as a subject, she is proposing to her addressees a reappraisal of autonomous feminine subjectivity.

Mary is described as "unmaidenly," "unpredictable," "a woman of discretion" (*FR*:13, 15, 35); it is said of her that "she had seen nobility herself at first hand," "nothing impressed her," "she simply didn't care," "she knew how to detach herself" (13), "like a child at a party, paid no attention" (21). These characterizations clearly endow her with a competence (will, and power to act) independent of, or even contrary to, her interlocutor's expectations. Kaspar's vision of the original state of mankind is triggered during his encounter with Mary and, in particular, by his looking at her loose hair—a salient aspect of her femininity. I would suggest that Kaspar's vision depends on his contemplation of Mary's autonomous subjectivity. The revelation he receives bears the mark of the feminine gender, the acknowledgment of which has made it possible.

By granting this vision to a male character like Kaspar, the author shows she is addressing not only women but also men, and confirms what she had already announced in *Tribute to the Angels* through the figure of the White Lady: namely, that the autonomy of the feminine subject and intersubjective acknowledgment of this autonomy form the basis of the radical renewal of our culture that she is urging.

Conclusions

H. D. builds up her own enunciating subjectivity, not as dependent on other socially recognized ones, but in dialogic interaction with them. Her competence becomes more and more authoritative as we move from the first book of the poem to the final part of the third book. In this progression she offers herself as an example of feminine autonomy, which is not to be intended as a separatedness of the individual, but rather as an attempt to seek one's own individual path, thanks to (and in spite of) intersubjective confrontations. She is not afraid to confront herself even with the Word of God, which she does not reject or dismantle, but recontextualizes, revealing deep consonances.

The knowledge she proves to be endowed with as a poet is grounded on various ways of sensing, such as feeling, seeing, and remembering. Although it would not be fair to count this as a textual marker for gender, it should be noted that it is consistent with a tendency detected in women in contemporary society by various authors (Gilligan; Belenky et al.).

As for the representations of genders, H. D., in *Trilogy*, does not propose a pursuit of the androgynous but, in accordance with her appreciation of differences, puts on stage definitely male and female characters, such as the White Lady, Mary, and Kaspar. Gender expectations, however, are often subverted, both in the attributes assigned to female and male characters or figures, and in the fact that the author, as a narrator in the third book of the poem, aligns herself with the perspective of a male character. This alignment is exploited to exemplify (and thus propose to the readers) the acknowledgment of that autonomous feminine subjectivity, which the author has pursued and practised throughout the poem.

Works Cited

Austin, John L. *How to Do Things with Words.* Oxford: Oxford UP, 2nd ed., 1975.

Belenky, Mary F., Blythe McVicker Clinchy, Nancy R. Goldberger, and Jill M. Tarule. *Women's Ways of Knowing.* New York: Basic Books, 1986.

Benveniste, Emile. *Problèmes de linguistique générale.* Paris: Gallimard, 1966.

———. "L'appareil formel de l'énonciation." *Langages* 17 (1970): 12–18.

Camboni, Marina. "Liberare l'anima. Ovvero il gioco delle parole possibili." In Mariella Pasinati, ed., *Parole di libertà.* Palermo, Ila Palma, 1992:73–90.

———. "Alchimie, miti, sogni, parole revisionarie," in *H. D. Trilogia. The Walls Do Not Fall (WDNF): Tribute to the Angels (TA); The Flowering of the Rod" (FR).* Original text and Italian translation. Ed. Marina Camboni. Caltanissetta: Salvatore Sciascia, 1993:253–84.

Ducrot, Oswald. "Analyse de textes et linguistique de l'énonciation." In O. Ducrot et al., *Les mots du discours.* Paris: Minuit, (1980): 7–56.

Gilligan, Carol. *In a Different Voice. Psychological Theory and Women's Development.* Cambridge, MA: Harvard UP, 1982.

Greimas, Algirdas J. *Du sens II.* Paris: Seuil, 1983.

———. and Joseph Courtes. *Sémiotique. Dictionnaire raisonné de la théorie du langage.* Paris: Hachette, 1979.

H. D. *Trilogia. The Walls Do Not Fall (WDNF); Tribute to the Angels (TA); The Flowering of the Rod (FR).* Original text and Italian translation. Ed. Marina Camboni. Caltanissetta: Salvatore Sciascia, 1993.

Jakobson, Roman. *Shifters, Verbal Categories, and the Russian Verb.* Cambridge, MA: Harvard University Department of Slavic Languages and Literatures, Russian Language Project, 1957.

Levinson, Stephen C. *Pragmatics.* Cambridge: Cambridge UP, 1993.

Mühlhäusler, Peter & Rom Harré. *Pronouns and People: The Linguistic Construction of Social and Personal Identity*. Oxford: Blackwell, 1990.

Sbisà, Marina. "On Illocutionary Types." *Journal of Pragmatics* 8 (1984): 93–112.

———. *Linguaggio, ragione, interazione. Per una teoria pragmatica degli atti linguistici*. Bologna: Il Mulino, 1989.

———. "Speech Act Theory." In *Handbook of Pragmatics*. Ed. J. Verschueren, J. O. Ostman, and J. Blommaert. Amsterdam: John Benjamins, 1995.

Tannen, Deborah. *You Just Don't Understand*. New York: Ballantine, 1990.

Binding Words and Feelings: Nominal Compounds in the *Trilogy*

Patrizia Lendinara

This study of the compounds occurring in H. D.'s *Trilogy* does not aim to discover new meanings in a work that has been so often studied and so widely appreciated.[1] Its purpose is rather to attempt to discover some linguistic features whose systematic analysis may contribute to the elucidation of the *Trilogy*. The sections of the three books that constitute the single long poem *Trilogy* cannot be examined in isolation: one must keep in mind the relationship between the parts and note recurrent elements.

H. D. spent the years of the Second World War in London where she had returned, at the outbreak of the conflict, to stay with her daughter in a flat in Lowndes Square. The separate parts of the *Trilogy*—*The Walls Do Not Fall*, *Tribute to the Angels*, and *The Flowering of the Rod*—were published respectively in 1944,[2] 1945, and 1946.[3] The

---

1. See Michael Boughn, *H. D. A Bibliography*.
2. In the same year, H. D. wrote *Tribute to Freud* (except for its afterword, subtitled "Advent"). On the relationship between this work and the *Trilogy*, see Peter Revell (171–98).
3. The three books (henceforth, respectively, *WDNF*, *TA*, and *FR*) were republished in 1973 under the collective title of *Trilogy: The Walls Do Not Fall, Tribute to the Angels, The Flowering of the Rod*. The *Trilogy* has

devastation of the war, its meaning[4], and the conversion of this experience into hope form the matter of the *Trilogy*, which has been termed "one of H. D.'s most coherent and ambitious poetic narratives."[5] The poems show her indebtedness to Denis de Rougemont and Sigmund Freud as well as her continued interest in myth and classical themes.[6]

There are many compounds in the poems, indeed so many that they are a significant feature of the *Triology*. Here H. D. uses the hyphen to bind syntactic groups (for example, *lost-god, water-about-to-be-changed-to-wine*), to separate prefixes and suffixes (for example, *un-named, fruit-less*), and to create daring syllabifications and misspellings (for example, *O-sir-is* and *O-Sire-is*). According to H. D., every word, if subjected to long examination, will yield new meanings,[7] and this is what she seems to have intended when she bound and divided the words of her poems. The use of the hyphen both to join syntactic groups and to separate the elements of compounds is a device to be found in her prose as well.[8] In the *Trilogy*, as elsewhere, she uses a number of compounds that are not recorded in English dictionaries,[9] such as *art-craft, fishing-net,* and *star-whirl-pool.* But well-known compounds may also have multiple meanings that contribute to the significance of the poems.

---

recently been printed with a commentary and facing Italian translation by Marina Camboni, H. D. *Trilogia.*

4. H. D. had also experienced the First World War in London, suffering great emotional stress; her experience of the Second World War was less personal: she seemed this time to share the misery of war with the people of London, and indeed humanity in general.

5. Susan Gubar, "The Echoing Spell" (196–218). See also Michael Boughn, "Unity" (6–30).

6. Susan Gubar, "The Blank Page" (243–63).

7. "If you look at a word long enough, this peculiar twist, its magic angle, would lead somewhere": *Bid Me to Live* (162). All the quotations and references are to *Bid Me to Live.* With a New Introduction by Helen McNeil and an Afterword by Perdita Schaffner, (henceforth *BML*). See also the following lines from the *Trilogy:* "but if you do not even understand what words say, / how can you expect to pass judgment / on what words conceal?" (*WDNF:*8, 16–18).

8. I examined the *war*-compounds in her novel in my " 'War' e 'not-war' in *Bid Me To Live* di H. D." Some of the compounds in the novel, for example, *love-and-war sequence* (95) and *not-war* (115) belong to H. D.'s idiolect. On her use of language in her poetry, see Marina Camboni, "H. D.'s *Trilogy,*" (103–106); Patrizia Lendinara, "L'immaginario," (103–13).

9. The standard reference throughout this analysis of the language of the *Trilogy* is to *The Oxford English Dictionary,* 20 vols. Oxford: Clarendon Press, 1989 (henceforth *O.E.D.*).

The important role played by compounds in modern English poetry was noted by A. L. Binns, who examined James Joyce's use of the compound *sindark* in "Chamber Music" ('Night's sindark nave')[10] and showed how it would mean either "as dark as sin" or "dark with sin, for sin, by sin," significantly changing, according to one's choice, the interpretation of the line in question and the entire poem.[11]

Many of the compounds used in the *Trilogy* suggest more than one meaning, which serves to enrich the poems. Several compounds belong to specific semantic fields, such as names of colors, animals, plants, and the sea (see the appendix). What is remarkable, however, is the frequency[12] and repetitiveness[13] of the compounds, but also their use, which is both redundant and recherché. The relationship between stress and word-formation should be kept in mind, particularly in poetry: many of H. D.'s choices are undoubtedly dictated by her medium.

Syllabifications and Metaplasms

The alteration of words produced through incorrect syllabification (which is indicated by a hyphen) is noteworthy and comparable to

10. A. L. Binns, "Linguistic Reading" (118–34).
11. In her turn, Hildegard L. C. Tristram (*Linguistik* 49), after remarking that "Multiple Auflösbarkeit von Komposita ist ein Strukturierungsmittel besonders der modernen Dichtung zur Erweiterung des Sinnhorizontes," considers the compound *wring-world* used by Gerald Manley Hopkins in "Carrion Comfort" ("Thy wring-world right foot rock? lay a lionlimb against me?"), showing that a *wring-world* is either a "world that wrings" or a "world which is to be wrung (by the foot)"; *wring-world* could also be a copulative combination, like *king-emperor*; see Hans Marchand, *Categories* (§ 2.55. 1).
12. The three parts of the *Trilogy* contain about 300 different compounds. I exclude from my reckoning words with prefixes and suffixes, as well as compounds with locative particles, though I provide examples from these categories of words when they have irregular hyphenation (see below note 59). I also exclude all such word combinations as *marah-mar* (*TA*:8, 9), *Mary-myrrh* (*FR*:16, 10), and *Zeus-pater* (*TA*:42, 4).
13 Twenty-nine compounds occur twice: *bridegroom, city-gate, Fisherman, four-square, garden-pink, grandfather, grass-blade, great-grandfather, green-white, half-open, head-dress, honey-comb, market-place, may-tree, million-million, myrrh-tree, not-known, old-church, ox-stall, pillar-of-fire, present-day, sea-shell, sea-temple, sea-weed, seventy-times-seven, sun-rise, sun-set, two-*

H. D.'s handling of compounds and syntactic groups. She explains the technique in *Bid Me to Live (A Madrigal)*, where she writes that "the words themselves held inner words."[14] In these instances, the hyphen signals a division into syllables that may be etymologically incorrect. The word *devil* (from Old English *deofol,* a loan-word from Greek through Latin) is misspelled and syllabified as *dev-ill:* "Dev-ill was after us" (*WDNF:* 2, 5) in order to lay stress on *ill.* A similar effect is produced by dividing *egocentric* into *ego-centric* ("has its peculiar ego-centric / personal approach": *WDNF:* 38, 20–21), though, in this instance, the syllabification is etymologically correct; the position of the word at the end of the line accentuates the meaning "centred in the ego." Other syllabifications, such as *super-natural* (*TA:*26, 8), will be considered below.

Syllabification is applied to names of places, such as *Paris:* "Par-Isis"[15] and personal names: *Osiris* is split up into both *O-sir-is* (highlighting the word *sir*) and *O-Sire-is* (highlighting the word *Sire*)[16] (see also *Ge-meter* and *De-meter* [*FR:*25, 18]). The *Trilogy* contains a few (grammatical) metaplasms[17] that draw their expressiveness from their arbitrariness: [18] H. D. uses *father-god* side by side with the regular *God the Father* ("Theus, God; God-the-father, father-god": *TA:*42, 5); and chooses *maid-of-the-sea* as a variation of *sea-maid* ("a maid-of-the-sea, a mermaid": *FR:*22, 11).[19] A similar example is found in *BML:* "Breakfast. Break fast. They would break their fast" (20).

Clippings and Tautological Compounds

Some compounds are only hinted at by the use of a shortened form, such as *lapis* for *lapis-lazuli* (*WDNF:*1,7); her choice of a back clipping

---

way, and *wild-goose;* a few compounds appear thrice: *apple-tree, eye-lid, half-second, heart-beat, high-altar; butterfly* occurs four times.

14. *BML* 162. See above, note 7.

15. So Bar-Isis is Par-Isis? / Paris, anyway" (*H. D.,* I: 3, 5–6).

16. Both metaplasms occur in the same line: "Osiris equates O-sir-is or O-sire-is" (*WDNF:*40, 2).

17. That is, alterations of words by addition, removal, or transposition of letters and syllables; see Heinrich Lausberg (*Elemente* § 120).

18. Both metaplasms, while synchronically arbitrary, are etymologically correct.

19. In the *Trilogy,* H. D. uses the loan-word *siren* only once, in the (hyphenated) syntactic group: *Siren-song;* on the use of *siren* and *lady from the sea* in *BML,* see Lendinara, " 'War' e 'not-war' " (287).

is interesting, because, in modern literature, the usual shortened form of *lapis-lazuli* (also *lapis lazuli*) is *lazuli*.[20]

On the other hand, compounds such as *plum-tree* instead of *plum* (*WDNF*:5, 10) are tautological.[21] Her use of the compound *bone-frame* for *frame*, to refer to the human body (*WDNF*:1, 43) is both tautological and recherché. H. D. is extremely careful about the formal correctness of her language, and clearly also refers to a literary standard (her work is full of echoes of earlier poets); she always avoids a mechanical use of those words whose meaning has been worn out by over-use. Tautology is evident in compounds such as *garden-pink* (*TA*:29, 11, and 43, 21) instead of *pink; herb-basil* (*WDNF*:26, 6) instead of *basil; vein-path* (WDNF:38, 25) of *vein;* and *weather-vane* instead of *vane* (WDNF:32, 10). A further tautology is the compound *sand-print,* which appears together with *sand,* in the line "but wind blows sand-prints from the sand" (*WDNF*:5, 13).

Etymologic Writings

Compounds commonly written without a hyphen are split apart by H. D., who writes, for example, *sun-rise* and *sun-set.* The hyphen emphasizes the elements of the compound, forcing the reader to focus his / her attention on the fact that the sun "rises" and "sets" (encompassing the entire poem within its course). Another example is *mad-house* instead of *madhouse* (*BML* 167). The compounds listed below rarely obtain a similar effect, but their number demonstrates a constant effort to pinpoint the semantic value of each word of a compound and, at the same time, to load the lines of the poems with extra meanings:

candle-stick: "that in a candle on a candle-stick" (*TA*:6, 24)
cross-wise: "*cross-wise*" (*WDNF*:43, 11)
eye-lid: "or eye-lids half-raised; you find" (*TA*:29, 35)
eye-lid: "those eye-lids in the Velasquez" (*WDNF*:19, 3)
god-father: "or the Angel god-father" (*TA*:42, 6)[22]

---

20. *Lazuli* is a fore-clipping (see Marchand, § 9).
21. See Marchand (§ 2. 2. 5) "the second-word is the genus proximus while the first-word is the differentia specifica. . . . Common are compounds with *tree* for a second-word, as *oak-tree, palm-tree, plane-tree,* perh. on the analogy of *apple-tree* where the notional basis is different."
22. See also below. There is a possible word-play in the use of this compound.

hearth-stone: "he saw the many pillars and the Hearth-stone"
    (*FR*:32, 7)
honey-comb: "on the amber honey-comb" (*WDNF*:29, 6)—also
    honeycomb (*FR*:7, 5)
mid-winter: "and its mid-winter dawn-pattern" (*FR*:4, 12)
moon-light: "as of moon-light on a lost river" (*FR*:17, 7)—also
    moonlight (*FR*:27, 18)
sea-weed: "gather dry sea-weed" (*WDNF*:17, 9)
sea-weed: "and brittle burnt sea-weed" (*FR*:4, 19)
sun-rise: "Phosphorus at sun-rise" (*TA*:10, 13)
sun-rise: "like water at sun-rise and sun-set" (*FR*:28, 10)
sun-set: "Hesperus at sun-set" (*TA*:10, 14)
sun-set: "like water at sun-rise and sun-set" (*FR*:28, 10)

This also applies to particles, prefixes and suffixes:

after-thought: "as if his gift were an after-thought" (*FR*:42, 9)

out-flowing: "a little too porous to contain the out-flowing"
    (*WDNF*:31, 17)

over-come: "bent him down, as if over-come" (*FR*:42, 27)
over-night: "over-night, a million-million tiny plants" (*FR*:37, 3)
over-whelming: "she was not even over-whelming" (*TA*:40, 19)—also
    overwhelming (*FR*:42, 28)
over-wrought: "Simon though over-wrought and excited" (*FR*:23, 5)

pre-determined: "as in a mirror was pre-determined" (*FR*:40, 3)
pre-history: "depth of pre-history" (*FR*:40, 16)
pre-history: "with the drowned cities of pre-history" (*FR*:33, 19)

re-born: "the re-born Sun" (*WDNF*:22, 16)
re-create: "re-invoke, re-create" (*TA*:1, 17)
re-dedicate: "re-dedicate our gifts" (*WDNF*:35, 3)
re-gathering: "the voice to quell the re-gathering" (*TA*:4, 9)
re-invoke: "re-invoke, re-create" (*TA* 1, 17)
re-light: "O swiftly, re-light the flame" (*TA*:11, 1)
re-light: "Swiftly re-light the flame" (*TA*:12, 1)
re-name: "he might re-name them" (*FR*:25, 17)
re-value: "now is the time to re-value" (*WDNF*:36, 9)
re-vivify: "re-vivify the eternal verity" (*WDNF*:35, 18)

In all these *re-* compounds, hyphenation emphasizes the idea of repetition; in normal use this prefix is written with a hyphen either when there is a homographic form of Latin or Romance origin, such as *re-cover—recover*, or when the main element begins with *e* (for example, *re-enter*).

sub-conscious: "Depth of the sub-conscious spews forth" (*WDNF*:32, 1)
sub-conscious: "sub-conscious ocean where Fish" (*WDNF*:30, 19)

un-cut: "and seen Jewels cut and un-cut that altered" (*FR*:28, 9)
un-lovely: "of this not un-lovely temple" (*FR*:26, 22)
un-maidenly- "but the un-maidenly woman did not take the hint" (*FR*:13, 14)
un-maidenly: "it was her hair—un-maidenly" (*FR*:15, 16)
un-maidenly: "the un-maidenly mermaid, Mary of Magdala" (*FR*:26, 11)
un-named: "another, deep, un-named, resurging bell" (*TA*:41, 12)
un-weaving: "she was busy; she was deftly un-weaving" (*FR*:21, 16)[23]

under-layer: "with under-layer of changing blue" (*TA*:13, 3)

paw-er: "paw-er of the ground" (*WDNF*:21, 4)
boy-hood: "after boy-hood and youth dedicated" (*FR*:29, 11)
fruit-less: "fruit-less on the field-edge" (*WDNF*:26, 11)[24]

The separation of suffixes, such as *-er*, *-hood* and *-less*, should be reckoned among the examples of H. D.'s poetic licence. The word *pawer*, a neologism from *to paw*, is divided into *paw-er* (*WDNF*:21, 4) and used to refer to a god, to stress the agentive role of Amon-Ra. The *Trilogy* abounds in substantives in *er* (the formative for

---

23. She uses it to mean unplaiting (hair), a rare, if not unique usage.
24. For words with the suffix *-less*, see below. See also the following examples, though, in these instances, the hyphenated form is also in use: *-a plenty*: "I am Mary—O, there are Marys a-plenty" (*FR*:16, 9); *to-day*: "in to-day's imagery" (*WDNF*:20, 10); "happiness; *to-day* shalt thou be" (*FR*:3, 25); "*to-day* shalt thou be with me in Paradise" (*FR*:11, 18); *drift-wood*: "heap drift-wood" (*WDNF*:17, 10); *egg-shell*: "can not crack me, egg in egg-shell" (*WDNF*:4, 27); *snow-flake*: "in the forest, as every snow-flake" (*WDNF*:38, 27); *wave-shape*: "shells to the wave-shapes? Gabriel" (*TA*:5, 10).

agent-nouns),[25] for example, *bearer, begetter, carrier, discoverer, fosterer, gambler, gatherer, giver, harvester, interpreter, keeper, painter, plasterer, ruler, seducer, spinner*. In several instances these words refer to leading characters of her poems, for example, to the intriguing figure of Kaspar, the male protagonist of *The Flowering of the Rod*.

Binding Words

Similarly, H. D. forms new compounds, which can have multiple meanings, out of syntactic groups: *coral-sea* (FR:6, 3), a combination that evokes the syntactic group *Coral Sea*, is both a "coral-coloured sea" and a "sea where coral can be found," and so on. Other combinations, such as *God-the-father* instead of *God the father* do not produce striking effects, but there are too many to be either fortuitous or used for metrical reasons:

almond-tree: "and the snow fell on the almond-trees" (FR:36, 9)
autumn-drought: "after the memorable autumn-drought" (FR:41, 13)
bedding-down: "inquiring perhaps as to bedding-down" (FR:42, 18)
bee-line: "resurrection is a bee-line" (FR:7, 2)
bell-note: "and I remembered bell-notes" (TA:15, 3)
bell-tower: "from the bell-towers, lilies plundered / with the weight of massive bees . . ." (TA:15, 9–10)
bird-claw: "bird-claw, scavenger bird-beak" (WDNF:6, 4)
bird-beak: "bird-claw, scavenger bird-beak" (WDNF:6, 4)
black-lead: "enclosed in black-lead" (WDNF:41, 5)
blue-goose: "Blue-geese, white-geese, you may say" (FR:4, 1)
blue-violet: "What is the jewel colour? / . . . / faint blue-violet" (TA:13, 1, 6)
bridge-head: "for even now, / the terrible banner / darkens the bridge-head" (FR:1, 15–17)[26]
built-up: "and the terraces and the built-up inner gardens" (FR:32, 6)
burnt-out: "that burnt-out wood crumbling" (TA:21, 9)
burnt-out: "this is the flowering of the burnt-out wood" (TA:43, 24)
burnt-out: "was in recognition of an old burnt-out / yet somehow suddenly renewed infatuation" (FR:20, 21–22)
carefully-braided: "the long, carefully-braided tresses" (FR:21, 17)

---

25. See Marchand (§ 4. 30. 1–26).
26. The *bridge-head* of the poem is merely the "head of a bridge," but the military overtones may be intentional.

coral-sea: "in the coral-seas; I would rather drown" (*FR*:6, 3)
dawn-pattern: "and its mid-winter dawn-pattern" (*FR*:4, 12)
deep-violet: "whose candle burns deep-violet" (*TA*:42, 9)
double-plume: "though these or the double-plume or lotus" (*WDNF*:8, 3)
dune-grass: "over sedge, over dune-grass" (*WDNF*:42, 2)
field-edge: "fruit-less on the field-edge" (*WDNF*:26, 11)
field-furrow: "In the field-furrow" (*TA*:10, 1)
flowering-grass: "and the flowering-grass; and he himself watched all night" (*FR*:38, 8)
fir-branch: "remembering—than rest on pine or fir-branch" (*FR*:6, 4)
God-the-father: "Theus, God; God-the-father, father-god" (*TA*:42, 5)
gold-piece: "some say she had nothing with her, / ... / no gold-piece or silver" (*FR*:12, 15, 17)
Great-hearth: "and the very fire on the Great-hearth" (*FR*:32, 8)[27]
great-mother: "the original great-mother" (*WDNF*:34, 13)[28]
he-himself: "he-himself was not here" (*FR*:34, 13)
high-altar: "as lamps on the high-altar" (*TA*:17, 5)
high-altar: "approach the high-altar?" (*TA*:20,4)
high-altar: "on the high-altar" (*TA*:34, 6)
high-priest: "as no high priest of Astoroth" (*TA*:19, 3)
house-money: "some say she took the house-money" (*FR*:12, 13)
house-work: "and not caring for house-work ... or was that Mary of Bethany?" (*FR*:12, 8)
latter-day: "Yet we, the latter-day twice-born" (*WDNF*:14, 1)
lost-god: "illusion of lost-gods, daemons" (*WDNF*:31, 23)
lower-gate: "as you pass through the lower-gate" (*FR*:13, 6)
lyre-note: "the indicated flute or lyre-notes" (*WDNF*:10, 7)
may-tree: "will you find the may-tree" (*TA*:17, 18)
may-tree: "was it may-tree or apple?" (*TA*:19, 14)
mountain-goat: "and he let the long-haired mountain-goats" (*FR*:38, 5)
new-church: "take what the new-church spat upon" (*TA*:1, 12)
new-world: "who have no part in / new-world reconstruction" (*WDNF*:14, 16–17)[29]
old-body: "till the new Sun dries off / the old-body humours" (*WDNF*:14, 10)

---

27. An allusion to the sacred fire, see also the compound *Hearth-stone*.
28. A loan translation of *Magna Mater*, the name of a goddess venerated in Rome, whose secret and licentious cult was introduced from Phrygia.
29. The compound does not refer to the Western Hemisphere.

old-church: "take what the old-church / found in Mithra's tomb,"
   (*TA*:1, 8–9)
old-church: "the old-church makes its invocation" (*TA*:33, 4)
old-self: "but the old self / . . . / cries out in anger" (*WDNF*:29, 6, 8)
optical-illusion: "whether it was a sort of spiritual optical-illusion"
   (*FR*:40, 13)
other-half: "but God in the other-half of the tree" (*TA*:23, 4)
palm-shadow: "I know the insatiable longing / in winter, for palm-
   shadow" (*FR*:4, 3–4)
papyrus-swamp: "there was One / . . . / in the papyrus-swamp"
   (*WDNF*:40, 20, 23)
river-reed: "where the mantis / prays on the river-reed"
   (*WDNF*:23, 7–8)
rose-vein: "green-white . . . / . . . / with rose-vein; . . ." (*TA*:13, 2, 4)
shadow-on-snow: "under the long shadow-on-snow of the pine"
   (*FR*:4, 22)
Siren-song: "and that a Siren-song was fatal" (*FR*:22, 13)
so-far: ". . . the deep deep-well / of the so-far unknown" (*FR*:40,
   14–15)
square-cut: "a circlet of square-cut stones on the head of a lady"
   (*FR*:28, 32)—also *square cut* (*FR*:28, 26)
stable-door: "when Balthasar had pushed open the stable-door"
   (*FR*:42, 11)
stable-floor: "for, as he placed his jar on the stable-floor" (*FR*:41, 10)
stained-glass: "without stained-glass, picture" (*WDNF*:18, 9)
stone-portal: "or a carved stone-portal entrance" (*FR*:22, 5)
storm-wind: "when storm-wind / tore it from its stem" (*WDNF*:6,
   7–8)
twin-horn: "with twin-horns, disk, erect serpent" (*WDNF*0 8, 2)
very-few: "and only the very-few could even attempt to do this"
   (*FR*:29, 10)
white-goose: "Blue-geese, white-geese, you may say" (*FR*:4, 1)
wild-almond: "are we wild-almond, winter-cherry?" (*WDNF*:27, 10)
wild-goose: "does the first wild-goose care" (*FR*:3, 13)
wild-goose: "does the first wild-goose stop to explain" (*FR*:3, 9)
winter-cherry: "are we wild-almond, winter-cherry?" (*WDNF*:27, 10)
winter-dawn: "opalescent winter-dawn; as the wave" (*FR*:4, 14)
winter-rain: "in the time of the sudden winter-rain" (*FR*:41, 12)
wood-smoke: "when, in the drift of wood-smoke, / will you say
   again, . . . " (*WDNF*:29, 17)
world-father: "he is the world-father" (*WDNF*:16, 3)[30]

---

30. See also the following examples, though in these instances both forms
   are in use: *at-home / at home*: "still half at-home in the world"

In some instances the hyphen generates ambiguous compounds, unrecorded elsewhere, whose interpretation remains an open question: the compound *black-lead* (*WDNF*:41, 5), for example, does not refer to (pencil) graphite, but rather to lead, the metal, and is a loan translation of the Latin *plumbum nigrum;* a *bee-line* ("resurrection is a bee-line," *FR*:7, 2) is not a "straight line," but simply a "line of insects."

Aggregations

At times more than two words are combined to form new compounds, producing neologisms, such as *pearl-of-great-price* (*WDNF*:4, 46), that receive, thanks to the process of aggregation, new strength and connotations that go beyond the meaning of the single words:

ash-of-rose: "we find not ashes, not ash-of-rose" (*TA*:43, 17)[31]
before-and-after: "bridge that before-and-after schism" (*WDNF*:40, 12)
fire-to-endure: "companion of the fire-to-endure" (*TA*:16, 9)
Hermes-thrice-great: "Hermes-thrice-great" (*WDNF*:35, 10)[32]
Holy-Presence-Manifest: before the Holy-Presence-Manifest" (*FR*:42, 24)
healing-of-the-nations: "what particular healing-of-the-nations" (*WDNF*:26, 4)
Leader-of-the-dead: "of Leader-of-the dead from Thoth" (*TA*:33, 2)[33]
life-after-death: "the first actually to witness His life-after death" (*FR*:12, 5); cf. *life-and-death*
nothing-too-much: "of nothing-too-much"(*WDNF*:4, 22)
paint-and-plaster: "paint-and-plaster medieval jumble" (*WDNF*:18, 4)
pearl-of-great-price: "that pearl-of-great-price" (*WDNF*:4, 46)
pillar-of-fire: "In no wise is the pillar-of-fire" (*WDNF*:36, 1)

(*WDNF*:29, 9); *snow goose / snow-goose*: "like the snow-geese of the Arctic circle" (*FR*:3, 18).

31. A possible allusion to the color *ash(es) of roses.*

32. A loan translation of *Trismegistus,* the name given to the Egyptian god Thoth by Neoplatonists (Lat. *Hermes ter maximum*); the loan translation is not exact because it should have been *Hermes-thrice-greatest*

33. I.e., *psychopomp* (a loan-word form Greek) "conductor of souls to the place of the dead." H. D. offers a loan translation of this word; see also *place-of-the-skull.*

pillar-of-fire: "different from the pillar-of-fire" (*WDNF*:36, 3)[34]
place-of-a-skull: "The place-of-a-skull" (*FR*:2, 17)[35]
self-out-of-self: "you beget, self-out-of-self" (*WDNF*:4, 44)
water-about-to-be-changed-to-wine: "of water-about-to-be-changed-to-wine" (*WDNF*:31, 18)[36]

Neologisms or Nonce-words

Some of the compounds in the *Trilogy*, though unrecorded elsewhere, have a regular structure and are transparent in meaning: [37]

Christos-image: "The Christos-image" (*WDNF*:18, 1); cf. *Christ-figure*
devil-ridden: "was devil-ridden or had been" (*FR*:25, 7); cf. *hag-ridden*[38]
dim-white: "nor porcelain; dim-white cloud" (*TA*:40, 11); cf. *dim-grey* and *dim-yellow*
death-symbol: "of pain-worship and death-symbol" (*WDNF*:18, 5); cf. *death-token*
ear-of-wheat: "a worm of the ear-of-wheat" (*WDNF*:6, 31); cf. *ear of corn*
ever-narrowing: "or fall from the innermost centre of the ever-narrowing circle?" (*FR*:5, 16); cf. *everblooming*
flower-cone: "a flower-cone" (*FR*:10, 17); cf. *flower-seed*
gorgon-great: "such as your gorgon-great" (*WDNF*:6, 21); cf. *gorgon-like*
grape-leaf: "no grape-leaf for the thorn" (*TA*:4,6); cf. *grape-stalk*
green-white: "green-white, opalescent" (*TA*:13, 2)

---

34. Biblical echoes are evident, see Ex. 13:21 and Rev. 10:1. Several compounds of the *Trilogy* have biblical overtones, for example *flesh-pot* (see Ex. 16:3).
35. I.e., *Golgotha*, the Aramaic word, meaning "place of the skull," which was borrowed by Greek and Late Latin, among others.
36. Once again, the biblical overtones are intentional and relevant. H. D. hyphenates also *Ancient-of-days*: "the original Ancient-of-days" (*WDNF*:35, 9).
37. The same can be said of the *half-* compounds: *half-burn-out* (*TA*:23, 13); *half-open* (*FR*:15, 4; *WDNF*:5, 11); *half-over* (*FR*:6, 17); *half-parted* (*FR*:30, 2; *FR*:31, 21, and *FR*:34, 2), cf. the more common *half-minute*.
38. The compound *devil-ridden* (*FR*:25, 7) has a parallel in *war-ridden* of *BML*, p. 40.

green-white: "so delicate, green-white, opalescent" (*TA*:17,1 9); cf. *yellow-white*

iris-bank: "between iris-banks" (*WDNF*:23, 4); cf. *rose-hedge*

head-band: "one head uncrowned and then one with a plain head-band" (*FR*:28, 21)

heal-all: "heal-all" (*FR*:10, 29); cf. *cure-all*[39]

lake-edge: "by the beached boats on the lake-edge" (*WDNF*:29, 16); cf. *lake-shore*

lily-head: "It is crowned with the lily-head" (*WDNF*:3, 5); cf. *lily-bud*

lotus-grove: "from the lotus-grove" (*WDNF*:27, 2); cf. *flower-grove*

mist-grey: "mist and mist-grey, no colour" (*WDNF*:1, 4); cf. *mist green*

non-utilitarian: "are not only 'non-utilitarian' " (*WDNF*:8, 13); cf. *non-utility*[40]

noon-heat: "in the noon-heat?" (*WDNF*:26, 14); cf. *noon-hot*

one-truth: "lead us back to the one-truth" (*WDNF*:35, 14); cf. *one-word*

rose-purple: "mulberry and rose-purple?" (*TA*:17, 16); cf. *rose-pink*

rose-red: "in green, rose-red, lapis" (*WDNF*:1, 7); cf. *rose-pink*

rose-thorn: "rose-thorn forest" (*WDNF*:6, 10); cf. *rose-petal*

sea-depth: "floundered, was lost in sea-depth" (*WDNF*:30, 18); cf. *sea-swell*

sea-drift: "and sand and burnt sea-drift" (*FR*:4, 5); cf. *sea-clay* and *sea-mud*

sea-rock: "rivers flowing and fountains and sea-waves washing the sea-rocks"(*FR*:32, 10); cf. *sea-stone*

sea-temple: "to a forbidden sea-temple" (*FR*:22, 6)

sea-temple: "from a forbidden sea-temple" (*FR*:25, 4); cf. *sea-idol*

shark-jaw: "orbit and the shark-jaws" (*WDNF*:4, 39); cf. *shark-mouth*

vine-leaf: "gorged on vine-leaf and mulberry" (*WDNF*:6, 26); cf. *rose leaf*

wheat-gatherer: "shade to the wheat-gatherers" (*WDNF*:26, 13); cf. *wheat-farmer* and *wheat-grower*

At times the distinction between a neologism and a nonce-word is rather tenuous. While a compound composed of *all* and a noun used adjectivally, such as *all-colour* ("but all-colour," *TA*:43, 5) may be considered admissible, several compounds in the *Trilogy* are examples of poetic license, whether in meaning, structure, or both: [41]

---

39. Cf. also the compound *all-heal*, different in structure and meaning.
40. The prefix *non-* is not currently hyphenated in English.
41. Unrecorded are also the compounds *bone-frame*, *garden-pink*, *herb-basil*, *plum-tree*, *sand-print*, *sledge-runner*, *vein-path*, and *wheather-vane* discussed above.

apple-russet: "or the apple-russet silk" (*TA*:30, 3); cf. *russet apple*
arbutus-fragrant: "arbutus-fragrant?" (*WDNF*:27, 14); cf. *rose-fragrant*
art-craft: "from its art-craft junk shop" (*WDNF*:18, 3); cf. *arts and crafts* and *arty-craft*
banner-stuff: "crumpled rags, no good for banner-stuff" (*WDNF*:12, 6)
centre-island: "about the lost centre-island, Atlantis" (*FR*:31, 16)
clock-hand: "the clock-hand, minute by minute" (*TA*:24, 3); cf. *hour hand* and *minute hand*
counter-coin-side: "she is the counter-coin-side" (*TA* 39, 3); cf. *other side of the coin*
credit-loss: "with credit-loss too starkly indicated" (*WDNF*:31, 11); cf. *debit and credit* and *profit and loss*
deep-deep: "Some call that deep-deep bell" (*TA*:42, 1)[42]
deep-well: "or whether he looked down the deep deep-well" (*FR*:40, 14)
dream-equation: "in a simple dream-equation" (*WDNF*:20, 14); cf. *dream-figure*
fishing-net: "among the fishing-nets" (*WDNF*:29, 15); cf. *fishnet*
garden-square: "in an old garden-square" (*TA*:20, 14)
gem-stuff: "of encrusted gem-stuff" (*WDNF*:6, 16)
grave-edge: "at the grave-edge" (*TA*:35, 3)[43]
ice-mirror: "in an ice-mirror" (*FR*:10, 14); cf. *ice-cube* and *ice-shelf*
incense-flower: "I am Mary, the incense-flower of the incense-tree" (*FR*:19, 1)
heart-husk: "whose roots bind the heart-husk" (*WDNF*:25, 12)
heart-core: "lodged in the heart-core" (*WDNF*:25, 15); cf. *bottom of heart*[44]
latter-born: "you are the younger brother, the latter-born" (*WDNF*:10, 12); cf. *lastborn*
leaf-spire: "the spear and leaf-spire" (*WDNF*:26, 7)
manna-beans: "stripped from the manna-beans, pulse, lentils" (*WDNF*:2, 8)
million-million: "over-night, a million-million tiny plants" (*FR*:37,3)
million-million: "and a million-million little grass-stalks" (*FR*:37, 5)
moon-crescent: "of the moon-crescent" (*TA*:28, 3)

---

42. See also the other reduplicative compound *million-million* and the remarks by Marchand (§ 2. 20): "In English, the use of repetition is almost completely restricted to expressive sound words."
43. See below for the three *edge*-compounds.
44. For these and the other *heart*-compounds, see below.

moon-cycle: "of the moon-cycle, of the moon-shell" (*TA*:28, 2)
moon-regent: "the moon-regent, the Angel" (*TA*:28, 6)
moon-shell: "of the moon-cycle, of the moon-shell" (*TA*:28, 2)[45]
mother-father: "what is this mother-father" (*TA*:9, 7)
no-colour: "is white and white is not no-colour" (*TA*:43, 3)
ocean-weight: "ocean-weight; infinite water" (*WDNF*:4, 26)
octopus-darkness: "the octopus-darkness" (*WDNF*:4, 32)
pain-worship: "of pain-worship and death-symbol" (*WDNF*:18, 5)[46]
red-death: "where the red-death fell" (*TA*:7, 2)
red-fire: "yet he, red-fire is one of seven fires" (*TA*:5, 14)[47]
right-spell: "for the true-rune, the right-spell" (*WDNF*:2, 15)
saffron-shape: "the saffron-shape of the sandal" (*FR*:39, 15)
Same-forever: "Fosterer, Begetter, the Same-forever" (*WDNF*:40, 22)
sea-incense: "of burnt salt and sea-incense" (*WDNF*:17, 13)
shell-jaw: "my shell-jaws snap shut" (*WDNF*:4, 24)
spectrum-blue: "The Presence was spectrum-blue" (*WDNF*:13, 1)[48]
star-whirlpool: "see—I toss you into the star-whirlpool" (*WDNF*:21, 10)
T-cross: "and the T-cross becomes caduceus" (*TA*:33, 3); cf. *T-shaped cross*[49]
tower-town: "I am Mary, she said, of a tower-town" (*FR*:16, 1); cf. *towered town* and *tower and town*
true-magic: "invoke the true-magic" (*WDNF*:35, 13)
true-rune: "for the true-rune, the right-spell" (*WDNF*:2, 15)
vine-flower (*TA*:4, 7): "no vine-flower for the crown" (*TA*:4, 7)
under-definitive: "over-sensitive, under-definitive" (*WDNF*:32, 13)
unobtainable-elsewhere: "what he had, his priceless, unobtainable-elsewhere myrrh" (*FR*:13, 9)
worm-cycle: "to those who have done their worm-cycle (*WDNF*:8,2 3)[50]

---

45. For the *moon*-compounds in the *Trilogy*, see below.
46. The two components form a surprising compound; see also *right-spell*, *sea-incense*, *shell-jaw*, *true-magic*, and *true-rune*.
47. *Red-fire* is neither a firework nor a color, but one of the names given to fire by H.D.
48. The compound (unrecorded in dictionaries) is noteworthy, because *spectrum* includes among its meanings the obsolete "apparition, spectre" and the current "coloured band into which a beam of light is split by means of a prism or diffraction grating." H. D. may have intended either meaning or both.
49. H. D. also uses the compound *tau-cross*: "that he, by his tau-cross" (*WDNF*:35, 12).
50. In this compound *cycle* means "a recurrent round or course of phenomena," "a round or series which returns upon itself" (for example, the

zrr-hiss: "*there is zrr-hiss*" (*WDNF*:43, 3)

Here use of *not* in combinations with a verb in quite interesting (for a parallel, in general use, cf. *do-nothing*):

did-not: "literally, as his hand just did-not touch her hand" (*FR*:30, 9)
is-not: "what men say is-not—I remember" (*FR*:6, 15)
was-not: "what was or was-not in those alabaster boxes" (*FR*:14, 13)

She also makes use of *not* as a prefix, not only with adjectives (instead of the negative prefix *un-*), but also with nouns:

not-fear: "she is not-fear, she is not-war" (*TA*:39, 5)
not-inconsiderable: "had inspired some not-inconsiderable poets" (*FR*:15, 14)
not-known: "lightning is a not-known" (*WDNF*:43, 4)
not-known: "of the not-known" (*WDNF*:43, 28)
not-there: "we were there or not-there" (*TA*:20, 11)
not-war: "she is not-fear, she is not-war" (*TA*:39, 5)

It is evident that several compounds were devised by H. D. to multiply the evocative quality of her lines: [51] the compound *apple-russet* (*TA*:30, 3), which is used in reference to the colour of a silk dress (described as *apple-green* in the preceding line of the poem), seems rather awkward, but is meant to convey, in addition to the reddish-brown colour, a striking contrast between the *silk* (a soft and precious cloth) and the coarse homespun reddish-brown woolen cloth called "russet." A further word-play is provided by the fact that the *russet* is also a variety of reddish-brown apple.

The compound *red-death* (*TA*:7,2) mimes and evokes the syntactic group *Black Death* (the name commonly given to the deadly plague that spread throughout Europe in the fourteenth century) and also echoes the "The Masque of the Red Death" by Edgar Allan Poe.

Several of the aforementioned compounds have a multiple meaning: for example, a *tower-town* is not simply a *towered town*, but rather a town looking like a tower, a town coinciding with a tower. In H. D.'s lines Mary of Magdala (a town on the Sea of Galilee,

---

metamorphosis or cycle of an insect), but also alludes to cycles such as the Arthurian cycle, a "series of poems collected round a central event or epoch of mythic history."

51. See Lendinara (" 'War' e 'not-war' " 281–89).

whose Hebrew name means "tower') becomes herself a tower.[52] The word *octopus-darkness* is reminiscent of English and German compounds such as *raven-black/Rabenschwarz*, but, in this instance, the poet does not look for parallels in a bird with black feathers, but in a marine creature, whose name evokes the darkness of the unfathomed deep, and the inkiness of the related mollusc, the cuttlefish.

The new or alternative meanings achieved by binding the words of a syntactic group prompt the reader to look for the "inner meaning" of the new words. This happens also in *BML*, where *plane-tree* is repeatedly used, in the hyphenated form, in part because the first word's homophone *plane* is a shortened form of *aeroplane* (or *airplane*, now chiefly North American), a word that never occurs in the novel.[53] In her book, H. D. intentionally avoids the use of military vocabulary, but continually refers to the war by means of several devices. One of her lexical strategies is the use of compounds whose members belong to the lexical field of "war," for example *plane-tree*, whose first element is *plane*. H. D. invites her readers to look inside the words, because "the words themselves held inner words" (162). Thanks to these as well as other lexical strategies (for example, the use of polysemantic words such as *shell* (96), which also means "cartridge case," *stripe* [31, 31], also "badge of rank"; *watch* [19 ff.], also "vigilance, guard") the war permeates every page of the novel, "creeping closer" to the reader, to use H. D.'s expression ("the war crept closer," 68). The evocative strength of the *plane-tree* is evident in a somber scene of the novel, when the branches of the trees become metallic: "the plane-trees stood stark metal. They lifted metallic branches to a near sky that loomed now with a sudden spit of fire" (109).

In the *Trilogy*, H. D. makes use of a few unrecorded copulative combinations such as *centre-island*, *leaf-spire*, and *mother-father*. The reader may interpret them as either additive or appositional compounds, according to which word he considers dominant. *Atlantis* is a fabled "island that sunk in the middle of the ocean," an "island that was the seat of an empire with a leading role," a *leaf-spire* is a "leaf with the features of a spire," and a *mother-father* is a "father who is at the same time a mother."

---

52. On Mary Magdalene, see Marina Camboni, "Hilda Doolittle" (18–20).
53. The word *air-plane* never occurs in *BML*, where we find, once, the word *plane*, meaning "flat surface" (118). The word *plane-tree* occurs at p. 79, 80 (× 39), 89, 109, 139, and 180.

Word-play

Word play is provided by neologisms such as *true-magic, true-rune,*
and *right-spell,* because both *magic* and *runes* (at least according to
H. D.'s interpretation of runic writing) may be considered "true"
only by a limited number of followers, and, similarly, a *spell* would
not be generally considered "right." H. D. speaks of *incense-flowers*
and *vine-flowers,* but neither of these compounds, rich in evocative
overtones (religious, iconographic, and so on), should be taken literally.

In other instances a couple or a string of compounds generates
word-play:

banner-staff: "from each banner-staff" (*WDNF*:6, 18)
banner-stuff: "crumpled rags, no good for banner-stuff"
    (*WDNF*:12, 6)

God-the-father: "Theus, God; God-the-father, father-god" (*TA*:42, 5)
father-god: "Theus, God; God-the-father, father-god" (*TA*:42, 5)
god-father: "or the Angel god-father" (*TA*:42, 6)

Compound Strategies

Besides common instances of verbatim repetitions that produce envelope patterns,[54] such as:

four-square: "but not four-square, I thought" (*TA*:2, 3)
four-square: "but it was not four-square" (*TA*:2, 18)
seventy-times-seven: "he of the seventy-times-seven" (*TA*:3, 9)
seventy-times-seven: "He of the seventy-times-seven" (*TA*:3, 11)

the language of the *Trilogy* includes doublets such as:

---

54. By envelope pattern I mean a repetition at the end of the same section
    of a poem of words or ideas that are employed at the beginning. In
    some instances the repetition is not identical: for example, *latter-day:*
    "Yet we, the latter-day twice born" (*WDNF*:14, 1) and *present-day:* "of
    present-day endeavour" (*WDNF*:14, 26); *bell-notes:* "and I remembered
    bell-notes" (*TA*:15, 3), and *bell-towers:* "from the bell-towers, lilies plun-
    dered" (*TA*:15, 9).

bird-claw: "bird-claw, scavenger bird-beak" (*WDNF*:6, 4)
bird-beak: "bird-claw, scavenger bird-beak" (*WDNF*:6, 4)

shell-fish: "the shell-fish" (*WDNF*:4, 7)
shell-jaws: "my shell-jaws snap shut" (*WDNF*:4, 24)

sun-rise: "Phosphorus at sun-rise" (*TA*:10, 13)
sun-set: "Hesperus at sun-set" (*TA*:10, 14)

stable-floor: "for, as he placed his jar on the stable-floor" (*FR*:41, 10)
stable-door: "when Balthasar had pushed open the stable-door" (*FR*:42, 11)

This applies also to prefixes when they are separated by a hyphen:

re-invoke: "re-invoke, re-create" (*TA*:1, 17)
re-create: "re-invoke, re-create" (*TA*:1, 17)

A compound may generate further nearby compounds. At times the "archetypal" compound does not occur in the poem, but serves as a reference for both poet and reader: for example, *moonlight* (or *moonshine*) is the model for the following—unrecorded—compounds:

moon-cycle: "of the moon-cycle, of the moon-shell" (*TA*:28, 2)
moon-shell: "of the moon-cycle, of the moon-shell" (*TA*:28, 2)
moon-crescent: "of the moon-crescent" (*TA*:28, 3)
moon-regent: "the moon-regent, the Angel" (*TA*:28, 6)

Similarly, the following series of neologisms can be thought to refer to the now-obsolete compound *heart-root*:

heart-shell: "my heart-shell" (*WDNF*:25, 4)
heart-husk: "whose roots bind the heart-husk" (*WDNF*:25, 12)
heart-core: "lodged in the heart-core" (*WDNF*:25, 15)

H. D.'s painstaking rewriting, "her lifelong fascination with the palimpsest," [55] often produces an accumulation, in the same poem, of

---

55. Gubar ("The Echoing Spell" 197).

compounds belonging to the same semantic field (see also appendix). In the poem on the shell (WDNF:4) there occur sea-shell, shell-fish, shell-jaws, egg-shell. The effect of her deliberate repetition is, as is often the case, striking.

A few compounds or elements of compounds recur several times: for instance, see occurs, as a first word, × 13; moon, as a first word, × 6; apple, as a first word, × 4; goose, as a second word, × 4; deep, as a first word, × 3;[56] edge, as a second word, × 3; beat, as a second word, × 2; church, as a second word, × 2; door, as a second word, × 2.[57] These repetitions help in linking the single poems of the three parts of the Trilogy. In several instances, word repetition highlights the central themes of the Trilogy. The three compounds grave-edge, "at the grave-edge" (TA:35, 3), field-edge, "fruit-less on the field-edge" (WDNF:26, 11), and lake-edge, "by the beached boats on the lake-edge" (WDNF:29, 16) emphasize the liminal features of grave, field, and lake, in a collection of poems in which liminality is one of the main themes.

Analogously, words that refer to some of H. D.'s principal motifs, such as cross, half, hearth, maid, sea, and shell, are used as both first and second words of compounds and, in some instances, appear in clusters within the same section of a poem:

sea-temple: "to a forbidden sea-temple" (FR:22, 6)
sea-shore: "seated on the sea-shore" (FR:22, 9)
maid-of-the-sea: "a maid-of-the-sea, a mermaid" (FR 22, 11)
mermaid: "a maid-of-the-sea, a mermaid" (FR:22, 11)

Crescendos

In Bid Me to Live the male character, Rafe, is described as a "hearty over-sexed . . . young officer on leave" (46), an "over-sexed officer

---

56. See also altar- × 2; bird- × 2; blue- × 2; death- × 2; garden- × 2; grass- × 3; half- × 6; head- × 2; heart- × 4; high- × 2; house- × 3; ice- × 2; incense- × 2; latter- × 2; life- × 2; lily- × 2; lotus- × 2; mid- × 2; new- × 3; not- × 5; old- × 3; rain- × 2; rose- × 4; sand- ×3; shell- × 2; snow- × 2; stable- × 2; sun- × 4; tide- × 2; water- × 3; wild- × 2 and winter- × 3.

57. See stable-door: "when Balthasar had pushed open the stable-door" (FR:42, 11); hut-door: "to a half-open hut-door" (WDNF:5, 11). Words referring to opening and closing are among the key words of the Trilogy.

on leave," "Rafe-on-leave" (55), and a "husband-on-leave" (70). There is talk of "officers on leave" (118) and of officers on sick-leave" (114). The *Trilogy* provides analogous examples of this incremental pattern,[58] for example:

grandfather: "his father had had from his grandfather" (*FR*:29, 5)
grandfather: "and his grandfather from his great-grandfather (and so on)" (*FR*:29, 6)
great-grandfather: "and is grandfather from his great-grandfather (and so on)" (*FR*:29, 6)

Crescendos and *decrescendos* also occur at a distance, as happens with *burnt-out* (*TA*:21, 9) and *half-burnt-out* (*TA*:23, 13).

Antonyms and Synonyms

In the poems of the *Trilogy* H. D. makes use of compounds with opposite meanings, such as *old-church*, "take what the old-church" (*TA*:1, 9) and *new-church*, "take what the new-church spat upon" (*TA*:1, 12), and *no-colour*, "is white and white is not no-colour" (*TA*:43, 3) and *all-colour*, "but all-colour" (*TA*:43, 5). She also employs compounds with similar or identical meanings, such as *heart-beat* and *pulse-beat*: "heart-beat, pulse-beat" (*TA*:14, 9).

Prefixes and Suffixes

Many words with prefixes[59] or suffixes[60] appear in the *Trilogy*. It is interesting to note that the suffix she uses most often is -*less*. In a

---

58. This kind of incremental pattern is a specialized extension of the parallel pattern. Progressive or degressive increase in effect is obtained by repetition of one or both elements of a compound.
59. See Marchand (§ 3. 1. 1). Among the many words with prefixes, the *un*-compounds are particularly frequent. The un- generally means "not," but she also uses it to reverse the result of the action expressed by the simple verb: *unknot, unlock* (see § 3. 64). In the foregoing analysis I have provided examples of words whose prefix is hyphenated by H. D. for example, *mid-winter, pre-determined, re-born.* She also hyphenates some compounds with locative particles as a first element (§§ 2. 39–52), for example, *after-thought, out-flowing, sub-conscious, under-definitive.*
60. See Marchand (§ 4). H. D. often uses -*ness* and -*less* suffixes.

few instances the suffix is hyphenated, apparently to highlight one
of its meanings, "devoid of," a significance utterly consonant with
one of the main themes H. D. grapples with in the *Trilogy*.

beardless: "beardless, not at all like Jehovah" (*WDNF*:16, 8)
defenceless: "our awareness leaves us defenceless" (*WDNF*:29, 13)
doorless: "passed through a frame-doorless-" (*TA*:20, 6)
fruit-less: "fruit-less on the field-edge" (*WDNF*:26, 11)
limitless: "at invasion of the limitless" (*WDNF*:4, 25)
nameless "we nameless initiates" (*WDNF*:13, 23)
numberless: "he was such a rich man, with numberless herds, cattle
      and sheep-" (*FR*:38, 4)
numberless: "and he had numberless children" (*FR*:29, 2)
pitiless: "pitiless, pitiless, let us leave" (*FR*:2, 16)
powerless: "is powerless against" (*WDNF*:4, 33)
powerless: "*we are powerless*" (*WDNF*:43, 6)
priceless: "what he had, his priceless, unobtainable-elsewhere
      myrrh" (*FR*:13, 9)
reckless: "reckless, regardless, blind to reality" (*FR*:6, 26)
regardless: "reckless, regardless, blind to reality" (*FR*:6, 26)
selfless: "selfless" (*WDNF*:4, 45)
senseless: "yours is the senseless wheeling" (*FR*:6, 10)
speechless: "though, remote, speechless" (*WDNF*:13, 15)
speechless: "and Melchior bent and kissed the earth, speechless"
      (*FR*:42, 36)
tasteless: "Good was the tasteless pod" (*WDNF*:2, 7)
timeless: "has abstract value, is timeless" (*WDNF*:15, 15)
useless: "poets are useless" (*WDNF*:8, 6)
worthless: "worthless in itself (those weighty rings of gold)"
      (*FR*:42, 35)

Appendix

Semantic Fields with a Large Number of Compounds

Colors

spectrum-blue: "The Presence was spectrum-blue" (*WDNF*:13, 1)

mist-grey: "mist and mist-grey, no colour" (*WDNF*:1, 4)

smoke-grey: "than any valuer over a new tint of rose or smoke-grey" (*FR*:28, 18)

rose-purple: "mulberry and rose-purple?" (*TA*:17, 16)

rose-red: "in green, rose-red, lapis" (*WDNF*:1, 7)

blue-violet: "faint blue-violet" (*TA*:13 6)
deep-violet: "whose candle burns deep-violet" (*TA*:42, 9)

dim-white: "nor porcelain; dim-white could" (*TA*:40, 11)
green-white: "green-white, opalescent" (*TA*:13, 2)
green-white: "so delicate, green-white, opalescent" (*TA*:17, 19)

Animals

butterfly: "of horns, as the butterfly" (*WDNF*:7, 3)
butterfly: "of the butterfly's antennae (*WDNF*:32, 20)
butterfly: "to hatch butterflies" (*WDNF*:39, 9)
butterfly: "she is Psyche, the butterfly" (*TA*:38, 19)
grasshopper: "where the grasshopper says" (*WDNF*:23, 9)
mountain-goat: "and he let the long-haired mountain-goats" (*FR*:38, 5)

blue-goose: "Blue-geese, white-geese, you may say" (*FR*:4, 1)
snow-goose: "like the snow-geese of the Arctic Circle" (*FR*:3, 18)
white-geese: "Blue-geese, white-geese, you may say" (*FR*:4, 1)
wild-goose: "does the first wild-goose stop to explain" (*FR*:3, 9)
wild-goose: "does the first wild-goose care"(*FR*:3, 13)

See also:

bee-line: "resurrection is a bee-line" (*FR*:7, 2)
bird-claw: "bird-claw, scavenger bird-beak" (*WDNF*:6, 4)
bird-beak: "bird-claw, scavenger bird-beak" (*WDNF*:6, 4)
king-cobra: "or the erect king-cobra crest" (*WDNF*:7, 5)
spider-snare: "persistence; I escaped spider-snare" (*WDNF*:6, 3)
worm-cycle: "to those who have done their worm-cycle" (*WDNF*:8, 23)

Trees, plants, and flowers[61]

almond-tree: "and the snow fell on the almond-trees" (*FR*:36, 9)
apple-tree: "a half-burnt-out apple-tree" (*TA*:23, 13)
apple-tree: "your Holy Ghost was an apple-tree" (*TA* 36, 5)
apple-tree: "remember the golden apple-trees" (*FR*:5, 23)
incense-tree: "*I am Mary, the incense-flower of the incense-tree* (*FR*:19, 1)
lotus-tree: "Is ours lotus-tree" (*WDNF*:27, 1)[62]
may-tree: "will you find the may-tree" (*TA*:17, 18)
may-tree: "was it may-tree or apple?" (*TA*:19, 14)[63]
myrrh-tree: "I am that myrrh-tree of the gentiles" (*FR*:16, 11)
myrrh-tree: "changed her to a myrrh-tree" (*FR*:16, 20)[64]
oak-tree: "before laurel or oak-tree" (*WDNF*:37, 6)
plum-tree: "from a plum-tree in flower" (*WDNF*:5, 10)
apple-russet: "or the apple-russet silk" (*TA*:30, 3)[65]
arbutus-fragrant: "arbutus-fragrant?" (*WDNF*:27, 14)
Christmas-rose: "or a face like a Christmas-rose" (*TA*:43, 22)
dune-grass: "over sedge, over dune-grass" (*WDNF*:42, 2)
fir-branch: "remembering—than rest on pine or fir-branch" (*FR*:6, 4)
flower-cone: "a flower-cone" (*FR*:10, 17)
flowering-grass: "and the flowering-grass; and he himself watched
    all night" (*FR*:38, 8)
grape-leaf: "no grape-leaf for the thorn" (*TA*:4, 6)
grass-blade: "clung to grass-blade" (*WDNF*:6, 5)
grass-blade: "up our individual grass-blade" (*WDNF*:14, 31)
grass-stalk: "and a million-million little grass-stalks" (*FR*:37, 5)
herb-basil: "herb-basil, or is ours" (*WDNF*:26, 6)
incense-flower: "*I am Mary, the incense-flower of the incense-tree*"
    (*FR*:19,1)
iris-bank: "between iris-banks" (*WDND*:23, 4)

---

61. See the passage in *BML* about the tree growing in the garden of Julia's
    London house, which Rico has called the *key-of-heaven* tree: "What did
    he tell you was the name of the tree in your garden?' I said. 'Key-of-
    heaven tree,' she said. Ridiculous, improbable, impossible. Did you
    make it up, the name of that tree?" (169).
62. Instead of *lote-tree*: the reference is not to the *lotus*, but to the plant
    represented by Homer and to be identified, probably, with the *jujube*
    tree.
63. I.e., the hawthorn.
64. That is, a tree that yields *myrrh*.
65. For this compound, see above.

leaf-spire: "the spear and leaf-spire" (*WDNF* 26, 7)
lily-bud: "or the lily-bud" (*WDNF*:3, 4)
lily-head: "it is crowned with the lily-head" (*WDNF*:3, 5)
lotus-grove: "from the lotus-grove" (*WDNF*:27, 2)
mulberry: "gorged on vine-leaf and mulberry" (*WDNF*:6, 26)
mulberry: "mulberry and rose-purple?" (*TA*:17, 16)
mulberry: "and the mulberries were domed over" (*FR*:36, 10)
new-grass: "crop me up with the new-grass" (*WDNF*:22, 12)
palm-shadow: "in winter, for palm-shadow" (*FR*:4, 4)
river-reed: "prays on the river-reed" (*WDNF*:23, 8)
rose-thorn: "rose-thorn forest" (*WDNF*:6, 10)
vine-flower: "no vine-flower for the crown" (*TA*:4, 7)
vine-leaf: "gorged on vine-leaf and mulberry" (*WDNF*:6, 26)
wild-almond: "are we wild-almond, winter-cherry?" (*WDNF*:37, 10)
winter-cherry: "are we wild-almond, winter-cherry?" (*WDNF*:27, 10)

Sea

sea-depth: "floundered, was lost in sea-depth" (*WDNF*:30, 18)
sea-drift: "and sand and burnt sea-drift" (*FR*:4, 5)
sea-floor: "from the sea-floor" (*WDNF*:30, 24)[66]
sea-incense: "of burnt salt and sea-incense" (*WDNF*:17, 13)
sea-maid: "of the marble sea-maids in Venice" (*TA*:31, 6)
sea-plant: "or sea-plant cell" (*FR*:9, 5)
sea-road: "he saw the ships and the sea-roads crossing" (*FR*:32, 4)
sea-rock: "rivers flowing and fountains and sea-waves washing the
      sea-rocks" (*FR*:32, 10)
sea-shell: "in every sea-shell" (*WDNF*:4, 2)
sea-shell: "*Annael*—and I remembered the sea-shell" (*TA*:16, 1)
sea-shore "seated on the sea-shore" (*FR*:22, 9)
sea-temple: "to a forbidden sea-temple" (*FR*:22, 6)
sea-temple: "from a forbidden sea-temple" (*FR*:25, 4)
sea-wave: "rivers flowing and fountains and sea-waves washing the
      sea-rocks" (*FR*:32, 10)
sea-weed: "gather dry sea-weed" (*WDNF*:17, 9)
sea-weed: "and brittle burnt sea-weed" (*FR*:4, 19)

See also:

coral-sea: "in the coral-seas; I would rather drown" (*FR*:6, 3)

---

66. The word is not used in its technical (geological) sense.

maid-of-the-sea: "a maid-of-the-sea, a mermaid" (*FR*:22, 11)
mermaid: "a maid-of-the-sea, a mermaid" (*FR*:22, 11)
mermaid: "some said, this mermaid sang" (*FR*:22, 12)
mermaid: "the un-maidenly mermaid, Mary of Magdala" (*FR*:26, 11)

Works Cited

Binns, A. L. "Linguistic Reading: Two Suggestions of the Quality of Literature." In *Essays on Style and Language*. Ed. Roger Fowler. London: Routledge and Kegan Paul, 1966:118–34.

Boughn, Michael. *H. D.: A Bibliography 1905–1990*. Charlottesville: UP of Virginia, 1993.

———. "Unity in H. D.'s War *Trilogy*." *Iron* 5 (1969): 6–30.

Camboni, Marina. "Hilda Doolittle, la donna che divenne il suo nome." *Versus* 76 (1997): 7–29.

———. "H. D.'s Trilogy, or the Secret Language of Change," *Letteratura d'America*, VI, 27 (1985): 87–106.

Gubar, Susan. "The Blank Page and the Issue of Female Creativity." *Critical Inquiry* 8 (Winter 1981): 243–63.

———. "The Echoing Spell of H. D.'s *Trilogy*." *Contemporary Literature* 19 (Spring 1978): 196–218. Reprinted in *Shakespeare's Sisters: Feminist Essays on Women Poets*. Ed. Sandra M. Gilbert and Susan Gubar. Bloomington: Indiana UP, 1979:153–64.

H. D. *Bid Me to Live*. With a New Introduction by Helen McNeil and an Afterword by Perdita Schaffner. London: Virago Press, 1984.

———. *Tribute to Freud*. With unpublished letters by Freud to the author. New York: Pantheon Books, 1956.

———. *Trilogia*. Edited, Translated, and annotated with "Breve biografia letteraria" and "alchimie, miti, sogni, parole revisionarie" by Marina Camboni. Caltanissetta-Roma: Salvatore Sciascia Editore, 1993.

———. *Trilogy: The Walls Do Not Fall, Tribute to the Angels, The Flowering of the Rod*. Foreword by Norman Holmes Pearson. New York: New Directions, 1973.

Lausberg, Heinrich. *Elemente der literarischen Rhetorik*. München: Hueber, 1967 (first ed. 1949). Italian trans. *Elementi di retorica*. Bologna: il Mulino, 1969.

Lendinara, Patrizia. "L'immaginario Linguistico di H. D." In *H(ilda) D(oolittle) e il suo mondo*. Atti della giornata di studio su H. D.,

Palermo (18 ottobre 1990). Ed. Marina Camboni. Palermo: U of Palermo, 1995:103–13.

———. " 'War' e 'not-war' in *Bid Me to Live* di H. D." In *Le aperture del testo. Studi per Maria Carmela Coco Davani*. Ed. Mirella Billi et al. Palermo: U of Palermo, 1995:281–89.

Marchand, Hans. *The Categories and Types of Present-Day English Word-Formation: A Synchronic-Diachronic Approach*. 2nd. ed. Wiesbaden: Harrassowitz, 1960.

Revell, Peter. "The Meaning that Words Hide: H. D.'s *Trilogy*." In *Quest in Modern American Poetry*. New York: Barnes and Noble, 1981.

Tristram, Hildegard L. C. *Linguistik und die Interpretation englischer literarischer Texte*. Anglistische Arbeitshefte 18. Tübingen: Niemeyer, 1978.

"And so remembrance brings us to this hour in which I strive to save identity" Figures of Memory in H. D.'s Late Poetry

Raffaella Baccolini

> I live convinced,
> instead, that memory's the thing to keep
> a place intact as is, *as was*,
> or to arrange it as it never was
> and never could be, which is what
>
> I'd much prefer.
> —Diane Raptosh, "Just West of Now"

Written in the spring of 1957 but only published in 1982, *Vale Ave* marks a break or a change in H. D.'s work. It is the first poem H. D. wrote after the composition of her epic masterpiece, *Helen in Egypt* (composed between 1952 and 1955 and published in 1961), and together with the other long poems she wrote in the last years of her life, namely *Sagesse* (June-winter 1957), *Winter Love* (1959), and *Hermetic Definition* (1960–61), it marks a shift toward a more openly autobiographical kind of poetry. Similarly, her prose of these years, especially her memoirs *End to Torment* (1958) and *Thorn Thicket* (1960), shares this shift toward autobiography. In particular, her poetry becomes *daringly* personal—one would be tempted to say almost confessional, a few years before confessional poetry became an acknowledged, even if controversial, movement in American poetry. From the composition of *Vale Ave* onward, in fact, H. D.'s poetry became openly autobiographical, with little or no use of the mythological mask that characterizes her early poetry. Its themes—for example, what Rachel Blau DuPlesiss has called the pattern of "romantic thralldom," desire in old age, and sexuality—are treated with unabashed candor, breaking with a traditionally established, if unwritten, code of decorum regarding themes appropriate to female poetry. Central to H. D.'s late production is the art of remembering in its link with her palimpsestic view of history, but also with such fundamental themes of her poetry as writing and identity. And yet, as often is the case, if *Vale Ave* marks a discontinuity with H. D.'s earlier production, it also signals a continuity, as memory, writing, and identity are central concerns in H. D.'s canon.

Divided into seventy-four numbered sections, *Vale Ave* is preceded by a brief prose introduction and is dedicated to Bryher: "To: *Amico*, Küsnacht, Spring 1957" (18). Written while H. D. was recovering from a broken hip, the sequence recapitulates a series of meetings and partings throughout history, starting with those of the archetypal lovers Lucifer and Lilith. As the poet herself writes, "The Lucifer-Lilith, Adam-Eve formula may be applied to all men and women, though here we follow the *processus* through the characters of Elizabeth and Sir Walter, meeting and parting, *Vale Ave*, through time—specifically, late Rome, dynastic Egypt, legendary Provence, early seventeenth-century England, and contemporary London" (*Vale Ave* 18). It is therefore in this larger context that H. D. inserts her own meeting and parting with Sir Hugh Dowding, Air Chief Marshal during the Battle of Britain. H. D. met Dowding in the 1940s and corresponded with him after having attended one of his lectures on spiritualism. News of her communication with his dead pilots, however, was badly received by Dowding, who ultimately rejected H. D. and her séances (Guest 261–62; Friedman, *Psyche Reborn* 173–175). Thus Dowding became for the American poet one more in the long list of men who, following a "different and yet the same" pattern—to use an expression dear to H. D.—rejected her. Among them were, for example, her first love and mentor Ezra Pound, her husband Richard Aldington, her spiritual companion D. H. Lawrence, and, during her last years, the Haitian journalist Lionel Durand.

A pattern of repudiation—meeting and parting, *Vale Ave*—is therefore central to this poem and to most of H. D.'s late long poems, like *Hermetic Definition* and, to a certain extent, *Winter Love*. Such a pattern must be confronted and remembered so that the poet can transcend its immediate destructiveness through an understanding of its larger meaning. To make sense of H. D.'s late poetry, we must read it in the light of H. D.'s interest in spiritualism, occultism, and heresy, as has been done, and also with regard to the function that love and desire fused with memory have in her quest for self-defini-tion.[1] Because of her interest in the recovery of the lost tradition of the Church of Love, however, "Dante's Notebooks," four little booklets H. D. wrote in Lugano in 1948 on the Italian poet, can be of particular help in understanding her late poetry. In most of H. D.'s late poetry, beginning with *Vale Ave*, love, in its sexual and spiritual connotations, represents both a personal and transcendental force that needs to be confronted during the heroine's quest for self-iden-tity. Similarly, memory figures not simply as a repository for images of the past, but as a power that allows H. D. and her female personae to reshape and interpret past experiences into a new and different form, and to see personal past experiences as part of a larger univer-sal design. H. D. derives this notion of memory primarily from psychoanalysis and her view of mythology, but also from Dante's *Vita Nuova*. If her analysis with Freud taught her to connect her personal history with universal history, Dante's interpretive mem-ory proved equally important. In turn, her "alchemy of memory" can be seen as her personal contribution to dealing with the dark vision of history that characterizes most of her modernist col-leagues' poetry.

Confessional Poetry and H. D.

Although it is not my intention to claim for H. D. a position as the unacknowledged founder of the confessional movement, it seems nonetheless that her post-*Helen in Egypt* poetry breaks with her pre-vious work and shares some features with confessional poetry.[2] As

---

1. The importance of spiritualism and occultism is central to Friedman's *Psyche Reborn*. See also Twitchell-Waas for a reading of *Vale Ave*.
2. It is also worth remembering that H. D. was an important figure for many post-World War II poets, among them Denise Levertov, Robert Duncan, and Adrienne Rich. Although the term "confessional" implies

Susan Stanford Friedman points out in the first chapter of *Penelope's Web*, throughout most of her life H. D. tended to confine autobiographical material to her prose, while in her poetry she operated on a more mediated lyrical and mythic level (25, 48–50, 55, 68–71). Beginning with *Vale Ave*, as Jeffrey Twitchell-Waas also recognizes, H. D. tends to bring the details of her life more directly into her poetry (203).

Autobiography figures prominently, however, even though in a highly encoded manner, in most of her poetic production. H. D.'s poetry has always been autobiographical to some extent, but she has often made use of the impersonal technique and a mythic mask to encode gender-related issues without explicitly addressing them. Such a feature has been persuasively demonstrated by several feminist scholars, although others have considered her use of Greece and mythology as a form of escapism. We owe to Norman Holmes Pearson, curator at Beinecke Rare Book and Manuscript Library at Yale and H. D.'s personal friend and literary executor, the first reappraisal of H. D.'s use of Greece and mythology:

> She used art in order to find herself. That constant search for identity marks twentieth-century American literature. You remember Cummings: "Why do you write?" "I write, I dare say, to become myself." Those more or less were his words. Or what does Pound call the hero, the protagonist of the *Cantos*? "A man of no fortune, and with a name to come." You could say that H. D. devoted her life to this kind of search, this question of, Who am I?; not any longer, What is an American?, nor even, What is man?, but, Who am I in my individuality? And yet again, paradoxically, *one is swept up into a knowledge of one's identity by the similarities in the patterns of other lives and other races.* When you said that she used Greek myth to find her own identity, you hit upon an aspect of H. D.'s poetry which, rather surprisingly, has gone unrecognized. She has been so praised as a kind of Greek publicity girl that people have forgotten that she writes the most intensely personal poems using Greek myth as a metaphor. That is, she can say these things better and more frankly about herself using these other devices than she could if she simply said, "I, I, I." To say "Helen " is to really free oneself.
>
> (Dembo, 441, emphasis mine)

The "similarities in the patterns of other lives and other races" become precisely the palimpsestic, structural device on which H. D.

---

the notion of sin and repentance, and thus may not seem appropriate to H. D.'s late poetry, it is the notion of confessional as *bold* and defying exposition of one's private and public matters that I take here to refer to H. D.'s poetry.

builds *Vale Ave*—the parallels between lovers meeting and parting through history, with her own personal story of thralldom. Despite Pearson's perceptive statement, however, it cannot be denied that H. D.'s poetry changes through the years and moves from the impersonal, encoded, and usually short lyrics of the 1920s to the long, narrative sequences of the Second World War years, of which *Trilogy* and *Helen in Egypt* represent her acknowledged masterpieces. The differences in length, structure, and genre are accompanied by a change in the treatments of the personal material, so that from the extinction of personality of the early years, H. D.'s poetry moves toward an increasingly autobiographical style in which the persona of the poet and the poet herself often seem to share the same voice. Moreover, as is often the case in modern poems that contain history, "the recurrence of past patterns in the present renders history and the poet's life inextricable" (Keller 552). These are some of the elements that H. D.'s late poetry share with confessional writing.[3]

The label "confessional," Diane Wood Middlebrook recollects, "was first applied, disapprovingly, to Robert Lowell's *Life Studies*, a collection of autobiographical prose and poetry published in 1959" (632).[4] It was a type of narrative and lyric verse that dealt with the facts and intimate experiences of the poet's life (Abrams 32) and violated the norms of decorum for subject matter prevailing in serious literature (Middlebrook 633). Together with Lowell, Anne Sexton, Sylvia Plath, and John Berryman are generally considered the most representative writers of this group. They all used personal, autobiographical material that they transposed in their poems with unabashed candor and with no inhibitions. Confessional, then, referred primarily to content, not technique, and as far as content

---

3. It is also true, however, that H. D.'s poetry has never shown a *total* extinction of personality; similarly, this can also be claimed for the Imagist movement, whose impersonal technique did not exclude the treatment of autobiographical events altogether. Moreover, it might be worth remembering that the rejection of impersonality that characterizes post-World War II poetry is already present in Pound's *Pisan Cantos* (1948), in which the active pursuit of memories and a minute observation of nature are a hold against madness—they function as resources for maintaining equilibrium under the pressure of disaster, imprisonment, and debilitating self-doubt.

4. As Keller states, however, among the poets who contributed to the development of confessional writing is also Allen Ginsberg, whose depiction of madness, sexual promiscuity, and a sexuality then widely regarded as deviant was rather daring for the time (550).

was concerned, "confessional poetry was not overtly political, but it participated in the protest against Impersonality as a poetic value by reinstating an insistently autobiographical first person engaged in resistance to the pressure to conform" (Middlebrook 635). Moreover, through the use of psychoanalysis, confessional poetry became more than autobiographical poetry. According to M. L. Rosenthal, a confessional poem has to achieve the "fusion of the private and the culturally symbolic" (81). Psychoanalysis becomes, then, for somebody like Sexton, an important literary source for her poetry, in which biographical events are transformed as to become an embodiment of her civilization.

Violation of the norms of decorum, unabashed candor, resistance to the pressure to conform, and psychoanalysis as an important source for poetry: these are the aspects of confessional writing that H. D.'s post-*Helen in Egypt* poetry may be said to contain. *Vale Ave* and all of her late poetry make use of personal material in a perspective that can thus be associated with confessional poetry. The shattering of the self and the painful labor of reconstruction are placed at the center of the poem in such a way as to make the poets' vulnerability—a central trope of confessional poetry—and the pattern of repudiation an embodiment of civilization. H. D. herself provides her readers with a key to interpret the pattern—a key that is only touched upon in the prose introduction, but that becomes clear to the poet herself (and to the readers) as the poem progresses. In fact, although we are told that the "formula may be applied to all men and women" throughout history, it is only in the poem itself that the meaning of the pattern of repudiation will be interpreted and the initial shattering of identity recognized as a conventional element of the Church of Love and a necessary step in the definition of the new life. But through the use of memory, both as a structural device and a redemptive force, H. D. transcends the much-too-personal aspect of confessional writing and writes a prophetic text, in which prophecy is nonetheless inextricably linked to her personal, gendered experience. And yet, despite the historical, palimpsestic structure of the poem, confessional moments spring up in some sections, particularly with regard to the poetic voice and the theme of romantic passion.

Vale Ave as Confessional Poetry

The poetic sequence is composed of seventy-four sections, each supposedly spoken by one of the different, historical female personae:

Elizabeth Dyer of seventeenth-century England, Julia of ancient Rome, two nameless women, a Provençal nun, and a young woman from dynastic Egypt, and the poet herself, speaking both from contemporary London (in the 1940s) and Küsnacht (in the 1950s). Although some sections are clearly distinguished and in the voice of one of the women, others seem to conflate the different historical periods by introducing images of one epoch into another. Each period is characterized in fact by recurrent images, like, for example, the purple tent in Rome, the lily in Egypt, and the broken vows in Provence. Thus *Vale Ave* appears as a multi-vocal text, where the sections in the voice of the poet become increasingly autobiographical. The long poem, therefore, combines features such as the personal and the historical, the lyric and the narrative, that situate it on the margins of any poetic genre—confessional or not. Section XLVII, in particular, marks a break in the poem's palimpsestic pattern and represents one of the most confessional moments in the poem, when the poet abandons all masks and gives an assessment of her own life and career:

> I transcribed the scroll, I wrote it out
> and then I wrote it over, a palimpsest of course,
>
> but it came clear, at last, I had the answer
> or the seven answers to the seven riddles,
>
> the why and why and why—the meetings and the parting
> and his anger—it took some time, though five years is
> not long
>
> to write a story, set in eternity but lived in—England;
> I left of course; I traveled to the Tessin from Lausanne,
>
> to Zürich and around and back again,
> and I wrote furiously; he got the last of this prose Trilogy,
>
> this record, set in time or fancy-dressed in history,
> five years ago, then I had five years left
>
> to break all barriers, to surpass myself
> with *Helen and Achilles* . . .
>
> an epic poem? unquestionably that,
> I would not trouble him to read the script.
>   (*Vale Ave* 51)

This section recapitulates the years between 1946 and 1957, marked by the composition of the prose trilogy, *The Sword Went Out to Sea*

(1946–47), *White Rose and the Red* (1947–48), and *The Mystery* (1949–51). The autobiographical writing of these years represent a "palimpsest," different versions, set in different times, of a similar story, primarily the story of Dowding's rejection. Similarly, *Vale Ave* concentrates in one long sequence six versions of the same story: the pattern of lovers meeting and parting at different historical moments. But the most significant element in this passage is H. D.'s own reading of *Helen in Egypt*, where she openly admits to her revisionist project and unbecomingly, because as a woman she is traditionally expected to be modest, praises her own poetry. It is "unquestionably" an epic poem, her masterpiece with which she "surpass[es her]self" and breaks all barriers, revises the epic genre, but also revises and rescues Helen's figure from tradition. In a manner that is typical of H. D.'s mature poet of the long sequences, this section, however, presents contradictory feelings on the poet's part. On the one hand, regardless of others' judgment, she dares to call her *Helen* sequence a masterpiece; on the other, she dimisses her work as trivial when she says she "would not trouble [Dowding] to read the script."

But it is in the treatment of desire and old age that the poem becomes most autobiographical. Another example of the movement away form her earlier highly encoded poetry and toward unabashed confessionalism is section XL, which presents the most explicit sexual passage in the sequence. This section bears no immediate reference to any specific place or time, so that this timelessness allows it to apply to all historical periods. But while thus suggesting that love—Eros is eternal and central to the definition of one's identity, this strategy also has a defensive function, in that the sexual scene described is personal but not necessarily autobiographical. And yet, compared to an earlier poem like "Leda," which offers an idyllic and mediated image of blissful love, section XL strikes one as "surprisingly and unsettlingly touched with aggression and animalism" (Twitchell-Waas 207).

Following the techniques and the tenets of Imagism, in fact, "Leda" presents the sexual intercourse of Leda and Zeus mediated by the image of the lily and the swan:

> where the low sedge is thick,
> the gold day-lily
> outspreads and rests
> beneath soft fluttering
> of red swan wings
> and the warm quivering
> of the red swan's breast.
> (*Collected Poems* 121)

Conversely, section XL of *Vale Ave* presents a much more direct treatment of sexuality:

> If there is urgency, there is no fear,
> hail, yes, but not farewell.
>
> *Amenti* flowered long before Eden's tree;
> his hand invites the *delta* underneath
>
> the half-transparent folds of the soft pleats,
> and does not tear but draws the veil aside,
>
> then both his hands grasp my bare thighs,
> and clutch and tighten, bird claws or a beast
>
> that would tear open, tear apart, but keep
> the appetite at bay, to gratify a greater hunger
>
> or to anticipate deeper enjoyment;
> yet his commanding knees keep my knees locked,
>
> even while his virility soothes and quickens,
> till in agony, my own hands clutch and tear,
>
> and my lips part, as he releases me,
> and my famished mouth opens
>
> and knows his hunger and his power;
> and this is the achievement and we know the answer
>
> to ritual and to all philosophy,
> in the appeasement of the ravished flower.
>
> (46–47)

Whereas in "Leda" H. D. presents sexual intercourse in a more mediated and lyrical way, in section XL of *Vale Ave* she employs openly sexual images and language. In "Leda," through the use of precise, hard language, the image of the lily can be read as an objective correlative for the woman, so that the climactic movement of the sexual intercourse between Zeus and Leda is encoded in the image of the "quivering" swan over the "outspread" flower. In *Vale Ave*, on the other hand, H. D. does not encode the female body in suggestive images of flowers, but literally talks of "thighs," "knees," "lips," and "mouth." But if the language describing the sexual act is direct, the overall feeling of the sexual encounter is far from definite. The images and the language employed waver between being simultaneously violent and satisfying to the woman. The scene describes what will become a familiar but puzzling situation of thralldom for the woman poet in H. D.'s late poetry, with its mixture of thrill and dangerous destructiveness.[5] Words such as "no fear," "invites," "soft," and "achievement," that can be said to belong to a *positive* sphere, are juxtaposed to others such as "grasp," "clutch," "tear open, tear apart," "claws," "beast" that seem to belong to the sphere of *violence*. Other words, such as "agony," "famished," "ravished," and "appeasement," do not fit in only one category and stand ambiguously in-between. In a sexual context, they suggest a romantic feeling of intense passion, but suggest, in each case, the idea of loss and, ultimately, metaphoric death. Pain, deprivation, violent sex, and giving in to someone's aggression seem dangerously linked to sexual fulfillment. Section XL, then, shows how love and desire are part of the poet's quest. They are instrumental to an understanding of the pattern, because the fulfillment of the sexual act, "the appeasement of the ravished flower," seems to lead to the discovery of "the answer / to ritual and to all philosophy."[6] Ecstasy is achieved, but at a much too high cost as the final image, suggesting the loss of one's self, the danger of displacement in the giving in to an aggressive, yet vital force, purports. Love reveals itself to be at once the source of thralldom and its answer, as its association with the Church of Love of the esoteric tradition will make clear. In this light, then, *Vale Ave* can be seen as a complex sequence that breaks with certain features of H. D.'s poetry, anticipates some, and continues still others. Among those that are recurrent in her late poetry are the assessment of her own poetry, the treatment of desire, sexuality, and old age.[7] Similarly,

5. Cf., for example, *Winter Love* and *Hermetic Definition*. For readings of the treatment of desire and sexuality in these poems, see Baccolini.

6. In an uncanny and somewhat disturbing way, H. D.'s passage seems to echo, and possibly address, W. B. Yeat's (in)famous question about Leda, "Did she put on his knowledge with his power" (115). The sexual act seems here to be connected with the acquisition of knowledge.

7. Another element that makes the poem autobiographical is its insistence on senility and the issue of desire in old age. Here, as she will also do in *Winter Love* and *Hermetic Definition*, H. D. plays with the notion of being old, particularly how scandalous it is considered by society to have sexual feelings after a certain age. Resistance to the pressure to conform represents another confessional element, as the poet decides

the issue of memory is employed continuously and discontinuously within H. D.'s canon.

H. D.'s Art of Memory

Memory constitutes, in its link with the past and history, a recurrent figure in modernist writing, not just as a theme, but also as a structural device. Modernist writers show a profound ambivalence toward the past and tradition. If it is true, as Hayden White argues in *Tropics of Discourse*, that the modernists have shown an intense "hostility" toward history (31), it is also true that they have shown a similar obsession with the past, its return and influence on the present. Stephen Dedalus's famous claim that "history . . . is a nightmare from which I am trying to awake" (Joyce, *Ulysses* 2.377) can be countered by H. D.'s insistence that "remembering . . . always, but remembering . . . differently" is indispensable for the artist (*By Avon River* 31). Ezra Pound's modernist imperative "make it new" in Canto LIII, Eliot's statement that "novelty is better than repetition" ("Tradition" 38), and Wyndham Lewis's scornful assessment of the past when he claims that "our vortex is not afraid of the Past: it has forgotten it's [sic] existence" (44), coexist with a pervasive use of memory and the mythic past in H. D., Joyce, Pound, and Eliot. Modernist culture has rightly been viewed as a deliberate break with Victorian norms and conventions, but although modernism celebrates a liberation from the past, this imperative desire for novelty exists side by side with a critical recovery of tradition and an obsession with the notions of time, memory, and hence, history and identity.[8] The consciousness of the past, Eliot reminds us in

---

to break all conventions and becomes more direct in her old age. In the poem she moves from recognition of old age and physical impairment, her "predicament" (57), through "rebellion" (53–54), to renewal (63).

8. Modernist art, in fact, openly displays an ambivalent attitude toward the past and tradition; while it expresses contempt for and, at times, hostility, toward much of the past, it also seeks to recover what it considers "the best tradition"—the *Dolce Stil Novo*, Arnaut Daniel and the troubadour love lyric, for instance. Modernist borrowing from past tradition, and myth in particular, is "a way of controlling, of ordering, of giving a shape and a significance to the immense panorama of futility and anarchy which is contemporary history" (Eliot, "*Ulysses*" 177). On the revisionist use of myth by women, see Ostriker.

"Tradition and the Individual Talent" (1919), is a necessary step in the progress of an artist and for his or her self-awareness, but does not entail a whole-hearted admiration for or acceptance of it (37–40); rather, this consciousness calls for critical awareness. The modernist critical search for the past displays a search for new values and for identity; it also unveils a fear that only through memory and fragments can we preserve the ruins of modern civilization. Fragments, recollections, and free associations become then the structural elements of much modernist writing.

Although the study of memory goes back to Plato and Aristotle, it emerges with renewed emphasis in much literature of the turn of the nineteenth century, where the past is often linked, negatively, to habits and, favorably, to the recognition spurred by memories.[9] Two types of memory have traditionally been identified in the debate: recall and recognition, voluntary and involuntary memory, habits and memory. Most of the fin-de-siècle philosophers and writers who deal with the issue of memory also maintain a distinction between different types of memory. In *Matter and Memory*, for example, Henri Bergson affirms that "*the past survives under two distinct forms: first in motor mechanisms; secondly, in independent recollections*" (87; emphasis in the original), where by motor mechanisms he means habits, and by independent recollections he means individual acts of recollection that come spontaneously to one's mind. For Bergson, as for the modernists, memory and the past are valuable and functional: they make one's perception understandable; they provide a means of interpreting the present or what is about to come; they form a valuable and desirable guide to life.[10]

---

9. For a comprehensive analysis of the art of memory up to the Renaissance, see Yates. The philosophical tradition has always distinguished recall from recognition: Plato, Aristotle, St. Thomas Aquinas, and St. Augustine, for example, have all identified two types of memories, of which the second involves judgment and leads to knowledge (Yates 1–81). On memory, forgetfulness, and the past, see also Rossi.

10. Although the distinction between voluntary and involuntary memory is not explicitly made, Bergson's theory clearly anticipates Proust's. By voluntary memory, Proust meant a kind of memory deliberately recalled in order to apply it to and interpret a present situation. By involuntary memory, on the other hand, he meant a kind of memory that comes spontaneously, unsolicited by the past, and that it usually displaces, unsettles, confounds the individual. Habits, on the other hand, were paralyzing and stifling forces for the individual.

Like many other modernists, H. D. makes extensive use of memory as a theme in, and a structural device of, much of her work. She enters the debate on memory especially after her psychoanalytic sessions with Freud, who worked out his own theory of memory in his 1914 essay "Remembering, Repeating and Working Through."[11] For the American poet, memory is also of two kinds, but as she develops her "art of remembering," she introduces a third kind of memory—revisionist remembering. By revisionist remembering I do not mean only the kind of revision she carries out on tradition—a critical attitude toward the past—but also the ability to mix memory with imagination, or, to say it with her own words from *Vale Ave*, to "mix [her] metaphors and history" (55), with regard to her own life, thus creating a version of the past that is strategic to her own empowerment.

Starting with her sessions with Freud, H. D.'s last productive years were characterized by a recurrent interest in the art of remembering. It was then that she began to develop what was to become her 1950s "aesthetics," based on the power of memory mixed with imagination and interpretation. Together, memory, imagination, and interpretation represent the source of writing and, thus, of survival for the aging poet. "The past is literally blasted into consciousness," says H. D. in the Vienna of the early 1930s, where, as Pearson notes, "she was putting together the shards of her own history" in a larger pattern ("Foreword" v). Through psychoanalysis, Freud helped her to remember, and to interpret what she remembered. The importance of memory is recognized by the poet, who, in *Tribute to Freud*, acknowledges the power of memory linked with imagination and interpretation—the strategies employed in most of her late poetry: "We travel far in thought, in imagination or in the realm of memory. Events happened *as* they happened . . . but here and there a memory or a fragment of a dream-picture is actual, is real, is like a work of art or is *a work of art*. . . . Those memories, visions, dreams, reveries—or what you will—. . . are healing. They are real" (35, second emphasis added). But memory or dream alone are not enough without interpretation; memories are "priceless broken

11. Freud believed the past could be a burden on the present and worked toward the assumption that the past could be known and transcended—in a certain way forgotten, done away with—through psychoanalytic cure (154–55). And yet, in Freud's work, as well as in modernists' writing, we find that ambivalent feeling—the disturbing suspicion that we can never be altogether free of the past.

fragments that are meaningless until we find the other broken bits
to match them," so that these fragments can function as an illumination (*Tribute to Freud* 35).

In addition to employing memory as a principal structural device
and pattern in her post-World War II poetry since *By Avon River*,
H. D. returned to the nature of memory in her memoir of Ezra
Pound, *End to Torment*. Again memory and imagination superim-
pose to form the work of art. As George Hart points out (163),
memory in *End to Torment* is of two kinds. It is an act of will, a
process that produces memories rather than recalling them: "It is
hardly a process of remembering, but almost . . . of 'manifesting' "
(*End to Torment* 46). It is also a more psychoanalytic kind of remembering, by which memory is not forgotten but becomes real when
she writes of it. With this kind of memory, "past, present and future . . . [come] together" (*End to Torment* 55).

In her poetry, on the other hand, memory is variously employed.
In *Trilogy*, for example, after the use of the alchemy of language has
given rise to the vision of the Lady, the poet affirms "remembering"
as one of the necessary values to counter the utilitarian, senseless
force of the nonbelievers, which is linked to the cycle of death
and destruction:

> So I would rather drown, remembering—
> than bask on tropic atolls
>
> in the coral-seas; I would rather drown,
> remembering—than rest on pine or fir-branch
>
> where great stars pour down
> their generating strength, Arcturus
>
> or the sapphires of the Northern Crown;
> I would rather beat in the wind, crying to these others:
>
> yours is the more foolish circling,
> yours is the senseless wheeling
>
> round and round—yours has no reason—
> I am seeking heaven;
>
> yours has no vision,
> I see what is beneath me, what is above me,
>
> what men say is-not—I remember;

I remember, I remember—you have forgot:

you think, even before it is half-over,
that your cycle is at an end,

but you repeat your foolish circling—again, again, again;
again, the steel sharpened on the stone;

again, the pyramid of skulls;
(*Collected Poems* 582–83)

Through a series of images developed in the first part of *The Flow-ering of the Rod*—the circling of the geese, one of the personae of the poet, versus the circling of the voices of reason, remembering versus forgetting—the poet shows the contrast between her vision of Atlan-tis, "heaven," and the "no[n]-vision" of the others, the materialists who scorn poetry in favor of war, of which the "steel" and the "skulls" are significant symbols. Using Freud's own terms, the poem shows how remembering is different from repeating: under-standing allows one to remember and not repeat; repeating is simi-lar to habits, to the "inferior" kind of memory, to memory without understanding and interpretation. Memory becomes, then, an im-portant element for surviving the war, although it is not yet explic-itly linked with the act of writing, as it will be in the 1950s.

In *By Avon River* memory becomes one of the strategies of empow-erment for H. D.'s poet, as the act of "remembering differently" becomes the place of self-definition for the woman poet (31). Re-membering Shakespeare differently means transforming the English poet from a threat for her into a possible source of inspiration. Shakespeare's figure is neutralized by making him a follower of the Cathar heresy; thus revisionist remembering changes woman's place in tradition from object of man's poems to subject of her own poetry.[12] Memory also functions as revelation or epiphany for the imagined Shakespeare of the prose section. Through a series of asso-ciations between Judith, Juliet, and Queen Eleanor of Aquitaine, who introduced the troubadour tradition into England, and with it the cult of the doctrine of love, H. D.'s Shakespeare remembers his affiliation with the Church of Love. It is the memory of his daughter Judith, and of his love for her that makes him—and the read-ers—realize he is a follower of the Cathar heresy (*By Avon River* 96).

---

12. On the use of revisionist memory, see Baccolini, and Friedman's "Re-membering."

This final revision provides an empowering message for the woman poet and a further way for her to identify with Shakespeare without feeling threatened.

The importance of memory in the search for identity is further enriched in *Helen of Egypt,* where Helen needs to remember the past in order to make sense of it and fight for her identity: "If she forgets . . . she is lost" (*Helen in Egypt* 37).[13] Helen's quest for wholeness after the destruction wrought by the war parallels the act of reconstruction out of fragments and memories typical of modernist texts like T. S. Eliot's *Waste Land* or Pound's *Pisan Cantos:*

> remember these small reliques,
> as on a beach, you search
> for a pearl, a bead,
>
> a comb, a cup, a bowl
> half-filled with sand,
> after a wreck.
> (*Helen in Egypt* 164)

H. D.'s project, however, differs, in that the remembered story is not traditionally epic; rather, it is personal and is the story of love:

> the million personal things,
> things remembered, forgotten,
>
> remembered again, assembled
> and re-assembled in different order
> as thoughts and emotions,
>
> the sun and the seasons changed,
> and as the flower-leaves that drift
> from a tree were the numberless
>
> tender kisses, the soft caresses,
> given and received; none of these
> came into the story,
>
> it was epic, heroic.
> (*Helen in Egypt* 289)

"Thoughts and emotions" epitomize H. D.'s process of remembering. It is a mixture of logic and feeling, free association and events,

---

13. On H. D.'s use of memory in *Helen in Egypt* see Hart.

recollection and imagination, where "the million personal things" —the "tender kisses" as well as "the soft caresses, / given and received"—find their place together with the larger pattern of history. It is a revisionist project that transforms and transcends the confinement of genre—a revisionist epic—and of societal norms for women—a project that is fundamental to the redefinition of her identity.[14] In her post-World War II work, then, memory together with writing and love become central to the poet's quest for identity and knowledge, whereas forgetting represents a loss, as it did for the Greeks. To be bereft of memories means to lack knowledge and to lose oneself; to remember is to gain oneself.

Memory in *Vale Ave*

In *Vale Ave* and the post-*Helen in Egypt* poems, memory becomes the main structural device and theme. Its centrality is certainly derived from psychoanalysis, but also from her reading of Dante as a member of the Church of Love. In "Dante's Notebooks," H. D. recorded her interpretation of Dante's work, the *Vita Nuova* and *Paradiso* in particular, and in accordance with a vast body of criticism that reads Dante's work as belonging to an esoteric tradition, H. D. interpreted the events in the *Vita Nuova* as coded messages. Dante's *Vita Nuova* represents his book of memory; composed between 1292 and 1295 it narrates, first in prose and then in verse, remembered events, followed by a discussion of the lyrics themselves. H. D. had already adopted and adapted Dante's structure in *Helen in Egypt*, with prose sections preceding and discussing the lyrics, and in the late poetry, beginning with *Vale Ave*, where the poems contain recollected events; each recollection, in turn, is interpreted.[15]

The first forty-two sections can be, for the most part, attributed to one of the female personae, even though a few of the sections seem to incorporate different voices within the same poem. Starting with section XLIII, on the other hand, the poems recreated H. D. and Dowding's meeting and parting in London, but after a few such sections, the setting changes to Küsnacht, and the events are not

---

14. On H. D.'s revisionist epic, see Friedman's "Gender and Genre."
15. Compare, for example, the structure of *Hermetic Definition*, where the third part is an explanation of the previous two. On *Hermetic Definition*, see Baccolini.

presented, but recollected and simultaneously interpreted.[16] But H. D. not only borrows from Dante's *Vita Nuova* the pattern of recollection and interpretation, she also finds in it the confirmation that her personal story acquires its true meaning when set in a larger, historical context—a lesson her sessions with Freud had also emphasized. In keeping with its medieval spirit, in fact, the *Vita Nuova* is a quest for knowledge, where knowledge is understood as the interpretation of an experience that acquires its true meaning when it is viewed as part of a universal design. By fusing the lesson of psychoanalysis with that of the Italian poet, H. D. recovers Dante on her own terms; this, in turn, allows her to find an answer to the destructive pattern of personal thralldom and the disorder of wartime, as well as to elaborate her own vision of Paradise.

Using memory as a central device, H. D.'s poet is able to interpret the meaning of the pattern of repudiation; H. D.'s reading of Dante's *Vita Nuova* offers a possible key to interpretation. The sequence of events establishes a situation of thralldom for the different female personae; memory forces them to face the crisis and also offers an answer to the threatened sense of identity. The very act of parting is read as a rejection of love; in turn, separation brings about a loss of identity: "O, do not tear yourself away, / for if they take you, I am lost again" (26). It also brings a devaluation of the woman both as a poet and as a fellow-alchemist: "I do not care for modern poetry" says Dowding to the poet (55), while he also dismisses her spiritual messages as "frivolous" (66). Simultaneously, the poem establishes another kind of entrapment due to her "predicament," the broken hip (57), but even more to the poet's age: "O, I am old, old, old, and my cold hand / clutches my shawl about my shivering shoulders, / I have no power against this bitter cold, / this weakness and this trembling, I am old" (44). But the physical entrapment and the emotional and spiritual thralldom also reveal a fear of another possible crisis in the poet's creativity: "Does writing equate walking?" asks the poet at one point, showing how the different issues are inextricably linked.[17] By introducing, in section LXVII, the

---

16. Compare, for example, section XLVI, where H. D. represents one of her meetings with Dowding, his actions, his words, and section LXI, where she remembers the past and her quest in the Kabbalah.

17. The passage appears in section LXVII, which is inadvertently omitted in the New Directions edition. This edition also switches around the ordering of sections LXV and LXVI; however, since it remains the most readily accessible edition, it is the one I quote from; I have integrated section LXVII from the MS copy at Beinecke.

figure of Freud, H. D. creates another layer where the image of physical impairment is superimposed on that of the writer's block for which she sought Freud's help. Memory, love, writing, and identity are thus indissolubly linked.

The memory of the lovers, their rejection, and the consequent shattering of self forces the female personae to recognize their crisis: "and so remembrance brings us to this hour / in which I strive to save identity," says the poet in section LIX, a section in which the persona of Elizabeth Dyer fuses with that of the poet (60). But memory, in its association with conjuring, also serves to lead the female personae to embrace the esoteric tradition. Such a choice empowers the woman in the poem with occult powers and, thus, with an interpretation of the rejection pattern: "I would recall the symbols, name the Powers, / invoke the Angels, Tetragrammaton" (30). Memory, in fact, allows for a better vision: "remembering . . . she can see / further than we can see, can conjure up, / invoke, entreat, implore" (54–55). Finally, memory makes a broken fragment meaningful once the pattern is interpreted, so that "the memory of a little room" becomes "one of the aspects of eternity," and the personal becomes one with the eternal through memory (39). Each individual woman's memory forms part of a larger design, and the pattern of rejection takes on a meaning in connection with the esoteric tradition. Far from being erased or forgotten, the particular and the personal are instead worked through and interpreted as being part of a larger pattern, and are thus connected with history and eternity. Memory and writing enact the understanding process so that the poem becomes, as Twitchell-Waas notes, the moment when eternal and personal intersect (207).

By reading the pattern of repudiation on a religious level, the poet is able to transcend its destructiveness and, in turn, to write about the experience. Memory mixed with interpretation allows her to recognize the importance of love and the message of the spiritual quest. The message derived from the poet—Elizabeth's engagement with alchemy and the Kabbalah reveals that the message spelled by the different letters-symbols H. D. found in Robert Ambelain's *Le Kabbale practique*, the book on the Kabbalah she was reading at the time—is "one story, / and only one, Love is the altar that we burn upon" (33). Elsewhere, H. D. links memory and love through Dante, when she says "It needed fire to generate remembrance, / Love was the *primum mobile*" (38). The ninth or Crystalline Heaven, seat of the highest order in the hierarchy of Angels, is the last and swiftest

sphere in Dante's vision of Paradise; it is also the heaven that generates the motion of the whole universe and is, therefore, life's primary force. Through echoes of Dante's work, the poet is able to
associate romantic with spiritual love, in a reading supported by
H. D.'s own work on Dante.[18]

H. D.'s reading of the *Vita Nuova* emphasizes, in fact, the pattern
of repudiation and its consequences, at the same time that it places
her personal thralldom within a larger, more meaningful pattern.
If, on the one hand, she interprets repudiation on a romantic level,
she also reads it on a religious one. An example of what she perceives as romantic rejection is Beatrice's denying her "dolcissimo
salutare"—her most sweet greeting—to Dante (*Vita Nuova* 120;
"DN" IV: 18). But the images of death—that of Beatrice's father,
of a young lady, and of Beatrice herself—are also interpreted as
metaphors for Guido Cavalcanti's repudiation of and "estrange-
ment" from Dante ("DN" I: 7, 8, 21, 27). The love story disguises a
religious message as well, and Cavalcanti's repudiation becomes a
symbol of the failure of secret communication between the members
of the sect ("DN" VI 18–20, 35—43). Another important element in
H. D.'s interpretation is Dante's final acceptance of Beatrice's death
as signifying an acceptance of Guido's final repudiation. Dante returns, alone, to practical affairs in order to regain balance and to
write his *Commedia* ("DN" I: 8). In one of the notebooks, H. D. writes
that the "story, drama (Commedia) requires the meeting (14) and
the repudiation of messages.... But without this repudiation,
D[ante] would not have known the *nova condizione*" ("DN" IV: 43).
A similar operation takes place in *Vale Ave*, where the poet accepts
her beloved's rejection once she understands that "his repudiation
was salvation," and goes on to write her own poem (60). Thus,
Guido becomes another "betrayer of *Cortezia*" for H. D. This reading
allows H. D. to see herself and Dowding as fellow questers, "*sembla-
bles*" in their exploration of occultism and search for knowledge. At
the same time it allows her boldly to place herself in Dante's position, as she associates her own rejection by Dowding with Dante's
by Cavalcanti.

Rejection recollected and interpreted provides the poet with an
answer, just as it did for Dante in the *Vita Nuova*. By going against
the traditional belief that "no woman / should explore these devi-
ous rites" (60), H. D. claims for herself and her female personae the

---

18. There are several other recurrent images in the poems, like the falcon
and the rose, that can be read as echoes of Dante.

role of quester. In section LXV, in fact, H. D. places herself in a long line of female questers that starts with Lilith and includes Helen, Guinevere, and Semiramis, and finally Elizabeth and the poet herself. These women are invoked as "Graces, even Virtues, / not for their beauty only, but for their implacable search / for the *semblable*, . . . / the *primum mobile* that gave both Hell and Paradise to Dante" (64). This claim revises women's traditional roles as beautiful objects of love and desire and empowers them to become "implacable" questers. Thus, the woman poet studies the symbolism of the Kabbalah, and finds an answer to the pattern of thralldom. In section LXVI, she recapitulates her journey, which "with a breath from Paradise," has brought her to seize her pen and write "of the enchantment and the purple tent and how / following inexorable destiny, we met" (58):

> I should be too old for exaltation,
> I am too old, but inexplicably,
>
> spring threatens with enchantment
> and I almost fear redemption through its beauty;
>
> doors open, one door shut inexorably,
> but I had sensed the depth and I was spared;
>
> I traveled, I was happy, even although
> the path had led from darkness
>
> on through darkness, back to illumination,
> and from illumination, to despair,
>
> and from despair to inspiration,
> and as answer to a prayer,
>
> the VALE AVE and the thought beyond the fear,
> perhaps there'll be a miracle, after all.
>   (63)

The writing of the poem becomes the answer; through its writing she conjures up the image of Dowding, the soldier-lover who, with his repudiation, initiates her "new condition." And her new condition is the "Resurrection and the hope of Paradise" she mentions at the end of the prose introduction (19). Dowding, the repudiation, and their common membership in the Church of Love foster the creativity of the aging poet; the image of "spring" in the above

passage brings "enchantment" and "redemption," "spare[s]" the
poet and leads her from darkness through illumination to inspiration. The transformation of the entrapment of thralldom in darkness
and despair into illumination and inspiration suggests the break-
up of a destructive cycle and a further movement away from the
merely personal toward the historical and political.

The final vision of hope restored and deliverance from iniquity
and distrust derives, once again, from revisionist remembering, the
combination of memory with imagination:

> I like to think, to make the almost unbearable story
>   bearable,
> that Hugh was there, I like to think that the *Seaspray*
>   returned,
>
> with other phantom ships, to hail them as they fell,
> and gather them together on that one mysterious Ship
>
> that brought *Alla* and *Teli* together, that the miracle
> extended through all time, but that eternity
>
> was not a vast conception of philosophy,
> but a simple plane, a near extension of our common time,
>
> where clocks tick and where no evil forces
> shatter the continuity of your lives,
>
> and where courtesy controls humanity,
> and where the Master of the Air
>
> says simply, "pride failed—
> but all through time, I waited for you."
>   (62)

Although the poet is well aware that this section is only a version
of what she "like[s] to think," this passage is nonetheless central to
H. D.'s redefinition of philosophy, that is, her own vision of eternity
and time. From now on, her "high philosophy" will be "remembrance" (63); similarly, her vision of time is one of incarnation. Time
is simultaneously unique and universal as embodied in the different
historical periods in *Vale Ave* and in the intersection of the personal
and the eternal. Elizabeth's Hugh is conflated with Dowding, and
seventeenth-century England becomes one with contemporary London and Küsnacht. But if it true that in this way the story—and

history—is different and yet the same, that in past, present, and future the pattern is identical—and thus, by implication, that there is no progress in time, no evolutionary change possible for the future—it is nonetheless true that through the use of revisionist remembering H. D. breaks the hold the past had on her: that is, she creates a different past that allows her to transcend thralldom and envision resurrection and the hope of Paradise. Through the creative function of memory, her vision and her writing provide an answer to the violence of thralldom and war. Her utopian vision of a world where "no evil forces shatter the continuity" of one's life is in accordance, once again, with the tradition of the Church of Love: "courtesy," *cortezia*, but also love, are the governing principles, the principal attributes of humanity. In H. D.'s revised utopia, then, there is no place for rejection, thralldom, or violence.

But if this is her imagined Paradise, the world as she would like it to be, the last section of the poem provides a different and yet consistent reality. Her vision may be "at best inadequate, fragmentary" but it is her own, and it conjures up all the meaningful people in her life (68):

> There is *Alla, Teli* and our Indian friend, *Alli*,
> there is *Zaka* unquestionably, and Amico
>
> who sent me your last picture, is *Dieh,*
> with the attribute, *Dieu qui délivrez des Maux,*
>
> there are all the others, on earth, a "cloud of witnesses,"
> as in heaven; may these deliver us
>
> from all iniquity, questioning and distrust,
> and at the last (I know they'll understand),
>
> I ask for this, the blessing of the Ship, of the "Parole,"
> in remembrance of the seven times we met.
> (68)

Out of the personal disorder of thralldom and the historical destruction of World War II, order is reestablished in the convocation of those most important to H. D.'s life-story: Dowding (*Alla*), herself (*Teli*), the medium Arthur Bhaduri (*Alli*), Freud (*Zaka*), as well as the inseparable Bryher (Amico—*Dieh*).[19] But given H. D.'s palimpsestic

---

19. Compare. Twitchell-Waas for the identification of some of the characters (223).

method, where one historical period is superimposed on another, and one lover-betrayer conflated with the others, one should not forget all the unnamed "others, on earth, a 'cloud of witnesses,' / as in heaven," the various Pounds, Aldingtons, Lawrences, Durands, as well as others who figured importantly in her life. This recollection was to become a recurrent motif in H. D.'s late poetry, intent as she was on reviewing her own life and the role of certain people in it. Such a confessional, personal urge suggests the need to reorder, *remember*, and reinterpret one's fragments into a larger, more meaningful picture that will stand the test of time.[20] Her vision of peace is transformed into a request for deliverance "from all iniquity, questioning and distrust" as well as for the blessing and the respect for her vision and her method, represented here by the symbols of the "Ship" and the "Parole." Both are inextricably linked with memory, her writing, and the message of love. Whereas the "Parole" is clearly linked to the message of love and the Kabbalah, and therefore to her own poetry, the "Ship" is associated with her spiritual work, but less clearly so. A Viking Ship, in fact, usually "appeared in H. D.'s war-time séances" (Twitchell-Waas 220). But the Ship is also a recurrent, palimpsestic image that connects the female personae of the poem to Dowding and to the poet herself—"that one mysterious Ship / that brought *Alla* and *Teli* together" (62). Thus, throughout *Vale Ave*, the Ship becomes the symbol of the meeting and parting of lovers (especially Elizabeth and Hugh), but it is also a symbol of love, particularly of love remembered, and a further symbol of the conflation of the personal and the historical. The Ship, in fact, as Twitchell-Waas also suggests, is the answer to the "unbearable story" of personal thralldom and the various historical periods of violence and war that appear throughout the poem, but particularly in section LXIII (221). Just as the poet likes to think that the Ship gathers together all the victims of thralldom and war, she provides for herself and the others a shelter from psychological and physical violence, a monument—her own writing—by which to remember them and transcend, once again, the destructiveness of time and violence, but also to read her story into a larger pattern (*Vale Ave* 62). Compassion, love and

---

20. It also recalls Pound's attempt to ease the pain of imprisonment and disorder by recollecting people from his earlier years through the *Pisan Cantos*. In H. D.'s canon, *Winter Love* and *Hermetic Definition* are some such poems.

remembrance, once again, form H. D.'s philosophy, and are, together with writing, at the basis of her struggle for identity.

Vale Ave is, then, an early but important text for any assessment of H. D.'s post-World War II aesthetic of remembrance. In it, memory is not only recollection but also recognition, imagination, and prophecy. On an autobiographical level, memory recovers old age, and also death, as part of a continuous reconstruction of identity; on a religious and philosophical level, it reinscribes the notion of time and history as "processus" and "aspects of eternity." In this way, H. D. moves away from the merely personal to a more political and gendered vision of history and time. She places the personal, almost confessional elements of the poem within a historical pattern, and thus creates a sort of community to which the woman poet belongs—a community composed of all the people and cultural elements that have mattered in the course of the poet's life.

Works Cited

Abrams, M. H. *A Glossary of Literary Terms.* New York: Holt, Rinehart and Winston, 1981.

Ambelain, Robert. *Le Kabbale pratique.* Paris: Éditions Niclaus, 1951.

Baccolini, Raffaella. *Tradition, Identity, Desire: Revisionist Strategies in H. D.'s Late Poetry.* Bologna: Patron, 1995.

Bergson, Henri. *Matter and Memory.* Trans. N. M. Paul and W. S. Palmer. 1896. Reprint, London: Allen, 1911.

Dante Alighieri. *Vita Nuova.* Ed. Marcella Ciccuto. Milano: Garzanti, 1977.

Dembo, L. S. "Norman Holmes Pearson on H. D.: An Interview." *Contemporary Literature* 10 (1969): 435–45.

DuPlessis, Rachel Blau. "Romantic Thralldom in H. D." *Contemporary Literature* 29 (1979): 178–203.

Eliot, T. S. "Tradition and the Individual Talent." *Selected Prose of T. S. Eliot.* Ed. Frank Kermode. New York: Farrar, 1988:37–44.

———. "*Ulysses,* Order and Myth." *Selected Prose of T. S. Eliot.* Ed. Frank Kermode. New York: Farrar, 1988. 175–78.

Freud, Sigmund. "Remembering, Repeating and Working-Through." *The Standard Edition of the Complete Psychological Works of Sigmund Freud.* Trans. J. Strachey. London: Hogarth, 12 (1958): 147–56.

Friedman, Susan Stanford. "Gender and Genre Anxiety: Elizabeth Barrett Browning and H. D. as Epic Poets." *Tulsa Studies in Women's Literature* 5 (1986): 203–28.

———. "Hilda Doolittle (H.D.)" *Dictionary of Literary Biography: Modern American Poets, First Series, 1885–1945.* Vol. 45. Ed. Peter Quartermain. Detroit: Gale Research, 1986:115–49.

———. " 'Remembering Shakespeare always, but remembering him differently' ": H. D.'s *By Avon River.*" *Sagetrieb* 2 (1983): 45–70.

———. *Penelope's Web: Gender, Modernity, H. D.'s Fiction.* Cambridge: Cambridge UP, 1990.

———. *Psyche Reborn: The Emergence of H. D.* Bloomington: Indiana UP, 1981.

Guest, Barbara. *Herself Defined: The Poet H. D. and Her World.* Garden City: Doubleday, 1984.

H. D. *By Avon River.* New York: Macmillan, 1949.

———. *Collected Poems, 1912–1944.* Ed. Louis Martz. New York: New Directions, 1983.

———. "Dante's Notebooks." (1948). Collection of American Literature, Beinecke Rare Books and Manuscript Library, Yale University.

———. *End to Torment: A Memoir of Ezra Pound.* Ed. Norman Holmes Pearson and Michael King. New York: New Directions, 1979.

———. *Helen in Egypt.* New York: New Directions, 1961.

———. *Hermetic Definition.* New York: New Directions, 1972.

———. *Sagesse. Hermetic Definition.* New York: New Directions, 1972.

———. *Tribute to Freud.* New York: Pantheon, 1956.

———. *Trilogy. Collected Poems, 1912–1944.* Ed. Louis Martz. New York: New Directions, 1983: 505–612.

———. *Vale Ave. New Directions in Poetry and Prose 44.* Ed. James Laughlin. New York: New Directions, 1982.

———. *Winter Love. Hermetic Definition.* New York: New Directions, 1972.

Hart, George. " 'A memory forgotten': The Circle of Memory and Forgetting in H. D.'s *Helen in Egypt*" *Sagetrieb* 1–2 (1995): 161–77.

Joyce, James. *Ulysses.* New York: Vintage, 1986.

Keller, Lynn. "The Twentieth-Century Long Poem." *The Columbia History of American Poetry.* Ed. Jay Parini and Brett C. Miller. New York: Columbia UP, 1993: 534–63.

Lewis, Wyndham. "Our Vortex." *A Modernist Reader: Modernism in England, 1910–1930.* Ed. Peter Faulkner. London: Batsford, 1986: 44–46.

Middlebrook, Diane Wood. "What Was Confessional Poetry." *The Columbia History of American Poetry*. Ed. Jay Parini and Brett C. Millier. New York: Columbia UP, 1993: 632–49.

Ostriker, Alicia Suskin. "The Thieves of Language: Women Poets and Revisionist Mythmaking." *The New Feminist Criticism*. Ed. Elaine Showalter. New York: Pantheon, 1985.

Pearson, Norman Holmes. "Foreword," *Tribute to Freud*. New York: Pantheon, 1956: v–xiv.

Pound, Ezra. *The Cantos*. New York: New Directions, 1952.

Proust, Marcel. *Remembrance of Things Past*. Trans. C. K. Scott Moncrieff, T. Kilmartin, and A. Mayor. New York: Random, 1981.

Rosenthal, M. L. *The New Poets: American and British Poetry since World War II*. New York: Oxford UP, 1967.

Rossi, Paolo. *Il passato, la memoria, l'oblio*. Bologna: Il Mulino, 1991.

Twitchell-Waas, Jeffrey. " 'Set in eternity but lived in': H. D.'s *Vale Ave*." *Sagetrieb* 1–2 (1996): 203–27.

White, Hayden. *Tropics of Discourse*. Baltimore: Johns Hopkins UP, 1978.

Yates, Frances. *The Art of Memory*. Chicago: U of Chicago P, 1966.

Yeats, William Butler. *Collected Poems*. New York: Macmillan: 1956.

PART III

"I escaped spider-snare, bird-claw, scavenger
bird-beak": **The Poet's Legacy**

The Blank Page: H. D.'s Invitation to Trust and Mistrust Language[1]

Kathleen Fraser

we know no rule
of procedure,

we are voyagers, discoverers,
of the not known

the unrecorded;
we have no map . . .
H. D., "The Walls Do Not Fall"

With an authentic sense of beginning at Zero, a poetically mature H. D. could write in the war years of the early 1940s: "we know no rule / of procedure." Yet her contemporary readers know that rules of procedure did exist at almost every level of her early life. Even in

---

1. This essay was originally written as a talk, at the invitation of Donna Hollenberg, who chaired the H. D. panel at the American Literature Association meetings in May, 1997, in San Diego. She asked me to look at my writing practice in relationship to the work of H. D. and to speculate on any influence. Later, Hollenberg developed that idea with a number of other American women poets into a collection of essays to be called *H. D. and Poets After.* The essay is also included in Fraser, *Translating the Unspeakeable.*

that nontraditional world of literature she leaned toward, achieved forms stood in place. Nevertheless, she refused the finality of the already filled page. For while others' writings often thrilled her, they did not speak for the unsaid that burned in her.

Born from doubt and extreme privacy, her own tentative language slowly invented itself out of silence. Her gift was an ability to see the empty page waiting to be inscribed and to imagine—beyond the parchment metaphor of "palimpsest"—a contemporary model for the poem that would recover a complex overlay of erotic and spiritual valuings variously imprinted, then worn away, then, finally, rediscovered and engraved inside her own lines. Her vision lay in the conviction of plurality—that the blank page would never be a full text until women writers (and their reader-scholars) scrawled their own scripts across its emptiness.

Even within Pound's mentoring embrace, H. D. felt a certain cautionary guardedness around the unfolding, if uneasy, project of her own work. "Ezra would have destroyed me and the center they call 'Air and Crystal,' " she admits in 1958, in her journal entry from *End to Torment.* A month later, she writes: "To recall Ezra is to recall my father. . . . To recall my father is to recall the cold blazing intelligence of my 'last attachment' of the war years in London. This is not easy" (from H. D.'s journal entries for April 9 and May 15, 1958).

She had survived two major wars and the tyranny of gender stereotype. But fifty years later she was still trying to sort out the impact of this strange, impassioned outsider Ezra Pound who identified and constellated her early poetic identity, while at the same time limiting its very stretch by his defining, instructive approval.

That a strong push-pull dynamic progressively marks her writer-relation to Pound and her position "on the fringes of the modernist mainstream" seems evident from passages in her fictional works and in bits of letters and journals (Friedman and DuPlessis). Her artistic progress is marked by self-initiated shifts in attitude and ambition—notably, her decision to try to shed the once-useful but finally limiting description of "Imagiste" given her by Pound as her poet designator. It is instructive to mark her ambivalence toward—and discomfort with—male value judgments vis-à-vis her own work and to see how she climbed, repeatedly, out of these silencing effects to recover again her own voice and to trust its foraging instincts.

We read the following words written to Pound, anticipating his criticism, in a note H. D. sent along to him in 1959 with a copy of her complete *Helen in Egypt*: "Don't worry or hurry with the Helen—don't read it all—don't read it yet—don't bother to write of it" (Friedman and DuPlessis). One hears the echo and ricochet of her wariness traveling all the way back to Pound's first decisive claim on her poetic gifts, the swift and confident slash of his editor's pencil, and his literal initialing—or labeling—of her for purposes of identification and value in the poetry marketplace.

In H. D.'s life, this style of "help" manifested itself in various powerful guises, notably in encounters with big-affect literary friends such as D. H. Lawrence, whose charismatic male authority was often as much a source of anxiety as support. The delicate yet powerful mythic terrain wisely appropriated by H. D. afforded protection from a merely personal accounting of her highly volatile emotional life—the more personal lyric, so liable to deliver her into the hands of male "correction." Myth finally provided a route of independent travel, a large enough page on which to incise and thus emplace her own vision of the future, spiritually enlivened by values retrieved from female life.

When she directs our attention, in *Trilogy*, to the "blank pages / of the unwritten volume of the new," H. D. is issuing a literal invitation of breathtaking immensity and independence to contemporary women poets. Once perceived, the page is there and yours to remake. No more alibis. The challenge is at once freeing and awesome.

•

As a contemporary writer, I have been called back to this blank page again and again. Let me attempt to describe a largely intuitive gathering-up of poem materials for a serial work of mine, "Etruscan Pages" (Fraser 1998, 97–118), in which the layerings of old and new inscriptions were built from accretions of literal archeological remnant bound together into current pages of language, visual figure, and event (present-time dreams and letters).

I believe it was H. D.'s profound connection to the contemporary relevance of ancient cultures—as well as her Egyptian experience with hieroglyph as a kind of telegram from the atemporal—that opened me and prepared me for my journey (May, 1991) to the sites of three Etruscan necropoli—Tarquinia, Vulci, and Norchia—scattered north of Rome along the Maremma coast, each site marked on the map with an almost illegible triangle of black dots. Having deferred a long-held intellectual curiosity, early prompted by reading D. H. Lawrence in the sixties and an early draft (1979) of Rachel Blau DuPlessis's ground-breaking essay "For the Etruscans"

(1–19)—and thinly veneered with bookish obligation—I finally took the occasion of a friend's visit to propose a journey to these three sites, and we set off early one morning with map and guidebook.

There was nothing that could have prepared me for the impact these places had on me—their absence informed by presence. The cliff tombs of Norchia might well have been entirely nonexistent if one were dependent only on visual clues or signs along nearby roads. By guesswork we found ourselves climbing down through rough rock passages overgrown with foliage that seemed to have been there forever. The lack of any other car or human allowed the presence of birds, local wild flowers, and the more apparent ruins of Roman conquerors—planted just across the ravine from the Etruscan cliff tombs—to resonate powerfully. I felt as if dropped through time, less and less able to talk casually of our surrounds.

Days later, the poem slowly began to rise to the surface of my listening mind. And during that time a startling convergence of dreams and events worked to push the limits of the poem into something much more layered and much less personal than any account of my own private experience could have provided. A week after the Maremma trip, I returned to the Villa Giulia, the major Etruscan museum in Rome, to see again the dancers lavishly flung across urns and the sculpted bodies of husband and wife entwined sensuously on the limestone lid covering an elongated sarcophagus. It was then I could finally begin to piece together their celebratory moment on earth with utterly changed eyes. H. D.'s invitation had allowed me to step out of the skin of verbal overlay and late twentieth-century gloss, rendering me available to the palpable presence of these women and men.

Here are several passages from a letter, early embedded in my "page," that narrate a dream and then an archeological episode, both given to me during the weeks of the poem's writing, as if invented for the layered record I was attempting to rewrite:

> The night after you left for Paros, I dreamt I was lying on a stone slab at the base of the cliff tombs at Norchia, preparing to make my transition from "this world" to "the other." I was thinking about how to negotiate the passage, when it came to me—the reason for all the layers of fine white cloth arranged and spread around me. I said to you (because you were with me), "You just keep wrapping yourself with white cloth and eventually you are in the other place."
>
> (*Il Cuore: The Heart* 111)

and this, from an unexpected conversation—days later—with an archeologist:

The other source [referring to etymological studies] is the "mummy wrapping," linen originally from Egypt (probably hauled on trading ships) covered with formulaic and repetitious Etruscan religious precepts—written "retro" (right to left). Even though there are over 1,200 words covering it, the total lexicon is barely 500. The mummy text is preserved in the museum in Zagreb, thus "The Zagreb Mummy." When they found her in Etruria, her body had been wrapped in this shroud made of pieces of linen, written on through centuries [with Phoenician, Greek, and, finally, Etruscan characters], used as "pages" for new writing whenever the old text had faded. Her family had wrapped her in this cloth, this writing, because it was available.

(Il Cuore: The Heart 111–12)

With these interventions, the actual making of the poem became immensely absorbing. H. D.'s exhortation to heed "the blank pages of the unwritten volume of the new" was pulling me away from her "air and crystal" language. My page wanted to be inscribed as if it were a canvas, my own linguistic motion and visual notation appropriating the Etruscan lexicon and alphabet as subject and object—inventions suggested directly from contact with tomb inscriptions and the beaten-gold tablets at Villa Giulia, covered with the elusive remainders of their language.

For example, a passage on the imagined origins of the letter "A" is juxtaposed with a miniature lexicon composed of words that already existed throughout the larger poem's text, a word hand-scrawled in Etruscan letters (meant to resemble those scratched into burial stones) and a bit of quoted speculation by D. H. Lawrence. I wanted to place a close-up lens over particular words, as well as to foreground the hand and mind at work making language through history.

Without H. D.'s precedent, it is very unlikely that I would have trusted my own particular rendering of the historic clues and layers of the Etruscan culture, nor understood the urgency of articulating another reading of it in the face of all the officially recognized studies preceding me—including Lawrence's narrative. While my poem, "Etruscan Pages," intentionally acknowledges Lawrence's 1932 travel memoir, *Etruscan Places,* it writes the new word PAGE over the old word PLACE to tip the reader's attention in the direction of an alternative reading introduced through a formal shift of perception. Mine is a document meant to record an alternative vision of the predominantly male archeological point-of-view already well-installed.

Having given Lawrence's account a rather perfunctory skim in the sixties, I was curious to go back to it—once I had a fairly realized draft of my own—just to see what had occupied him. I was pleased, but not that surprised, to find that there were a number of physical details and baffling absences we'd noted in common—although sixty years apart—even to particulars of asphodel (he must have been there in May), and the "nothing" that seemed to be so present in the barren fields and shut tombs around Vulci, where a sensuousness of daily life had once been so radiantly apparent.

I decided to incorporate several fragmentary phrases from Lawrence's text as a way of marking our meeting in parallel time—a kind of palimpsest dialogue. But I was deeply relieved to find that he'd not been to Norchia, the site that most profoundly spoke to me. I didn't want his brilliant voice-print preceding me everywhere. Its definite authority and well-installed literary history might have in some way inhibited me from capturing my own barely visible version.

•

I'd like to return now to the issue of asserted literary dominion versus self-confirmation, as it impinges on the working life of the woman poet. For in spite of her strategies for empowerment, we recognize in H. D.'s 1959 note to Pound a residual mistrust based on the tension between her deep desire for his approval and the necessary self-affirmation of her own unmediated—and thus uninhibited—vision and writing method. Even after fifty years, a lurking fear of not meeting his standards still seems to hover in her. It isn't a simple fear of critique, for she was obviously strong-willed and utterly conscious of her aesthetic choices by then; rather, it is more like the dread of having to tangle with the absolute ego of the beloved but intrusive father-judge, forever looming in the shadow just over her shoulder, and to risk the loss of his admiration.

Reviewing H. D.'s progress toward the trust of her own "page," a contemporary woman poet might well identify with this struggle to circumvent the tremendous pressure of prevailing male ideology that has so conveniently persisted, historically viewing women contemporaries as "receptacle-like muses rather than active agents," thus reinforcing long-dominant "notions of what was properly and naturally feminine" (Friedman and DuPlessis).

Recently, reading through a selection of letters between Pound and the young Louis Zukofsky, exchanged between 1928 and 1930, I was generally amused until I came across such bits of Pound-heavy advice as his urging Zukofsky to form a new literary group of serious, high-energy writers, but exhorting him: "NOT too many women, and if possible no wives at assembly. If some insist on accompanying their *mariti* [husbands], make sure they are bored and don't repeat offense." Later, advising Zukofsky about the selection of work for a new magazine, he says: "AND the verse used MUST be good ... preferably by men (sic) under 30" (Pound and Zukofsky).

In these tossed-off bits of pecking-order jocularity are found the not-very-subtle codes of selection and disenfranchisement that were practiced to various degrees in the literary world I entered as a young poet in the early sixties. A primary difference between my world and H. D.'s was that nine-tenths of the once published writing by modernist women was out-of-print, leaving very few female texts as models for the nontraditional poetics one felt compelled to explore.

Fortunately, change was in the air. By the early Seventies, women scholars had begun to talk to each other about this problem and to investigate it in print.

This brings us again to the shaping hand of influence and the prevailing authority of installed standards of judgment, and how the effects of gender-specific valuing, editing, and explication can make a radical difference in the continuing life of the working poet.

Thinking about particular writers who shaped my early writing sensibility, I cannot find any direct H. D. imprint on my poetics or practice, yet I know that somewhere along the line my mature writing has been significantly touched by her traces, even though in the first decade of my exposure to modernist American poetry there was the now documented, measurable obstacle blocking access to her writing.

I would guess that I first saw the initials "H. D." at the end of an anthologized poem sometime at the end of the sixties. No doubt, that poem was one of the few safe and untouchable Imagist poems that editors began recirculating around that time to represent her work. We would later discover a much more complex, fecund, and demanding literary production. But for the moment, lacking any particular professor's or admired poet's passion for this mythic and (what seemed to me) very austere and impersonal voice, and swarmed as I was by every possible kind of innovative or jazzy poetic example, I was not available to H. D.'s spiritual and generative gift. I suspect that even if *Trilogy* or *Helen in Egypt* had been waved in my face at this time, I lacked sufficient conscious appetite for her alchemical and mythical vocabularies of transformation.

Eventually, in the mid-eighties, I had the opportunity to read *Trilogy* aloud with a small group of women poets and could finally hear H. D.'s voice, as if there were no longer any barrier. By then, my inevitable share of human loss had prepared me.

In the sixties, I was in love with everything that promised a fresh start and quite ready to shed a dominating mainstream "poetics of Self," imposing its confessional hypnotic trance on readers and young American writers. I was chafing at the confines of the typical "I"-centered, mainstream American poem that so theatrically and narcissistically positioned the writer at the hub of all pain and glory; it seemed reminiscent of pre-Renaissance science, before Galileo announced the radical news of his telescopic discovery:

<u>Man is no longer at the center of the universe.</u>

H. D. understood this afresh. The hierarchies forever asserting themselves were again toppled.

Physics, action painting, field poetics, and new music—as well as fuller readings of Woolf and new encounters with Richardson, Moore, and Stein, the New York school, the Black Mountain poets, and the Objectivists—had all been registering a different dynamic involving energy fields, shifting contexts, and a self no longer credibly unitary, but divided and subdivided until uncertainty called into question any writing too satisfied with its own personal suffering or too narrowly focused on cleverness and polish.

My devotion and intellectual curiosity had been claimed instead by a dozen highly inventive, nontraditional sorts of poets. I imagined, then, that I was equally open to all poetry but, in fact, I was a young reader and writer, prone to the excitement of what I thought of as a high-modern tone and syntax, one whose surface diction and visual field promised to carry me away from what had begun to feel like the dangerous trap of lyric habit, and ever closer to my own increasingly idiosyncratic compositions. I did not want to write within a language tradition too easily understood, too clearly part of the agenda rubber-stamped by most mainstream journals, but I had not yet articulated for myself the reasons for my resistance, nor the power relations dictating the limits of what I felt antagonistic toward.

The contemplative, as a desired place of knowledge, was beyond me; the contemporary implications and uses of myth hadn't yet hit—I mean, the understanding that myth is ahistoric, breathing in us, and not merely confined to a narrative of the ancient past.

The seventies and eighties revealed a different grid, a detour meant to flaw the convenient, intact, uniform story of influence. As it turned out, H. D.'s linking of "hermetic" assignations with "secret language" and her conscious rejection of single-version narratives would become central in helping to define my own poetic process. It was not that I wanted to write *like* her, but rather, that I began hearing her urgency and experiencing in her work a kind of female enspiriting guide that I'd been lacking.

•

Constructing and *re*constructing this episodic moment across the space of my own blank pages, I finally understood that H. D. had used the scaffolding of locked-up myth to regenerate lopsided human stories with a new infusion of contemporary perspective. This meant the possibility—for herself and her readers—of being more fully included in the on-going pursuit of knowledge, and thus less personally stuck in the isolation of private anguish. There was, as it turned out, a place in language—even in its zero beginnings—to put one's trust.

Works Cited

DuPlessis, Rachel Blau. "For the Etruscans." In *The Pink Guitar: Writing as Feminist Practice.* New York: Routledge, 1990.

Fraser, Kathleen. *Il Cuore: The Heart. Selected Poems, 1970–1995.* Hanover: Wesleyan UP, 1998.

————. *Translating the Unspeakable: Poetry and Innovative Necessity.* Tuscaloosa: U of Albama P, 2000.

Friedman, Susan Stanford, and Rachel Blau DuPlessis, eds. *Signets: Reading H. D.* Madison: U of Wisconsin P, 1990.

H. D. *Trilogy: The Walls Do Not Fall, Tribute to the Angels, The Flowering of the Rod.* Foreword by Norman Holmes Pearson. New York: New Directions, 1973.

Hollenberg, Donna Krolik, ed. *H. D. and Poets After.* Iowa City: U of Iowa P, 2000.

Pound / Zukofsky: Selected Letters of Ezra Pound and Louis Zukofsky. Ed. Barry Aheam. London: Faber 1987.

Selected Bibliography

Published Works by H. D.*

Poetry

Sea Garden. London: Constable, 1916; Boston and New York: Houghton Mifflin, 1917; London: St. James Press; New York: St. Martin's Press, 1975.

Hymen. London, Egoist Press, 1921; New York: Henry Holt and Company, 1921.

Heliodora and Other Poems. London: Jonathan Cape, 1924; Boston and New York: Houghton Mifflin, 1924.

Collected Poems of H. D. New York: Boni & Liveright, 1925 [1940].

Red Roses for Bronze. London: Chatto & Windus, 1931; Boston and New York: Houghton Mifflin, 1931 (extended edition); New York: AMS Press, 1970.

The Walls Do Not Fall. London, New York: Oxford University Press, 1944.

Tribute to the Angels. London, New York: Toronto: Oxford University Press, 1946.

What Do I Love. London: Brendin, 1944.

---

* For a chronology of composition see Susan Stanford Friedman's *Penelope's Web* in "Selected Critical Studies."

By Avon River. New York, Macmillan, 1949; Redding Ridge, CT: Black Swan Books, 1989 (Afterword by John Walsh, "Remembering Shakespeare Always, but Remembering him Differently" by Susan Stanford Friedman).

Selected Poems of H. D. New York: Grove Press, 1957.

Helen in Egypt. Introduction by Horace Gregory. New York: Grove Press, 1961; New York: New Directions, 1974; Manchester: Carcanet Press, 1985.

Two Poems ("Star by day," "Wooden animal"). With illuminations by Wesley Tanner. San Francisco: Arif Press, 1971.

Hermetic Definition. Foreword by Norman Holmes Pearson. New York: New Directions, 1972; Carcanet Press: Oxford, 1972.

Temple of the Sun. Berkeley: Arif Press, 1972.

Trilogy: The Walls Do Not Fall, Tribute to the Angels, The Flowering of the Rod. Foreword by Norman Holmes Pearson. New York: New Directions, 1973; Manchester: Carcanet Press, 1988; new edition with Introduction and reader's notes by Aliki Barnstone. New York: New Directions, 1998.

The Poet and the Dancer. San Francisco: Five Trees Press, 1975.

Collected Poems 1912–1944. Ed. and introd. by Louis L. Martz. New York: New Directions, 1983.

Priest & Dead Priestess Speaks. Port Townsend, WA: Cooper Canyon Press, 1983.

Selected Poems. Ed. and introd. by Louis L. Martz: New York: New Directions, 1988.

Vale Ave. Ed. by John Walsh; Illustrations by David Finn. Redding Ridge, CT: Black Swan Books, 1991.

Drama and Translations

Choruses from Iphigeneia in Aulis. Translated by H. D. *The Egoist* 2.11 (1 Nov. 1915): 171–72; The Poets' Translation Series, no. 3. London: Ballantyne Press, 1916.

Choruses from Iphigeneia in Aulis and the Hippolytus of Euripides. Translated by H. D. London: The Egoist Press, Ltd., 1919.

Hippolytus Temporizes. A Play in Three Acts. Boston: Houghton Mifflin, 1927. Corrected edition with Afterword by John Walsh. Redding Ridge, CT: Black Swan Books, 1985.

Euripides' Ion. Translated with notes by H D. London: Chatto & Windus; Boston: Houghton Mifflin, 1937. Corrected edition with Afterword by John Walsh. Redding Ridge, CT: Black Swan Books, 1986.

Songs and Musical Settings

H. D. and Walter Rummel. "Songs for Children" ("The Mill Fairy," "The Flower Fairy," "The Cricket," "The Leaves") in *Ten Songs for Children Young and Old*. London: Augener, 1914. Reprinted in *H. D. Newsletter* 3:2 (1990): 12–26.

Audio Tapes

Helen in Egypt. Selections from the poem read by H. D. Watershed Tapes, P. O. Box 5014, Washington, D.C. 20004.
Five American Women. New York: Random House Audio Pub., 2001.

Prose Works

Palimpsest. Paris: Contact Editions, 1926; Boston and New York: Houghton Mifflin, 1926; Carbondale, ILL: Southern Illinois University Press, 1968 (with Preface by Harry T. Moore, "Forewarned as Regards H. D.'s Prose" by Robert McAlmon, "A Note on the Text" by Matthew J. Bruccoli).
Hedylus. Boston: Houghton Mifflin, 1928. Corrected edition: Redding Ridge, CT: Black Swan Books, 1980 and Oxford: Carcanet Press, 1981 (both with Afterword by John Walsh, "The Egyptian Cat" by Perdita Schaffner).
"Narthex." *The Second American Caravan*. Ed. Alfred Kreymborg, Lewis Mumford, and Paul Rosenfeld. New York: Macaulay, 1928: 225–84.
The Usual Star. ("The Usual Star" and "Two Americans"). Dijon, France: Imprimerie Darantière, 1934. "Two Americans" reprinted in *New Directions* 51 (1987): 58–68.
Kora & Ka. Dijon, France: Imprimerie Darantière, 1934; Berkeley: Bios, 1978.
Kora and Ka with Mira-Mare. Introduction by Robert Spoo. New York: New Directions, 1996.
Nights. By John Helforth. Dijon, France: Imprimerie Darantière, 1934; New York: New Directions, fine press ed., 1986 (Introduction by Perdita Schaffner).
The Hedgehog. London: The Brendin Publishing Company, 1936; New York: New Directions, 1988 (Introduction by Perdita Schaffner, Woodcuts by George Plank).

By Avon River. New York: Macmillan, 1949; Redding Ridge, CT: Black Swan Books, 1989 (Afterword by John Walsh and "Remembering Shakespeare Always, but Remembering him Differently" by Susan Stanford Friedman).

Tribute to Freud. With Unpublished Letters by Freud to the author. New York: Pantheon Books, 1956. Oxford: Carcanet Press, 1971 (Introduction by Peter Jones). Second and revised edition (*Writing on the Wall and Advent*). Boston: David R. Godine, 1974 (Foreword by Norman Holmes Pearson, Introduction by Kenneth Fields); New York: McGraw-Hill, 1975; New York: New Directions, 1984 (Foreword by Norman Holmes Pearson); Oxford: Carcanet Press, 1985.

Bid Me to Live (A Madrigal). New York: Grove Press, 1960; Redding Ridge CT: Black Swan Books, 1983 (Afterword by John Walsh and "A Profound Animal" by Perdita Schaffner); New York: The Dial Press, 1983; London: Virago Press, 1984 (Introduction by Helen McNeil, Afterword by Perdita Schaffner).

The Mystery (chapters 3, 14–19). In *Images of H. D.* by Eric White. London: Enitharmon Press, 1976.

End to Torment: A Memoir of Ezra Pound. Ed. Norman Holmes Pearson and Michael King, New York: New Directions, 1979. Contains *Hilda's Book* by E. Pound; Manchester: Carcanet Press, 1980.

HERmione. New York: New Directions, 1981 (with "Pandora's Box" by Perdita Schaffner); London: Virago Press, 1984 (Introduction by Helen McNeil, Afterword by Perdita Schaffner).

The Gift. New York: New Directions, 1982 (with "Unless a Bomb Falls . . ." by Perdita Schaffner); London: Virago Press, 1984 (Introduction by Diana Collecott).

The Gift: The Complete Text. Edited and annotated, with an introduction by Jane Augustine. Gainesville: UP of Florida, 1998.

Notes on Thought and Vision & The Wise Sappho. Introduction by Albert Gelpi. San Francisco: City Lights Books, 1982. Reprinted in: *The Gender of Modernism.* Ed. Bonnie Kime Scott. Bloomington: Indiana University Press, 1990: 93–109.

"Saint Anthony." *Polis* 3 (1982): 5–7.

"H. D. by Delia Alton." *Iowa Review* 16 (Fall 1986): 174–221.

Within the Walls. Redding Ridge, CT: Black Swan Books, 1990.

Paint It To-Day. Edited by Cassandra Laity. New York: New York UP, 1991.

Asphodel. Ed. by Robert Spoo. Durham and London: Duke UP, 1992.

Pilate's Wife. Edited and with an introduction by Joan A. Burke. New York: New Directions Books, 2000.

Film and Film Criticism

H. D. acted in a number of films directed by Kenneth Macpherson and produced by POOL, a publishing and film company created by Bryher and Macpherson, in which H. D. was also involved. The only extant film is *Borderline* (1930); only fragments survive of *Wing Beat* (1927) and *Foothills* (1929). They are kept in the "Macpherson Material," Museum of Modern Art, New York. *Borderline* can also be seen at the British Film Institute, London, and in selected locations. See: Anne Friedberg. "The Pool Films: What They Are, Where They Are, How to See Them." *H. D. Newsletter* 1 (Spring 1987): 10–11.

H. D. *Borderline—A POOL Film with Paul Robeson.* London: Mercury Press, 1930. Reprinted in: *The Gender of Modernism.* Ed. Bonnie Kime Scott. Bloomington: Indiana UP, 1990:110–125; *Sagetrieb* 7 (Fall 1987): 29–50; *Close Up 1927–1933: Cinema and Modernism.* Ed. James Donald, Anne Friedberg, and Laura Marcus. London: Cassell, 1998:105–48.

Correspondence

"H. D., Hilda Aldington." Letter to Margaret Anderson. *Little Review* 12 (May 1929): 38–40. Reprinted in *Little Review Anthology.* Edited by Margaret Anderson. New York: Hermitage House, 1953.

"A Note on Poetry." H. D. to Norman Holmes Pearson (1937). *The Oxford Anthology of American Literature.* Ed. William Rose Benét and Norman Holmes Pearson. New York: Oxford University Press, 1938. Reprinted in *Agenda* 25 (Autumn-Winter 1987–88): 64–70.

"Selected Letters from H. D. to F. S. Flint: A Commentary on the Imagist Period." Ed. by Cyrena N. Pondrom. *Contemporary Literature* 10 (Autumn 1969): 557–86.

"A Friendship Traced: H. D. Letters to Silvia Dobson." Edited by Carol T. Tinker. *Conjunctions* 2 (Spring-Summer 1982): 115–57.

"Art and Ardor in World War One: Selected Letters from H. D. to John Cournos." Edited by Donna Krolik Hollenberg. *Iowa Review* 16 (Fall, 1987): 126–55.

"Across the Abyss: The H. D.-Adrienne Monnier Correspondence."
Edited by Caroline Zilboorg. *Sagetrieb* 8:3 (Winter 1989):
115–134.

*A Great Admiration: Hilda Doolittle-Robert Duncan: Correspondence
1950–1961.* Edited by Robert J. Bertholf. Venice, CA: Lapis
Press, 1992.

Richard Aldington & H. D.: The Early Years in Letters. Edited with an
introduction and commentary by Caroline Zilboorg. Bloomington, Indiana UP, 1992.

Richard Aldington & H. D.: The Later Years in Letters. Edited with an
introduction and commentary by Caroline Zilboorg. Manchester and New York: Manchester UP, 1995. New York: St. Martin's, 1995.

*Between History & Poetry: The Letters of H. D. & Norman Holmes Pear-
son.* Edited by Donna Krolik Hollenberg. Iowa City: U of Iowa
P, 1997.

Analyzing Freud: Letters of H. D. Bryher and their Circle. Edited by
Susan Stanford Friedman. New York: New Directions, 2002.

Manuscript Collections

The Beinecke Rare Book and Manuscript Library, Yale University,
owns the largest collection of H. D.'s published and unpublished manuscripts, books, and papers. See "The H. D. Papers"
in the Collection of American Literature. Items relating to H. D.
can be located through the National Union Catalog of Manuscript Collections (NUCMC).

Book Translations of H. D.'s Works

French

Visage de Freud. Translated by Françoise de Gruson. Paris: Denoël,
1977.

HERmione. Translated by Claire Malroux. Paris: Éd. de Femmes,
1986.

Dis-moi de vivre: un madrigal Translated by Claire Malroux. Paris:
Éd. de Femmes, 1987.

Le Don. Translated by Claire Marloux. Paris: Éd. de Femmes, 1988.

Fin du tourment. Suivi de *Le Livre de Hilda* par Ezra Pound. Translation, introduction, comment by Jean-Paul Auxeméry. Paris: Éd. de la Différence, 1992.

Hélène en Egypt. Translation and introduction by Jean-Paul Auxeméry. Paris: Éd. de la Différence, 1992.

Le jardin près de la mer. Translation and introduction by Jean-Paul Auxeméry. Paris: Éd. de la Différence, 1992.

German

Avon. Translation by Johannes Urzidil. Berlin: Suhrkamp, 1955.

Huldigung an Freud: Rückblick auf eine Analyse. Mit den briefen von Sigmund Freud an H. D. Introd. by Michael Schröter. Frankfurt/M: Ullstein, 1976.

Trilogie. Band I, Text. Band II, Ammerkungen und Kommentar. Translation and comment by Annemarie and Franz Link. Freiburg: i. Br., 1978.

Das Ende der Qual: Erinnerung an Ezra Pound. Translation of *End To Torment* by Andrea Spingler. Zürich: Arche, 1985.

HERmione. Translated by Anja Lazarowicz. München: Hanser 1987; München: Goldmann, 1989; Berlin: Wagenbach, 1998.

Greek

Introduction to the Trilogy by H. D. Text, Translation, Notes. Ed. Liana Sakelliou. Translation by Liana Sakelliou, Thanasis Dokos, and Thomas Stravelis. Athens: Guthenberg Publishers, 1999.

Italian

I Segni sul muro. Translation of *Tribute to Freud* by Massimo Ferretti. Roma: Astrolabio, 1972.

H. D. Selection of poems by H. D. and translation by Mary de Rachewiltz. Milano: Scheiwiller, 1986 (Strenna per gli amici).

Trilogia. Edited, translated, and annotated, with "Breve biografia letteraria" and "Alchimie, miti, sogni, parole revisionarie" by Marina Camboni. Caltanissetta-Roma: Salvatore Sciascia Editore, 1993.

Fine al tormento: Ricordo di Ezra Pound. Edited, translated, and annotated by Massimo Bacigalupo. With letters of Ezra Pound to H. D. Milano: Rosellina Archinto, 1994.

Japanese

Freud ni sasagu. Translation of *Tribute to Freud* and *Writing on the Wall* by Jûkichi Suzuki. Tokyo: Misuzu Shobo, 1983.

Norwegian

Freud: ei erindring. Translation by Brit Bildøen. Oslo: Pax, 1998.

Spanish

El espejo y el brazalete. Translation of *Hedylus* by Pilar Gilart Gorina. Barcelona: Seix Barral, 1994.
Definición hermética. Translation and presentation by Ulalume González de León. México, D. F.: Universidad Iberoamericana: Artes de Mexico, 1997.

Bibliography and Criticism

Bibliographies

Boughn, Michael. *H. D.: A Bibliography, 1905–1990.* Charlottesville and London: UP of Virginia, 1993.
Mathis, Mary S. *H. D.: An Annotated Bibliography, 1913–1986.* Boston: Garland, 1991.

Selected Critical Studies*:

Alfrey, Shawn. *The Sublime of Intense Sociability: Emily Dickinson, H. D., and Gertrude Stein.* Lewisburg: Bucknell UP, 2000.
Agenda 25 (Autumn Winter 1987) H. D. Issue.
Baccolini, Raffaella. *Tradition, Identiy, Desire: Revisionist Strategies in H. D.'s Late Poetry.* Bologna: Pàtron Editore, 1995.
Bloom, Harold, ed. *H. D.* New York: Chelsea House Publishers, 1989. Rpt. 2002.

---

* For a detailed critical bibliography see Michael Boughn. Here are listed monograph studies, collections of essays, recent books on H. D., and criticism relevant for an assessment of her poetry.

Bryher. *The Heart to Artemis: A Writer's Memoirs.* New York: Harcourt, Brace & World, 1960; London: Collins, 1961.

————. *The Days of Mars: A Memoir, 1940–1946.* New York: Harcourt, Brace & World, 1972; London: Marion Boyars, 1981.

Buck, Claire. *H. D. and Freud: Bisexuality and a Feminine Discourse.* New York and London: Harvester Wheatsheaf, 1991; New York: St. Martin's, 1991.

Burnett, Gary, *H. D. Between Image and Epic: The Mysteries of Her Poetics.* Ann Arbor: UMI Research Press, 1990.

Camboni, Marina, ed. *H(ilda) D(oolittle) e il suo mondo.* Palermo: Università degli Studi di Palermo, 1995.

Chisholm, Dianne. *H. D.'s Freudian Poetics.* Ithaca: Cornell UP, 1992.

Collecott, Diana. *H. D. and Sapphic Modernism, 1910–1950.* Cambridge: Cambridge UP, 1999.

Contemporary Literature 10 (Autumn 1969); 27 (Winter 1986). H. D. Issues.

Curry, Renée, R. *White Women Writing White: H. D., Elizabeth Bishop, Sylvia Plath, and Whiteness.* Westport, CT: Greenwood Press, 2000.

Dehler, Johanna. *Fragments of Desire: Sapphic Fictions in Works by H. D., Judy Grahn, and Monique Wittig.* Frankfurt am Main; New York: P. Lang, 1999.

DeShazer, Mary K. *Inspiring Women: Reimagining the Muse.* New York: Pergamon Press, 1986.

Dodd, Elizabeth. *The Veiled Mirror and the Woman Poet: H. D., Louise Bogan, Elizabeth Bishop, and Louise Glück.* Columbia: U of Missouri P, 1992.

Duncan, Robert. *The H. D. Book.* Parts and chapters of the book have been published in a number of journals and magazines. For a complete list see Michael Boughn 1993, under Bibliographies.

DuPlessis, Rachel Blau. *H. D. The Career of that Struggle.* Bloomington: Indiana UP, 1986.

————. *Writing Beyond the Ending: Narrative Strategies of Twentieth-Century Women Writers.* Bloomington: Indiana UP, 1985.

————. *The Pink Guitar: Writing as Feminist Practice.* New York and London: Routledge, 1990.

Edmunds, Susan. *Out of Line: History, Psychoanalysis, & Montage in H. D.'s Long Poems.* Stanford: Stanford UP, 1994.

Friedman, Susan Stanford. *Psyche Reborn: The Emergence of H. D.* Bloomington: Indiana UP, 1981.

————. *Penelope's Web: Gender, Modernity, H. D.'s Fiction.* New York: Cambridge UP, 1990.

————. and Rachel Blau DuPlessis, eds. *Signets: Reading H. D.* Madison: U of Wisconsin P, 1990.

Fritz, Angela DiPace. *Thought and Vision: A Critical Reading of H. D.'s Poetry.* Washington, D.C.: Catholic UP, 1988.

Gelpi, Albert. *A Coherent Splendour: The American Poetic Renaissance, 1910–1950.* Cambridge: Cambridge UP, 1987.

Gilbert, Sandra M., and Susan Gubar. *No Man's Land: The Place of the Woman Writer in the Twentieth Century.* Vol. III: *Letters from the Front.* New Haven: Yale UP, 1990.

Gregory, Eileen. *H. D. and Hellenism: Classic Lines.* Cambridge: Cambridge UP, 1997.

Guest, Barbara. *Herself Defined: The Poet H. D. and Her World.* New York: Quill, 1984.

H. D. Newsletter, 1987–1991.

Hanscombe, Gillian, and Virginia L. Smyers. *Writing for Their Lives: The Modernist Women, 1910–1940.* London: Women's Press, 1987.

Hollenberg, Donna Krolik. *H. D.: The Poetics of Childbirth.* Boston: Northeastern UP.

————. *H. D. and Poets After.* Iowa City: U of Iowa P, 2000.

(HOW)ever 3 (October 1986). H. D. Issue.

Hughes, Glenn. *Imagism and the Imagists.* Stanford: Stanford UP; London: Humphrey Milford, Oxford UP, 1931.

The Iowa Review 16 (Fall 1986). H. D. Issue.

Kenner, Hugh. *The Pound Era: The Age of Ezra Pound, T. S. Eliot, James Joyce and Wyndham Lewis.* London: Faber, 1972.

Kerblat-Houghton, Jeanne. " 'Ce que recèlent les mots' in *The Walls Do Not Fall.*" *Revue Française d'Etudes Américaines* 7 (November 1982): 373–81.

King, Michael, ed. *H. D.: Woman and Poet.* Orono, ME: The National Poetry Foundation, 1986.

Kloepfer, Deborah Kelly. *The Unspeakable Mother: Forbidden Discourse in Jean Rhys and H. D.* Ithaca: Cornell UP, 1989.

Korg, Jacob. *Winter Love: Ezra Pound and H. D.* Madison: U of Wisconsin P, forthcoming 2003.

Kreis-Schinck Annette. *"We Are Voyagers, Discoverers": H. D.'s Trilogy and Modern Religious Poetry.* Heidelberg: Carl Winter Verlag, 1990.

Laity, Cassandra, *H. D. and the Victorian Fin de Siècle: Gender, Modernism, Decadence.* Cambridge: Cambridge UP, 1996.

Lazarowicz, Anja. *Schreiben heilt die Seele. Über Hilda Doolittle.* Munich: Hansesr, 1986.

Link, Franz H. *Zwei Amerikanische Dichterinnen: Emily Dickinson und Hilda Doolittle.* Berlin: Duncker & Humblot, 1977.

Lowell, Amy. *Tendencies in Modern American Poetry.* New York: Macmillan, 1917.

Morris, Adelaide K. *How to Live / What to do: H. D.'s Cultural Poetics.* Urbana: U of Illinois P, forthcoming 2003.

Pettipiece, Deirdre Anne. *Sex Theories and the Shaping of Two Moderns: Hemingway and H. D.* New York: Routledge, 2002.

Poesis: A Journal of Criticism 6 (Fall 1985). H. D. Issue.

Pondrom, Cyrena N. "Marianne Moore and H. D.: Female Community and Poetic Achievement." In *Marianne Moore: Woman and Poet.* Ed. Patricia C. Willis. Orono, ME: National Poetry Foundation, 1990: 1–32.

———. "H. D. and the Origins of Imagism." In *Signets: Reading H. D.* Ed. Susan Stanford Friedman and Rachel Blau DuPlessis. Madison: U of Wisconsin P, 1990: 85–109.

Ostriker, Alicia. *Writing like a Woman.* Ann Arbor: U of Michigan P, 1983.

Quinn, Vincent. *Hilda Doolittle.* New York: Twayne, 1967.

Rado, Lisa. *The Modern Androgyne Imagination: A Failed Sublime.* Charlottesville: UP of Virginia, 2000.

Rainey, Lawrence S. *Institutions of Modernism: Literary Elites and Public Culture.* New Haven: Yale UP, 1998.

Riddel, Joseph N. *The Turning Word: American Literary Modernism and Continental Theory.* Edited with an introduction by Mark Bauerlein. Philadelphia: U of Pennsylvania P, 1996.

Riding, Laura, and Robert Graves. *A Survey of Modernist Poetry.* London: William Heinemann LTD., 1929.

Robinson, Janice S. *H. D. The Life and Work of an American Poet.* Boston: Houghton Mifflin, 1982.

Rosenthal, M. L., and Sally M. Gall. *The Modern Poetic Sequence.* Oxford: Oxford UP, 1983.

Sagetrieb: A Journal Devoted to Poets in the Pound-H. D.-Williams Tradition 6 (Fall 1987); 14 (Spring & Fall 1995); 15 (Spring and Fall 1996). H. D. Issues.

San José Studies 13 (Fall 1987). H. D. Issue.

Schweik, Susan. *A Gulf So Deeply Cut: American Women Poets and the Second World War.* Madison: U of Wisconsin P, 1991.

Scott, Bonnie Kime. *The Gender of Modernism: A Critical Anthology.* Bloomington: Indiana UP, 1969.

Swann, Thomas Burnett. *The Classical World of H. D.* Lincoln: U of Nebraska P, 1962.

Sword, Helen. *Engendering Inspiration: Visionary Strategies in Rilke, Lawrence, and H. D.* Ann Arbor: U of Michigan P, 1995.

Taylor, Georgina. *H. D. and the Public Sphere of Modernist Women Writers, 1913–1946: Talking Women.* Oxford: Clarendon Press; New York: Oxford UP, 2001.

Trigilio, Tony. *Strange Prophecies Anew: Rereading Apocalypse in Blake, H. D., and Ginsberg.* Madison, NJ: Fairleigh Dickinson UP; London: Associated University Presses, 2000.

Tylee, Claire. *The Great War and Women's Consciousness.* Iowa City: Iowa UP, 1990.

Notes on Contributors

RAFFAELLA BACCOLINI teaches English and American Literature at the University of Bologna, Italy. She is the author of *Tradition, Identity, Desire: Revisionist Strategies in H. D.'s Late Poetry* and has published several articles on modernist writers (H. D., Pound, Ford, Loy, Joyce), women's writing (Levertov, women's theater, female autobiography, feminist criticism), and dystopian literature (Atwood, Orwell, Burdekin, Butler). She is currently working on "critical dystopias" and the function of memory in twentieth-century women's literature.

MARINA CAMBONI is Professor of Anglo-American Literature and Language and directs the Poetry Center POESIS at the University of Marcerata, Italy. She has translated H. D.'s *Trilogy* in Italian, edited the volume *H. D. e il suo mondo*, and contributed a number of essays on H. D.'s work to journals and volumes. She has written on Virginia Woolf, Gertrude Stein, Adrienne Rich, Anne Sexton, Allen Ginsberg, and Walt Whitman, and on American English; her fields of research are literary semiotics, contemporary poetry, and feminist theory and criticism. She is the editor of the series "Esperidi" of Anglo-American poetry for the Publisher Salvatore Sciascia.

DIANA COLLECOTT teaches British and American Literature and codirects the Basil Bunting Poetry Centre at the University of Durham, England. She edited the special H. D. issue of *Agenda*, introduced the Virago edition of H. D.'s *The Gift*, and has contributed essays on H. D. to other centennial publications and symposia. She has also written on other American writers, such as Henry James, William Carlos Williams, and Denise Levertov. Her latest published book is *H. D. & Sapphic Modernism*, Cambridge University Press, 1999.

KATHLEEN FRASER is an award-winning poet, prose writer, and editor-publisher of the journal *HOW(ever)* and the new on-line journal *HOW2*. Fraser was Professor of Creative Writing for twenty years at San Francisco State University, where she directed the Poetry Center and founded the American Poetry Archives. Her most recent book of poems is *il cuore: the heart*. Her latest published book is a collection of essays, *Translating the Unspeakable: Poetry and the Innovative Necessity*, University of Alabama Press, 2000.

EILEEN GREGORY has published essays on H. D. and is the founding editor of the *H. D. Newsletter*. She has also written on mythic themes in *Summoning the Familiar: Powers and Rites of Common Life*, as well as articles on Southern literature. An Associate Professor of English at the University of Dallas, Texas, she has recently published *H. D. and Hellenism: Classic Lines* with the Cambridge University Press.

PATRIZIA LENDINARA is Professor of Germanic Philology at the University of Palermo, Italy. She has published works on Old English language and literature and a number of essays on Old Frisian, Gothic, and Medieval Latin literature, and on lexical inferences between Germanic and Rumanian. She has also published essays on modern English literature, specifically on H. D., and edited *La lingua inglese e il suo sviluppo nel tempo e nello spazio*. Her present research focuses on Germanic glosses dating from the Anglo-Saxon period: her works have been recently republished by the variorum in the volume *Anglo-Saxon Glosses and Glossaries* (1999).

MARINA SBISÀ is Associate Professor of Philosophy of Language at the University of Trieste, Italy. Her research fields are speech act theory, discourse analysis, and women's studies, particularly with respect to female subjectivity. Besides a number of essays published in international journals, her publications include: *Che cosa ha veramente detto Wittgenstein* and *Linguaggio, ragione, interazione. Per una teoria pragmatica degli atti linguistici.* She has edited the revised edition of J. L. Austin's *How to Do Things with Words* (with J. O. Umson); *Gli atti linguistici, Come sapere il parto. Storia, scenari, linguaggi.* She is advisory editor of the *Journal of Pragmatics* and of the series "Pragmatics and Beyond" (John Benjamins, Amsterdam).

PAOLA ZACCARIA is Professor of Anglo-American Literature at the University of Bari, Italy. Her research fields are literary semiotics, cultural and feminist studies, contemporary and modern poetry. She has written a number of books on different authors: *Virginia Woolf: trama e ordito di una scrittrice; Forme della ripetizione di E. A. Poe, i deficit di Samuel Beckett; Cartografie letterarie dal Modernismo al transnazionalismo.* She has edited (with P. Calefato) *Segni eretici. Scrittura di donne tra autobiografia, etica e mito,* and *Sguardi in movimento 1902–1995. Donne-Cinema.*

Index

199

Index

Index of Works by H.D.